Global Corruption

Lawrence Cockf.
2/2013

Global Corruption

Money, Power, and Ethics in the Modern World

Laurence Cockcroft

PENN

University of Pennsylvania Press
Philadelphia

Published in the United Kingdom in 2012 by
I.B.Tauris & Co. Ltd.
6 Salem Road, London W2 4BU
www.ibtauris.com

Published simultaneously in the United States of America by
University of Pennsylvania Press
Philadelphia, Pennsylvania 19104-4112
www.upenn.edu/pennpress

A catalogue record for this book is available from the Library of Congress

ISBN 978-0-8122-4502-8

Designed and typeset by 4word Ltd, Bristol, UK
Printed and bound by TJ International Ltd, Padstow, Cornwall

To Jasmine, Jacob and Joshua

Contents

Illustrations and Charts

Preface

I first witnessed the real rural poverty of subsistence farmers in Nigeria in 1962 while working as a volunteer at a Training Centre devoted to promoting responsible leadership, as the newly independent country embarked on a new phase of its complex history. At that time, in the rolling hills of the northern Plateau, it was possible to think that the country's patchwork of more than 300 ethnic groups would easily grow into a unified nation within a generation. A stable, reasonably democratic government, fortified by the oil revenues which were already in sight, would manage this process, ending the grinding poverty of subsistence farmers, and relying for manpower on some of the many competent young Nigerians who came to the Centre.

Later in that year I went to Cambridge University where African issues continued to be my great interest, and from 1966 I had the opportunity to work as an agricultural economist for the governments of Zambia and Tanzania. There were many issues in those years surrounding the governments of Kenneth Kaunda in Zambia and Julius Nyerere in Tanzania: corruption was a minor question amongst these. Subsequently, as a consultant to the FAO, I worked in Ghana in the mid-1970s and could see an economy and society on its last legs as a result of the corruption sponsored by a military government.

Afterwards, I worked for ten years for a British agribusiness company with a good record in business ethics, but the experience taught me that in many developing countries forms of bribery were never far away, and I could see that its effect was always negative. But other factors in Africa's development still seemed more important at that time – such as the resolution of ethnic rivalries, the recurrent drift to a one-party state, and badly judged nationalizations. I wrote a book about these issues – *Africa's Way: A Journey from the Past* – which I.B.Tauris published in 1989. But by this time the role of corruption in the majority of African countries could hardly be disputed, and Kenya provided some of the most glaring examples.

A similar perception fuelled the views of a Kenyan friend and colleague, Joe Githongo, who was also a friend of the director of the World Bank in eastern Africa, Peter Eigen. We met in Nairobi in 1991 and sketched the basis for a possible international non-governmental organization which would seek to combat corruption, recognizing that its tentacles stretched across both the 'industrial' and the 'developing' world. By the intensive use of his already formidable network of colleagues and contacts in many parts of the world, Peter Eigen was able to turn this vision into the reality of Transparency International (TI) within two years. I joined both the initial international board of TI, and of its UK chapter, later serving as its Chairman.

The launch of TI in 1993 struck a chord in many places and within ten years the organization had chapters in more than 90 countries. Through this association over 20 years I have learned much about the incidence of corruption, the forms it takes, the roadblocks to reform, and possible solutions to the problem. One of the key roadblocks has certainly been resistance to reform by governments of both north and south. The British government proved to be one of the strongest 'resisters', perpetually responsive to lobbying by big business, and one of the biggest challenges in the UK has been to persuade successive governments that bribery really is a threat to a level playing field in international markets. In other parts of the world, governments apparently committed to the reform of corruption – such as those elected in Mexico in 2000 and Indonesia in 2004 – have seldom achieved their apparent goals. On the other hand, in 'aid and development' circles, the argument that corruption is a major threat to development has been won, though the consequences for policy are unresolved.

This book is an attempt to bring together the many and complex lessons I have learned over 20 years in sharing in an attack on corruption which has the potential to change the lives of many millions, but which faces immense challenges and whose success is far from secure. I remain convinced, however, that stability in our world, the reduction of huge inequalities, and the marginalization of the poorest, depends on rolling back the forces of corruption which, in one guise or another, retain immense power.

Acknowledgements

In writing this book I drew on the inspiration and advice of many individuals who work in the global anti-corruption network, or whose work runs parallel to it. The book has a long genesis, and over that time I have received invaluable support and encouragement from Roger Riddell, a development economist with a wide view of the world; Christopher Beauman, an economist with an expert view on eastern Europe and an invaluable analyst of international affairs; Frank Vogl, a colleague in the founding of TI, whose sense of balance in analysing the origins of corruption (and capacity for speed reading) is always full of insight; and Inese Voika, a founder of TI-Latvia, whose courage in the face of glaring corruption has always been inspiring. Their willingness to comment on successive chapter drafts has been invaluable, rivalled only by that of my wife, Shamshad, always my most analytical but supportive critic, and Jasmine, Jacob and Joshua Cockcroft, who have each advised on both themes and readability, always for the better.

I have made many references to the character of corruption, to specific cases in a range of countries, and to initiatives in fighting it. In doing so I have drawn on discussions with Patrick Alley and Simon Taylor, two of the founders of Global Witness; John Bray, the director of several international surveys on corporate sector corruption and a consultant to the Control Risks Group; Francesc Vendrell, former Special EU Representative in Afghanistan and Head of the UN Special Mission for Afghanistan; Dr José Ramón López Portillo, Centre for Mexican Studies, Oxford University; Dev Kar, lead economist at Global Financial Integrity in Washington, DC; William Hughes, former Director General of the UK's Serious Organized Crime Agency (SOCA); Nicholas Shaxson, author of *Treasure Islands*, a study of offshore financial centres; Juvenal Shiundu, an authority on Somali pirates; Sir Tim Lankester, former director of the School of Oriental and African Studies in London and President of Corpus Christi College, Oxford; Phil Mason, a senior civil servant in the UK's Department for International Development (DFID) with past responsibility for its anti-corruption agenda; Patrick Wilmot, a long-time resident in, and expert on, Nigeria; and David Bevan, economist and Fellow of St John's College, Oxford. Discussions with Sir Mark Moody-Stuart, former chairman, Royal Dutch Shell's Committee of Managing Directors and Anglo-American PLC on corporate initiatives, and Clare Short, former Secretary of State for International Development and currently chair of the Extractive Industries Transparency Initiative (EITI), have also been very helpful.

At an early stage I was given excellent research assistance by Mathew Gieve, and at a later stage by Susannah Kinghan – my sincere thanks to them both. In-depth reading and commenting on a nearly final draft is a demanding task and in this respect I am particularly indebted to Prof. Susan Rose-Ackerman; Henry R. Luce, Professor of Jurisprudence at Yale Law School; Victoria Brittain, formerly a senior editor at *The Guardian*; and Fritz Heimann, former chair of TI-USA and Senior Counsel to General Electric. Their incisive comments were invaluable. Any errors in the text which follows are entirely my own. Special thanks are due to the Rockefeller Foundation which awarded me a Residency at its Bellagio Centre in 2011, where the opportunity to progress the book and share ideas with co-residents was invaluable.

Finally, I am grateful to Iradj Bagherzade, the chairman of I.B.Tauris, for his encouragement, support and insights into the theme of the book, and to Jo Godfrey, my editor, for her very clear focus and guidance as the book took its final shape.

Abbreviations

AMF	Afghan Military Force
ARV	Anti-retroviral drugs
AVC	Autodefensas Unidas de Colombia
BPJ	Bharatiya Janata Party
BDI	Confederation of German Industry
BPI	Bribe Payers Index
BPL	Below the poverty line
BRIC	Brazil, Russia, India, China
CBI	Confederation of British Industry
CCP	Chinese Communist Party
CDM	Clean Development Mechanism
CIJ	Court of International Justice
CNOC	Chinese National Oil Corporation
COST	Construction Sector Transparency Initiative
CPI	Corruption Perception Index
CPIA	China Pharmaceutical Industry Association
DoJ	Department of Justice
DPJ	Democratic Party of Japan
DRC	Democratic Republic of the Congo
EFCC	Economic and Financial Crimes Commission

EITI	Extractive Industries Transparency Initiative
ETS	Emissions Trading Scheme
FARC	Fuerzas Armadas Revolucionarias de Colombia
FATF	Financial Action Task Force
FCPA	Foreign Corrupt Practices Act
FDI	Foreign Direct Investment
GCB	Global Corruption Barometer
GE	General Electric
GFI	Global Financial Integrity
HDZ	Croatian Democratic Union (*Hrvatska demokratska zajednica*)
HIV	Human immunodeficiency virus
IAMB	International Advisory and Monitoring Board (Iraq)
ICC	International Chamber of Commerce
IIG	Iraq Inspector General
IMF	International Monetary Fund
IRRF	Iraq Relief and Reconstruction Fund
KPK	Komisi Pemberantasan Korupsi
LDP	Liberal Democratic Party (Japan)
LNG	Liquefied natural gas
LRITE	Long-range information tracking equipment
Mcm	1000 cubic metres (of natural gas)
MDG	Millennium Development Goals
MNC	Multinational company
MPLA	Movimento Popular de Libertação de Angola
NNPC	Nigerian National Petroleum Company
NRM	National Resistance Movement
NRP	National Revolutionary Party
OECD	Organisation for Economic Co-operation and Development
PAN	Partido Acción Nacional
PDP	People's Democratic Party (Nigeria)
PRI	Partido Revolucionario Institucional (Mexico)
PWC	Price Waterhouse Coopers

RCD	Rassemblement Congolais pour la Democratie
REDD	Reducing Emissions from Deforestation and Forest Degradation in Developing Countries
SEC	Securities and Exchange Commission (USA)
SFDA	State Food and Drug Administration
SNI	Société Nationale d'Investissement (Cameroon)
SOCA	Serious Organised Crime Agency
TI	Transparency International
TPK	Travis Perkins plc
TSKJ	Consortium of Technip SA, Snamprogetti, Kellogg Brown Root & JGC Corp.
UNCAC	United Nations Convention Against Corruption
UNCTAD	United Nations Conference on Trade and Development
UNITA	União Nacional para a Independência Total de Angola
UNOCAL	Union Oil Company of California
UNODC	United Nations Office for Drugs and Crime

1

What is Corruption?

It is scarcely possible to look at a news website or pick up a newspaper anywhere in the world which does not carry a story about a corruption scandal. The news story will usually be written at face value, revealing what is often the tip of the iceberg rather than exploring the dense mass below. When Prime Minister Putin orders President Medvedev to step down, is that really a fight between two individuals, or between the interest groups, primed by corruption, which support each of them? When the Liberal Democratic Party in Japan lost office in 2008 after 60 years in power, was that because the *yakuza* mafia had finally decided that it could avoid criminal harassment by supporting the Democratic Party of Japan which then took office? When President Omar al-Bashir of Sudan agreed to the secession of Southern Sudan, was that because he believed that the north could retain the income from the oil-rich enclave of Abyei, straddling the border between north and south? Was the support which the media giant Rupert Murdoch gave to David Cameron and his Conservative Party in the UK election of 2010 the key to his later interest in enabling the company to gain full control of BSkyB, the country's biggest satellite TV station (later undone by the 'hacking' scandal within his own organization)? When Zheng Xiaoyu, the secretary of the Chinese Communist Party in Shanghai, was prosecuted for corruption in 2006, was that primarily a political struggle between Shanghai and Beijing, and less a part of the Party's nominal 'war on corruption'?

Corruption may not only underlie these events and situations, but also be responsible for many of the world's even deeper sores, and particularly the poverty and inequality which typify so much of the developing world. Its scale is huge, notably where political regimes are seeking to extend their tenure; or in a specific industry, such as defence and construction, where market share can be won by bribes; or in the total breakdown of health services where counterfeit drugs dominate a health system. Sometimes this propensity has been checked by religion, or the power of justice, or widespread public revolt, as was the case in Egypt and Tunisia in 2011. More often it has gone unchecked as vast fortunes have been accumulated illegally at the expense of society as a whole, creating huge pools of unregulated money which cycle in and out of formal economies. In the second decade of the twenty-first century such networks are operating on an unprecedented scale, are taking full advantage of globalization, and are often more resilient than the institutions, such as anti-corruption agencies, put in place to curb them. Their interaction with organized criminal networks, such as those that control the international drugs trade, is a source of further strength.

Formal definitions of corruption range from the decay of society to the single act of bribery. The corruption discussed in this book always involves the acquisition of money, assets or power in a way which escapes the public view; is usually illegal; and is at the expense of society as a whole either at a 'grand' or everyday level. Personal enrichment is nearly always a key objective, although corruption may be engineered by a group with the intention of achieving or retaining political power, so that these motives can become closely entwined.

Personal Enrichment
+ Political Power

The consistency of these themes across countries is striking, although different institutional frameworks may disguise the reality. In Russia, the corruption associated with the oligarchs in the 1990s set the scene for widespread manipulation of the political system to ensure that those in power could build up large personal fortunes. In Nigeria, the misuse of state funds for private gain has absorbed most of the growth of the economy over the last 30 years. In the USA, the corporate frauds that coincided with the bankruptcy of Enron and the accelerated expansion of the sub-prime mortgage market, including extensive deception about the value of underlying assets, have been driven by personal greed. In China, the high-profile cases that have exposed the corruption of very senior managers of state-controlled companies and Politburo members have similarly been driven by the accumulation of personal fortunes.

Since nearly all corruption is clandestine it easily escapes detection by investigative agencies. Its 'illegality' is more controversial: the 'mispricing'[1] of exports and imports may not contravene a specific law, though it will contravene formal accounting standards, which require traded products to be valued at world market prices. The risks taken in the banking sector on Wall Street and elsewhere were not, in principle, illegal: they became so when risks were deliberately misrepresented by the originators of mortgage packages sold by one bank to another.[2] So, while corruption is usually illegal, there are also forms of corruption which are technically 'legal', but which most of society regards as corrupt. The cost of this failure to curb corruption on a global basis is very high: its impact is profound at the level of individual livelihoods, national economic progress, the environment, and the credibility of the political system.

Where corruption is endemic, it is the poorest that pay the highest price. Corrupt behaviour at the top, which is often recognized and identified by the public, is readily used to justify corrupt behaviour at the lowest level. Without a bribe, a policeman may hold a vehicle at a roadblock for half a day, an irrigation manager may deny water to a small farmer, or a secondary school headmaster may prevent entry to a promising primary school leaver. Whilst such behaviour is frequently excused by reference to abjectly low incomes, it is in fact often the outcome of elaborate scams, orchestrated at a higher level, where a condition of the job is the payment of a commission at a higher level. When governments change, such mutually dependent relationships can easily survive under a new regime.

The UN General Assembly meeting in 2000 resolved to launch a series of measures designed to bring the poorest people of the world out of extreme poverty. They included a target of halving the number of people suffering from hunger, enabling all children to attend primary school, and halving the number of people without access to drinking water or sanitation. These measures were christened the Millennium Development Goals (MDGs). Although progress has been made, corruption has been a major impediment to their achievement. In India, the national food distribution programme targeted at the rural poor is based on an entitlement certifying that citizens are below the poverty line: such entitlements are themselves the subject of bribery.[3] Emergency food programmes, run by agencies such as the World Food Programme of the UN, have been subject to seizure by governments such as those of Zimbabwe and Myanmar, or by warlords in countries with long-running civil wars such as Somalia and the Democratic Republic of the Congo (DRC). The construction and maintenance of primary schools has been the subject of a major diversion of funds at central and local level. Access to drinking water has been beset with problems related to corruption. In cities such as Jakarta, Lima and Manila, the urban poor pay private water retailers between five and ten times as much for their water as the rich pay for piped water.[4]

In the many countries where corruption is a key or determining factor in the national economy, the costs to economic growth have also been high. In Nigeria, for example, corruption has condemned a majority of people to an income of less than US$2 per day in a country with an average income per year from oil of US$30 billion (one thousand million) since 1970. In Peru, corruption in the 1990s under Alberto Fujimori diverted resources to such an extent that only about half of the expected revenue reached the government.[5] In Kenya, the Anglo Leasing scandal, although spread over several years, accounted for about 12 per cent of annual government expenditure in a single year. In the DRC, the pattern of gigantic corruption initiated by Mobutu from 1961 to 1997 was synonymous with the diversion of resources away from the state to fund a patronage system, which eliminated any serious investment in health, education and basic infrastructure.

There are direct costs, too, to the corrupt management of natural resources such as timber, marine fisheries, and oil, which have implications well beyond the frontier of the country where they are found. In Indonesia, the value of timber cut illegally but traded on the world market has been as high as US$5 billion per year, or four and a half times the value of legally cut timber.[6] In Russia, the export of gas at a fraction of the world price to an intermediate company, which resold it to neighbouring countries at a higher price, deprived the Russian economy of up to US$50 billion per year from 2000 to 2008.[7] In the case of the 'pirates' operating from Somalia, it was the fact that international commercial trawlers were taking advantage of the absence of a marine control system which prompted the pirates to begin taxing and later taking hostage trawlers and eventually larger ships of diverse nationality. In China, the control, through corrupt means, of privatized small-scale coal mines by local Communist Party elites has been characterized by the serious negligence of the control of carbon emissions, with negative implications for China's total environmental programme.

However, the costs of corruption go beyond the individual, the coffers of the state, and the performance of the economy.

Raising funds for political parties in high-income countries has long been permeated by corruption. Business leaders polled by the World Economic Forum in 2003[8] stated that illegal donations were 'rare' in only 18 per cent of countries, and 'common' in 40 per cent. In Germany, Helmut Kohl, who had been the architect of the unification of Germany, ultimately retired in semi-disgrace as the result of party funding scandals involving the Christian Democratic Union (CDU). This extended to a deal with President François Mitterrand of France to claw back commissions for his party from the sale of Leuna, the former East German oil-refining company. In Japan, the political system developed after World War II has depended on the expenditure of up to US$10 billion over the cycle between general elections. A significant part of this has been provided by the *yakuza*, a mafia group who move in and out of the legal economy, buying protection from elected politicians through massive donations. In Italy, the 'clean hands' campaign launched by Milan's magistrates in 1994 found that thousands of municipal contracts were overpriced by as much as 50 per cent, with most of the margin flowing to the coffers of political parties, including both the Christian Democrats and the Socialists. In Russia, post-Communist multiparty elections have involved huge outlays by candidates and their backers. Between 1997 and 2000, a regional election campaign could involve expenditure on behalf of the candidate of US$2–5 million (and much more in an oil-rich region).[9] In the 2003 election it is reported that Mikhail Khodorkovsky, in a move which triggered his jail sentence, put up US$100 million in support of 100 of the Duma's 450 deputies – rivalled only by the similar sum spent by Gazprom in support of a different set of candidates. In 2010 the US Supreme Court, as a result of intensive lobbying by the pressure group Citizens United, lifted restrictions on corporate donations to political parties, further increasing the leverage corporations could exercise in their own interests on the legislative agenda.

Yoweri Museveni has been the president of Uganda since he took power in 1986; a new-look constitution limited him to two five-year terms in 1995. He succeeded in 2005 in having the constitution changed to allow a third term. In 2010 his National Resistance Movement (NRM) needed to secure a clear majority in parliament and it proved expensive, with individual MPs receiving up to US$10,000 each. In the presidential and parliamentary elections of 2011 at least 10 million voters received cash handouts which are reported to have totalled US$200 million. This was not an easy sum to raise through the budget. A convenient Russian arms deal solved the problem: two months after the election, Uganda's Central Bank lent the government US$750 million to buy 14 Sukhoi Su-30 fighter planes from Russia. The real cost was reported to be US$330 million, and the remainder was recycled to replenish the sources which had been used to fund the election.[10]

The use of corruptly gained funds by political parties is matched by broader forms of political finance, which are designed to buy support for the specific allocation of public funds, or a new piece of legislation. In the World Economic Forum survey of 2003, business leaders stated that in only 27 per cent of countries could 'bribery designed to influence policy' be described as 'rare'.

This book explores these issues in depth, particularly asking: what drives the process of corruption, and how might it be rolled back? Chapter 2 examines the threads that are common to large-scale corruption around the world, taking Nigeria, Peru, Indonesia, China, Russia and Mexico as examples that reflect the proximity of the motives of political power and personal wealth.

Chapter 3 points out that 'secret trades' are often integral to the process of corruption, and shows how the movement of products from 'illegal' to 'legal' channels is orchestrated by both traders and organized crime groups with strong links to politicians.

Chapter 4 captures the impact of corruption at three levels: the individual; the national economy; and the environment. It shows how corruption prolongs widespread poverty in many low-income countries, and how it can destroy national economic growth or distort its impact. It recognizes the fact that some fast-growing Asian economies have achieved rapid growth with corruption, but argues that they have paid a high political price.

Chapter 5 shows how each of the major religious traditions has recognized corruption as an issue and how the rejection of corruption is widely recognized as an ethical goal, though one which is only seldom incorporated into the political and social standards of the day. It goes on to explore the ways in which attitudes to corruption change over time – both for better and worse – and asks why this happens.

Chapter 6 shows how the international policies of Western governments during the Cold War tolerated corruption on a huge scale, on the grounds that an anti-Communist position trumped all others. The legacy of this thinking continued up to the 1990s, when the World Bank and other aid agencies increasingly came to regard corruption as an impediment to growth, while more 'realpolitik' foreign policy experts continued to support regimes that were corrupt but had major strategic value.

Chapter 7 identifies the main drivers of corruption as being party political funding; the problem of survival for those on very low salaries; organized crime; and multinational companies as they seek to expand market share in countries where corruption is endemic.

Chapter 8 describes some of the courageous individuals who have fought corruption head on; civil society organizations that have set out to confront corruption; initiatives involving companies and governments; international conventions; and anti-corruption systems at the company level, assessing how much they have achieved.

Chapter 9 identifies three crucial problems which are critical to the resilience of corruption: the prevalence of 'shadow economies' in which a third or even half of transactions are unrecorded; the existence of 'black holes' in the form of secrecy jurisdictions in which corruptly gained funds can hardly be traced; and ambiguity in the position of governments of importing countries whose need for energy supplies may override any concern about corruption.

Chapter 10 addresses the specific issue of climate change and the ways in which international strategies to address it are premised on disbursements from a series of very large funds susceptible to corruption, and through complex carbon trading systems which are susceptible to fraud.

Taking account of the roadblocks to reform, Chapter 11 assesses the strength of popular reaction against corruption in a range of countries, and particularly the impact of the social media as experienced in north Africa in 2011, and asks whether the public reaction against corruption will outweigh the intransigence of governments.

Summarizing the prospects for change, Chapter 12 identifies four major reforms which are conditions for real progress at both the international and national level if corruption is to be rolled back, and goes on to identify five more specific steps which would be decisive in moving forward – and identifies those individuals and organizations who can be critical to moving forward.

This book will show that, in spite of some progress, all forms of action in combating corruption have a long way to go. The international community needs to recognize that reform of corruption to date has been extremely limited, that momentum needs to be maintained, and that the challenges of this century can only be met successfully if the corruption dimension is built into policy and action. Without this, action to combat it at country level will be flawed, and progress on the issues of the twenty-first century will be hostage to the many and burgeoning forces of corruption.

2

The Corrosive Power of Corruption

On the night of 23 June 1996, the middle-aged Paulo César Farias and his 26-year-old girlfriend, Suzana Marcolino, were found shot dead in bed in a beach house in Guaxuma in the state of Alagoas in north-eastern Brazil. The local police immediately announced this to be a 'crime of passion': the public, the media and the Federal Chief Prosecutor were unconvinced. There were good reasons to be suspicious. Paulo César Farias, or 'PC' as he was generally known, had been the fundraiser and financial fixer for Fernando Collor de Mello in the early phases of his rise to power as a Federal Congressman in 1984 and Governor of the state of Alagoas in 1987 – and for his successful campaign for the Brazilian presidency in 1989. Collor was president from 1990 until his impeachment in 1992. PC not only raised US$100 million to invest in this campaign, he also raised an additional US$60 million for subsequent business purposes, and managed to raise a further US$30 million after the election from the same corporate sources.

Once Collor was ensconced in power, PC was able not only to fund the lavish lifestyle of the president and his flamboyant wife, Rosane, but also to build his own fortune of close to

US$1 billion managed through nine separate companies located in Europe, the USA and the Caribbean. Some of these were devoted to drug smuggling: five and a half tonnes of cocaine later detected by Italian police in Turin were traced to PC.

Collor was impeached in 1992 on the basis of evidence provided by his brother, Pedro Collor, about trading in influence schemes run by PC. A congressional inquiry concluded:

> The honourable president of the republic has been receiving throughout his term of office illicit financial gain in the form both of bank deposits … and of material goods and services … has failed in his institutional responsibility to maintain public morality and prevent third parties from using his name for personal enrichment without cause from practices at the outer limits of morality and decency.

PC was the third party. After his impeachment Collor and Rosane left the country. Shortly afterwards a judge ordered PC's arrest. Escaping by private plane to Uruguay and Argentina, PC made it via Europe to Bangkok, where a misjudged row with another Brazilian led to his arrest. Returned to Brazil he faced 41 charges and was sentenced to 11 years in jail. The evidence centred on 17 'phantom' accounts: 52 Brazilian companies had paid into these accounts and 49 had been paid out of them. But his prison sentence was effectively not only commuted to little more than a year, but enhanced by the nightly company of Suzana Marcolino, who for the subsequent two years was his regular girlfriend.

However, PC's restitution to life outside prison was to be accompanied by a major fight with his own brother, Augusto Farias, himself a Congressman, who claimed the fortune PC had built as 'family property'. Later, Augusto was named by a Congressional committee as one of four leaders of a mafia devoted to drug dealing and small arms trading. His fight with PC in 1996 coincided with the apparent demise of Suzana Marcolino, as PC developed a relationship with a widow with greater social cache. On the night of 23 June, Suzana, still a welcome visitor at the Guaxuma beach house, was armed with a Rossi 38 revolver. The police statement reported that Suzana had shot PC before committing suicide, ascribing the motive to a quarrel between the two. In fact, all the later evidence indicated that Augusto had planned PC's death as a strategy to retain control of the 'family funds'. He was indicted for the murders in 1999, but by 2002 the Chief Prosecutor had dismissed the charges for lack of evidence.

Although the impeachment proceedings against Collor led to his exclusion from politics for eight years, the Supreme Court found him not guilty of a criminal offence, on the basis that the evidence-gathering process was tainted. Collor successfully re-entered politics when the eight-year ban was over, and was elected to the Senate (for Alagoas) in 2006, a position he continued to hold in 2011.[1]

The murders were the climax of a saga which had transfixed Brazil on and off for four years as the fallout from the disastrous Collor presidency appeared to bring the country – so glad in 1989 to have escaped 25 years of military rule – back into a political mire. Political finance had been at the heart of Collor's fall after only two years in office, and triggered the beach house murders in Guaxuma. Political finance would continue to dog the subsequent presidencies of Fernando Henrique Cardoso and Luiz Inácio Lula da Silva.

Elements of this story are common to many countries where corruption is or has been at a very high level. The shared ingredients often include the need for political finance either to fight an election or to secure a regime in power; the personal enrichment of a head of state and his close family and associates; and the continued expansion and success of networks which depend on political cover from the state but work towards personal enrichment. In many cases members of the network have close relations with organized crime; may be engaged in illegal trade; and are able to deposit their corruptly gained funds in 'secrecy jurisdictions' from where it may be recycled into the domestic economy.

This chapter shows how these elements are present in six countries: Nigeria, Peru, Indonesia, Russia, China and Mexico. In the cases of Nigeria and Peru (under Fujimori), a type of kleptocracy which undertakes 'grand looting' has held power in which the principal beneficiaries were the President's family and supporters whose loyalty depended on their enrichment. In Indonesia, President Suharto allowed his family and a limited circle of trusted supporters to invest in businesses at his discretion and in captive niches where returns were very high, while ensuring payments to key lieutenants in his Golkar party. In post-Soviet Russia, the boundaries between the state and a state-sponsored oligarchy have varied over time, but ensure that individual gains through forms of corruption accrue to a small elite. In China, liberalization has paved the way for the creation of very large personal fortunes, often by officials and executives with very close ties to the Communist Party; the resulting fortunes have also been used to secure political loyalty. In each of these cases, organized crime has also been a driver of corruption as mafia bosses have sought cover for their activities. In the case of Mexico, the rival gangs which control the drugs trade into and from the USA have bought regional and national political support with serious consequences for the country. These cases show the nature of systems where corruption is endemic and how difficult it is to dismantle corrupt networks once they are established.

Nigeria: no escape

Nigeria has been synonymous with corruption for several decades, to an extent which is so extreme that observers often regard it as irrelevant to a wider international debate about corruption. Nigeria's first coup in 1965 was justified by its architect, Lieutenant Chukwuma Nzeogwu, as being to reverse the corruption which had set in since independence. Between independence in 1961 and the death of President Sani Abacha in 1998, the country experienced seven changes of government, only one of which (electing Shehu Shagari to the presidency in 1980) was through the ballot box. The pattern of corruption from 1986 onwards was set by General Ibrahim Babangida, who was in power for seven years, and allowed a sum of US$12 billion to accumulate in secret accounts which he controlled. Babangida envisaged handing over power to an elected politician who would favour his own network of northerners. In fact, the election of 1993 was won by a southern business tycoon, Mashood Abiola, but he was never allowed to take office and was almost certainly poisoned some months after the election.

Within six months, General Sani Abacha had taken power and proceeded to initiate a new low in presidential practice, combining a political reign of fear with a very high level of personal corruption. The key leaders of resistance to alleged human rights abuses by oil companies in the Niger Delta – Ken Saro Wiwa and eight others – were executed by hanging in 1995 on the erroneous charge of murdering four Ogoni chiefs; the wife of Mashood Abiola, Kadirat, was shot dead in Lagos traffic in 1996; ex-President Olusegun Obasanjo and his close northern associate, Shehu Yar'Adua, were imprisoned for failing to report knowledge of an attempted coup for three years from 1995 to 1998, and the latter was poisoned while in jail.

The largest single investment during the Abacha regime, for the production of liquefied natural gas (LNG), became notorious on both the domestic and international front as a prime example of corruption involving multinational companies, independent lawyers and government ministers. The LNG investment was commissioned by Nigerian LNG, a company jointly owned by the Government of Nigeria and Royal Dutch Shell. The contract to develop the project was awarded to TSKJ, a company domiciled in Madeira and jointly owned by M.W. Kellogg, a subsidiary of Halliburton of the USA, Technip of France, Snamprogetti of Italy and the Japan Gasoline Corporation, TSKJ employed a London-based lawyer, Jeffrey Kesler, as an 'agent' through his company, Tristar. Under this contract Kesler received a total of US$171 million[2] from 1995 to 2002, paid to accounts in Switzerland and Monaco, a significant part of which was destined to reach key figures in the Abacha government. A full-scale investigation by the US Department of Justice ultimately resulted in fines totalling US$578 million levied in February 2009,[3] and the imprisonment for five years of the chairman of Kellogg, Albert Jack Stanley. Kesler was extradited from the UK to the USA in 2010, and in March 2011 pleaded guilty to violating the US Foreign Corrupt Practices Act and agreed to pay US$148 million in fines.[4]

Abacha died from a heart attack in 1998, apparently experienced while engaged with two Egyptian prostitutes, who were flown out of Nigeria within 12 hours of his death. His low-key journey from the capital Abuja to Kano, and burial there, indicated how little he would be missed.

His death was the cue for Obasanjo to be released from jail. General Obasanjo had been close to the plotters of Nzeogwu's coup in 1966[5] and always claimed to have an anti-corruption stance at heart. He had served as president for a five-year military term from 1975 to 1980, which had been dominated by the need to restore Nigeria from the ravages of the Biafran civil war, when corruption was certainly muted. His resignation in favour of a civilian regime in 1980 earned him national and international plaudits, as did his impressive subsequent work as chairman of the Africa Leadership Forum. The work of the Forum and the fact of his imprisonment (charged with knowing of a planned coup but not reporting it) created very high expectations when his People's Democratic Party (PDP) was elected to government in 1999.

Obasanjo made important institutional moves in addressing corruption during both of his four-year terms in the presidency, including securing Nigeria's full membership of the Extractive Industries Transparency Initiative (EITI). Although these steps were widely acclaimed by the international 'development' community, there were always dissident voices within Nigeria that spoke of different moves which served the financial interests of Obasanjo, his own family and closest associates. Ministers in Obasanjo's government were clearly implicated in other scams: in 2004 seven former ministers and civil servants were found guilty of taking bribes of US$214 million from the French company Sagem SA, which had a contract to produce an ID card scheme for the whole population. Governors of Nigeria's individual states were charged by the Economic and Financial Crimes Commission (EFCC) in Obasanjo's second administration, the most conspicuous being Diepreye Alamieyeseigha, Governor of Bayelsa State, who was charged in both the UK and Nigeria, and who eventually pleaded guilty to stealing US$17 million.

However, it was the mechanics of support to change the constitution to allow a presidential third term which fatally undermined Obasanjo's reputation, in an uncanny parallel with the comparable move of Fujimori in Peru (see p.21). The attempt was a widely unpopular move which required extensive bribing of members of Congress, but which was finally not enough to gain the requisite support. The consequent selection by the PDP of a weak alternative presidential candidate – Umaru Yar'Adua – represented a major setback for Obasanjo. Subsequent investigations by parliament have uncovered further cases of alleged corruption closely linked to the energy and oil sectors, leading to Obasanjo's 'indictment' for misconduct by parliament in 2008. The government of Yar'Adua played down the role of the EFCC, ensuring the resignation of its tough director, Nuhu Ribadu, and that state governors were not pursued by his successor. However, when Yar'Adua died in 2010 his successor Goodluck Jonathan reinvigorated the judicial processes which had been held back and even allowed the Babangida case to go forward in 2011.

Why has the reduction of corruption in Nigeria proved so intractable? Two main reasons suggest themselves: first, the sheer scale of riches in the oil business; and second, the development of a 'twin-track' economy. In the first case, it is important to recognize the scale of the wealth generated by oil – at US$1.2 trillion from 1980 to 2010 (or US$10,000 per head of the current population). The temptation to the elite to acquire a slice of this for personal use has proved to be irresistible. But some of this access has been shared much lower down the social scale in a process known as 'bunkering', by which oil is siphoned off the major pipelines (laid and controlled by the big companies such as Shell and Chevron in partnership with the Nigerian National Petroleum Company (NNPC)), taken out to sea and transferred to waiting ships for transport to the international wholesale market. Nigeria loses 6 million barrels of oil per year through this method, worth perhaps US$1.5 billion,[6] in a racket from which the 'big men' receive huge benefit, and workers far down the scale are kept 'on side'.

The second reason for the indestructibility of corruption is the strength and durability of the 'twin-track' systems which sustain it. A key example of this is the domestic distribution of petrol, which is supposed to be refined from four large regional refineries, majority-owned by NNPC, which in turn has bought oil at a heavily subsidized price. This subsidy has operated as an incentive for traders to sell at least a third of total supplies on regional export markets at world prices. As a consequence, the 40-year-old refineries have been consistently short of supplies, and have a severe maintenance problem – so that even when operating they are prone to recurrent breakdown. However, oil traders and the 'big men' behind them have prospered greatly from this arrangement, and it has proved politically impossible to abolish this alternative oil and petrol economy. The twin-track economy operates in such a way that the presumed norms of a mixed economy, in which prices are set by a regulated market, exist only side by side with a larger informal economy, in which prices are set by a strategy geared entirely to maximize the income of a very small elite.

Although the Nigerian political stage has been populated by very different figures in the last 50 years, the constant thrust has been the drive by successive presidents to accumulate large fortunes for themselves and their immediate family and political network. It remains to be seen whether President Goodluck Jonathan, elected to the presidency in 2011, will break the cycle of corruption, or whether the networks which have sustained it continue to have a life of their own.

Peru: full circle

In Peru the decade from 1990 to 2000 saw the presidency of Alberto Fujimori, of Japanese descent, morph from one nominally committed to rolling back Peru's endemic corruption,[7] to one which was designed to perpetuate it on an even larger and more systematic scale. In fact, under the previous presidency of Alan García, interest groups in military and intelligence circles had prospered and wished to see a 'safe pair of hands' elected to the presidency, since a powerful leftist candidate, the famous novelist Mario Vargas Llosa, was regarded as the front runner.

The presidential potential of Fujimori to run in the service of existing corrupt interest groups had been spotted by Vladimiro Montesinos, a veteran of military intelligence and a well-established but secretive political fixer. One of the first supporting acts of Montesinos was to broker a US$1 million campaign contribution to Fujimori from Pablo Escobar, leader of Medellín, the Colombian drugs cartel. Fujimori was welcomed both locally and internationally as a competent middle-of-the-road reformer with a commitment to pragmatic economic reform. The World Bank and the International Monetary Fund (IMF), who had strongly rejected a strategy of bank nationalization proposed by García, welcomed Peru back into their fold. However, once in office the duo of Fujimori and Montesinos unleashed a perfect model of the modern corrupt state – raising funds from privatization, arms dealing and drug trafficking to keep themselves and a network of close associates in power.

Montesinos knew all of the military echelons, their needs and their price. He was also adept at diverting resources committed to one role for quite another. Thus, in 1991, within a year of taking office, he had assumed control of a joint Peruvian/US anti-drugs programme, budgeted at about US$40 million per year in 1991 and 1992, and succeeded in diverting most of this to fund political assassinations, phone taps and party finance. However, the initial strength of the Fujimori regime was its apparent, though illusory, commitment to a no-nonsense clearout of Peru's labyrinthine corrupt networks, and later its willingness to take on the terrorist Shining Path guerrilla movement. Both of these positions enabled it to maintain considerable public support in its first term, securing a 95 per cent public approval rating for the abolition of the two-house Congress of 240 members in 1992, and its replacement by a one-house Chamber of Deputies with 80 members. The new Chamber was skilfully manipulated by Montesinos with the key objective of approving unconstitutional decrees, the majority of which facilitated the continuing acquisition of large personal fortunes amongst a small elite in military, political and corporate circles.

Fujimori maintained close relations with Japan, both at government level and at civil society level. From 1991 onwards his immediate family was able to tap into Japanese non-governmental organizations (NGOs) and attract funds on a large scale to channel to the Peruvian NGOs under his control (APENKAI and AKEN), whose management systems were notoriously lax. Only about 10 per cent of these donations reached their intended beneficiaries, but about US$100 million reached the accounts of the Fujimori family.[8]

One of the government's strategic objectives was privatization, nominally as part of an anti-corruption drive. The proceeds of this totalled US$435 million between 1992 and 2000. Nearly 80 per cent of this was diverted away from the capital and recurrent budgets, and allocated to the re-purchase of government debt at heavily discounted rates (to be repaid at their original par value) and to arms purchases, ostensibly for a small-scale border war with Ecuador from 1995 to 1998. In the latter case a string of purchases of substandard equipment from Russia and Belarus contributed to defeat in the war but, through add-on fees of 15 per cent,[9] considerably increased the fortunes of Fujimori himself, Montesinos, the Comptroller General and 17 other ministers and former ministers. The account of the overseas bank which held these funds on behalf of Montesinos and his partners totalled US$246 million by 2001.

Drugs dealing was similarly a part of the Montesinos strategy: a much more lenient anti-narcotics judicial regime was introduced, replacing the special courts which had been set up to tackle the problem. This was a necessary move as Peruvian exporters of cocaine paste to Colombia and Peru were required to pay off Montesinos and commanders close to him. Testifying at his trial in 2001, the cocaine exporter Demetrio Chávez Peñaherrera confirmed that he had paid commissions of this kind at a rate of US$50,000 per month in relation to an average two flights per month between Peru and Colombia.

The local and international private sector were prepared to invest in this apparently liberalized economy run by an authoritarian regime. However, the system that was erected on this base was finally destroyed by the campaign to win a third term of office for Fujimori in 2000. The President's right to run for a third term involved a change to the constitution, achieved by the bribery of judges on the Constitutional Division of the Supreme Court. However, Fujimori failed in this election to win an overall majority in the Chamber of Deputies, and Montesinos subsequently increased the level of bribes available to key deputies to ensure their defection or clandestine support. Deputies with links to the media were particularly targeted: Jorge Polack, owner of Radio Libertad, accepted US$500,000 to deliver his support. But it was not to be enough. The level of electoral fraud carried out in the campaign – involving the forging of a million signatures – had undermined the support that Fujimori had once attracted. In September 2000, Montesinos fled Peru and in November Fujimori, on a visit to Japan, faxed the Chamber of Deputies to announce his resignation of the presidency.

The unique detail in the public domain surrounding this decade of particularly intense corruption in Peru was brought to light by the Commission to investigate it, led by José Ugaz, subsequently established by President Alejandro Toledo. The Commission had access to all the video tapes on which Montesinos had filmed the majority of the deals he made with Congress members, military officers and the private sector (notably the media). This was supplemented by findings in the USA provided by the detective agency Kroll, whose trawl through bank accounts confirmed the scale of individual assets earned through the system. The costs to the Peruvian economy were extremely high, and have been estimated at 50 per cent of revenue due to the government, and 4 per cent of GDP. This was a regime denuded of resources by its leadership, masquerading as a promoter of liberal democracy and an open economy, but actually designed from the beginning to serve only the interests of an embedded network in military circles who had chosen the President for this purpose.

Indonesia: a family business

The making of the legendary fortune of Suharto,[10] President of Indonesia from 1965 to 1998, was a mainly family business. By the time he fell from power his six adult children all owned major assets in the Indonesian economy, and also prime household and commercial blocks from Singapore to Los Angeles. These were strategic investments, and those in Indonesia had major significance for the economy, extending to toll roads, publishing, shipping, TV stations, chemical plastics, and hotels. The family's interests in airlines extended to a near monopoly in the air passage of Indonesians travelling to Mecca on *haj*. The first mobile phone concession issued – invaluable in a country of 200 million people – went to his son Bambang's company Satelindo. Suharto's second son, Tommy, was the most notorious of the family with a flamboyant lifestyle, the speed of which was matched by the pace of his acquisition of stakes in state-dominated enterprises. His sister Tutut was as resourceful as her brothers, establishing her own business group, Citra Lamtoro Gung, in 1983, which took major stakes in banking, toll road development, and educational television. These assets were largely funded through a series of Foundations to which companies had to make annual payments, as did any taxpayer assessed as having an income of over US$40,000. Collectively, they owned 3.6 million hectares of real estate in Indonesia, and about 40 per cent of the land area in annexed East Timor. The family regarded their financial position as one acquired by right of holding the presidency. After his father's fall, Tommy Suharto was found guilty on non-criminal charges of fraud, and obliged to divest himself of part of his assets. However, he was later condemned to jail for four years for hiring an assassin to kill the judge who had convicted him of graft (corruption).

In spite of the widespread public criticism of the ways in which the Suharto family accumulated its vast fortune, it has proved difficult to dismantle and to destroy the close networks which were associated with it. By the time he left office the total family fortune was estimated at US$15 billion – perhaps a record for a 'first family'.[11] How did Suharto succeed in accumulating this sum, holding the far-flung country together and presiding over a growth rate of GDP of more than 5 per cent throughout this period? The key to this success was the formation of Golkar, the political party which dominated the landscape under his presidency, and ensured his re-election five times between 1973 and 1998. The financial basis of Golkar lay in the deals which Suharto was able to facilitate, particularly in the forestry, power and banking sectors, which have been described as 'franchises', with rents paid to the president or his nominated agents – notably to the several Foundations which also directly enriched his family.

The forestry sector was vital to this strategy, but also representative of others. Two long-time associates of Suharto, 'Bob' Hasan and Liem Sioe Liong ('uncles' to his children), were critical. Hasan had been a trader in Semarang, central Java, in the 1950s, at a time when Suharto was a colonel in the post-independence army and needed additional revenue to keep his regiment afloat. The ties which were developed at that time were sustained and eventually enabled Hasan to become the dominant player in the forestry sector. During Suharto's presidency, concessions covering a total of 60 million hectares (out of a total forest area of 143 million hectares) were made available on long-term leases both to privately-owned companies and to state-owned enterprises. In the 1970s, the leaseholders were mainly joint ventures between Indonesian and foreign companies: Hasan's own close partner at this period was the American company Georgia Pacific. The timber industry was forced into a more concentrated pattern of ownership in the 1980s as part of a strategy to add more value within Indonesia. As a result, Hasan and a dozen other close associates came to be the effective owners of the whole forestry and forest products sector. Local communities were excluded from decision-making, and frequently from the means to subsistence which the forest had provided.

The surviving producers were pressured into forming the Indonesian Wood Panel Association (Akpindo) and were obliged to sell through import marketing bodies in South Korea and

Japan, which Hasan controlled. At the same time international concern about Indonesian deforestation grew. In response the government issued more and more regulations (there were 916 between 1967 and 1999) which 'in turn invited more bribes to circumvent them: indeed some policies seemed to be designed with this in mind'.[12] After Suharto's fall the impact of corruption on the industry was exposed to several inquiries, one of which, conducted by Ernst and Young, found that there had been a 50 per cent shortfall in the collection of forestry revenues from 1985 to 1995, with a total value of about US$5 billion, the result of an under-reporting of log production facilitated by bribes to inspectors. Land satellite imagery showed that 1.6 million hectares of forest was being lost each year. Falsification of data on reforestation eventually cost Hasan his freedom: in 2001, after Suharto's fall, he was convicted of deliberately defrauding the government of US$244 million through erroneous forest mapping, and was imprisoned for three years.

When Suharto resigned under public pressure in 1998 his vice president, B.J. Habibie, became president and the extent to which corrupt networks would be challenged was not clear. However, Habibie was himself forced out of power by his own party in 2001, as a result of a reaction from a reformist element in his Golkar Party. His exit ushered in an ostensibly more democratic era in which there have been three more or less fairly conducted presidential elections and two presidents (Megawati, a daughter of President Sukarno, and Susilo Bambang Yudhoyono). As a result of substantial institutional reform and the establishment of both a Corruption Eradication Commission (KPK) and a new investigative bureau (Tipikor), an impressive list of cases has been brought to the courts with the successful prosecution from 2004 to 2010 of 42 MPs and eight ministers. Nonetheless, there has been a limit to this process, and the networks established under Suharto have continued to exercise important economic power and a capacity to capture public resources.

The strength of these elements was demonstrated in late 2009 when the director general of the KPK, partly responsible for these successful prosecutions, was fired while investigating a major case involving the Auditor General. President Bambang had, in this case, sided with the Auditor General to widespread public criticism, culminating in massive demonstrations outside the KPK headquarters and a total of 1.5 million postings on Facebook. In 2010, an editorial in the Jakarta Post commented: 'All the laws needed to make anti-graft (*corruption*) reforms effective have been in place but their enforcement has been acutely devoid of leadership and political resolve.'[13]

When Suharto died in 1998, he was buried at his request in a mausoleum – in which his wife was already buried and in which there was plenty of room for his family – in a Javanese village close to the hilltop palace of a traditional king. He had certainly held Indonesia's diversity together, including maintaining a bloody grip on East Timor. But, as the KPK case revealed, the public wished to see the country's networks of corruption completely dismantled, while in reality they continued to have a life of their own.

Russia: merging public and private interests

In Russia, the dramatic privatization programme, which took place during the presidency of Yeltsin from 1991, created a group of business oligarchs who, for a relatively brief period, effectively controlled Russia's economy and derived huge profit from it. Their power was effectively undermined during the presidency of Putin, and much of the ability to cream off income and capital was eliminated and transferred to bureaucratic chiefs in government departments. President Dmitry Medvedev challenged this with some success, forcing the resignation of some key bureaucrats from corporate chairmanships. As these changes unfolded, the opportunities for corrupt personal enrichment shifted with them, but were never eliminated and continue to infiltrate Russian society. Surveys carried out within Russia confirm this. The Russian chapter of the anti-corruption advocacy organization Transparency International (TI) stated in 2005 that the post of a deputy minister could be sold for US$8 to US$10 million;[14] in 2006 parliamentary seats were estimated to be available for US$2 million;[15] the price of admission, in the form of a backhander, to the most prestigious universities was estimated at US$30,000 to US$40,000;[16] and the cost of avoiding the military draft was estimated at US$1,500 to US$5,000.[17] In 2005, the frequency with which bribes were requested was the third highest amongst ex-Soviet countries. These practices were greatly resented by the majority of the population: in fact, in a survey in 2000, 70 per cent of Russians said that taking a bribe is never justified.[18] Nonetheless, in parallel with these forms of corruption, organized crime has flourished. In 1991, a notorious St Petersburg gangster, Anatoly Vladimirov, made a large donation to an astronomy institute in the city, and in return the institute named a distant star 'Anvlad'. The Investigations Committee of the Prosecutor General's Office estimates that businesses pay up to US$33.5 billion in bribes annually.[19]

How did this scale of corruption come into being? The process of privatizing state assets, begun on a large scale in 1991, was the genesis of the current situation. The late Soviet period, notably under Brezhnev, was characterized by 'controlled corruption' in which the Politburo effectively licensed corruption, but on the basis of recognized norms and at a standard rate.[20] The partial liberalization initiated by Mikhail Gorbachev in 1985 began to erode these norms and sow the seeds of the 'competitive corruption' which exploded under the full-scale liberalization initiated by Boris Yeltsin from 1991 onwards.

The specific strategy for privatization was developed by Anatoly Chubais, appointed as Deputy Minister for Privatization in 1991. The chosen method was a universal voucher scheme allowing re-sale between individuals, which enabled well-placed and energetic individuals to scour the country for opportunities to buy up huge numbers of vouchers for cash. In this way young entrepreneurs who had been trading in imported computers and exporting modest quantities of oil were in a position to buy the 'commanding heights' of the economy. Nearly all of these were Muscovites, some in their early 30s, from highly-educated families, and who had studied at the best Russian universities. Boris Berezovsky had been Professor of Mathematics at the University of Moscow in 1991. One close observer has commented: 'Their outstanding talent was financial magic: to make money out of anything, by any means, and they changed their techniques of enrichment almost as often as their beautiful women changed their clothes.'[21]

The previously state-owned Gazprom was a key part of this process. In 1992 it was turned into a joint stock company, though with the state owning nearly all of the capital. In 1994, 40 per cent of this capital was privatized through a voucher scheme – for an implied price of US$100 million. In this case vouchers were distributed to 500,000 individuals, though unevenly and with Gazprom staff and management taking a disproportionate share. The price provided an opportunity to take a stake in a hugely profitable business: by 1999 Gazprom accounted for 8 per cent of Russian GDP, even though gas was sold on the domestic market for only about 20 per cent of the European imported price. In fact, this low price suited the management group within the company very well: it enabled them to sell gas at a low price to intermediary companies, of which they were the indirect beneficial owners, for re-export at a higher price. Thus, in the late 1990s, gas originating in Turkmenistan at a price of US$45 per 1,000 m^3 was sold to Ukraine through a US-registered intermediary company – ITERA for US$50 per 1,000 m^3. Mechanisms such as this earned ITERA and its shareholders several hundred million US dollars each year of its operations.

The acquisition of assets through the purchase of vouchers, which had enabled the oligarchs to become active in banking, was followed by the acquisition of assets through a 'debt for equity' swap in 1996, organized mainly by the banks which they controlled. In that year a banking consortium lent the government US$2 billion for one year for on-lending to companies against the collateral of the government's stakes: if the companies failed to repay, the banks could take voting stock of the same value. Since such a failure occurred, the bankers achieved control of five oil companies (including Yukos, Sibneft and Lukoil), two steel corporations and one oil trader. This process ensured that over half of the Russian economy was controlled from 1995 to 2001 by the new class of entrepreneurs who channelled large sums overseas to their personal accounts. It is no accident that capital outflows were estimated at US$20 billion per year in 1996, 1997 and 1998.[22]

But a financial crisis in 1998 had already shown that the peak years of privatization had failed to generate substantial revenues to the state, that deficit spending was high, and that the government could not meet its commitment to the IMF. Within a year, stock market values fell to one-fifth of their peak value, and the value of the rouble against the dollar fell to one-fifth of its previous value. Yeltsin's economic and political legacy appeared to be a disaster. His anointed successor, Vladimir Putin, was elected by more than 50 per cent of the vote in the presidential election of March 2000. Putin's strategy focused initially on excluding the oligarchs from playing a direct role in politics. At a meeting in July 2000 he is reported to have said to the assembled group of 21 oligarchs: 'You stay out of politics and I will not revise the results of privatisation.'[23]

In 2001, Putin re-asserted control of Gazprom, appointing future President Dmitry Medvedev as Chair of its Supervisory Board, but comparable levels of super profits continued to be earned. In that year, the vehicle for sales to Ukraine, ITERA, was replaced by Eural Trans Gaz,[24] designed to skim the same 'surplus' but with different target beneficiaries as defined by Putin on the Russian side and Yanukovych on the Ukrainian side.

The most conspicuous challenge to this reassertion of state control came from Mikhail Khodorkovsky, who had allegedly amassed US$15 billion by 2003. Although his Bank Menatep had failed, he was the dominant owner of the very profitable oil company, Yukos, which the bank had acquired in the debt for equity programme. This enabled him to adopt a highly active political strategy: in the October 2003 parliamentary elections, he put up US$100 million to ensure the support of 100 deputies (out of a total 450), rivalling a similar but not so politically challenging investment by Gazprom. This was a degree of political involvement which Putin found unacceptable: Khodorkovsky was found guilty of tax fraud in 2004 and sentenced to eight years in jail in eastern Siberia. The assets of Yukos were sequestrated, and most were sold off to the Baikal Financial Group – an unknown shell company – for only US$9.35 billion.

Whilst Putin's role in orchestrating this challenge to Khodorkovsky and others was clear, it was implemented by a group of state officials (the *siloviki*), who were keen to challenge the oligarchs and reassert their own capacity to siphon revenue from the corporate sector. The *siloviki* have captured for the state an increasing share of Russia's oil production, rising from 10 per cent in 2004 to 55 per cent in 2007. In parallel with this process, but not necessarily directly linked to it, the years from 2002 to 2006 saw a rising trend in 'illicit financial flows' from Russia, as measured by the difference in the recorded value of exports and the recorded value of imports in destination countries – rising from US$19 billion in 2002 to US$43 billion in 2006.[25] In 2011 this situation was challenged again by President Medvedev, who insisted that senior bureaucrats who sat on the boards of companies should step down, including those such as Igor Sechin, the chairman of Rosneft and a close associate of Putin.

Privatization in Russia has unleashed a process in which a small number of people inside and outside of government have been able to gain control of valuable assets and siphon off income and capital from them. But, as the major players in the system have changed over 20 years, there are many who have managed to maintain an individual interest in it. Thus the lines between business, government and politics have become very opaque. The commentator Andrei Piontkovsky has described the situation in the following terms: 'Today's Russia is unique. The businessmen, the politicians and the bureaucrats are the same people. They have privatized the country's wealth and have taken control of its financial flows.'[26]

It is this context which allowed officials in the Moscow Division of the Tax Commission to issue tax assessments for US$230 million on Hermitage Capital, an investment fund domiciled in the UK. The fund's lawyer, Sergei Magnitsky, exposed these assessments as false (being based on a fraud by criminal intermediaries), and as being part of a group of similar assessments on Russian-owned companies made by individuals in the Tax Commission for their own benefit. He was arrested, and after more than a year in jail died in November 2009, unleashing a stream of protests, initially by Russian and international civil society campaigners, but later by the EU Parliament and US Congress. The Moscow City Bar Association has commented that Magnitsky's death represents the systematic persecution of lawyers in Russia, adding: 'The perpetrators of the theft of budget funds have remained unpunished, while the lawyers who have attempted to report them have been subject to criminal prosecution.'[27]

This reality at an elite level has not altered the fact that most Russians perceive corruption as an issue in their everyday lives and one which has worsened over time. In the Global Corruption Barometer Survey of 2009,[28] more than 50 per cent of those interviewed in Russia said that they expected corruption to get worse in the future. The ability of Russian networks to morph but survive makes this fear credible, which has been further justified by the re-election of Putin to the presidency in 2012.

China: licensed graft, recurrent purges

When Mao Zedong waved the People's Liberation Army flag on the bridge of the entry gate to the Forbidden City in 1949, he and most of those who had survived the Long March believed that they were in a position to roll back centuries of corruption under the imperial Ming and Ching dynasties. The popularity of the Chinese Communist Party (CCP) with large swathes of China's population in 1949 owed a great deal to the perception that they were a more disciplined force than the exploitative Kuomintang, who had ruled large parts of China for the previous 20 years, and so was better able to address corruption. In fact, the CCP failed to defeat corruption right from taking power. Its campaigns have ranged across the peasant-dominated rural economy of the 1950s to the burgeoning industrial economy of today, with no apparent indication of a real diminution of corruption. It was described by Premier Wen Jiabao as one of the country's major problems in his keynote speech to the Party in March 2012.

The Party's early campaigns were largely based on invitations to denounce both local officials and surviving land owners. The first was in 1951, in the course of which it was reported that 1.23 million party members[29] (or a third of the total) had committed graft – of which 650 were given serious sentences. Fifteen years later, the Cultural Revolution (1966–9) swept aside both old bureaucrats and new leaders, but certainly did not wipe out corruption. Within ten years Deng Xiaoping had initiated the first stage of the agricultural and industrial reforms which were to transform China by re-introducing some of the major elements of a market economy. This threw up huge new dilemmas for the party leadership as they successfully induced local CCP bureaucrats to engage in market-based productive enterprises. For the most part this was in the form of 'guided assistance' to enterprises rather than direct ownership, which was rewarded by personal pay-offs. This form of *guanxi* (personal reciprocity) between local party leaders and a new generation of entrepreneurs characterized the economy of the 1980s, generating new opportunities for corruption.

The system exploded at the 15th Party Congress held in 1997, when it was determined that most state-owned assets would be fully privatized. This made it more difficult to quietly remunerate local officials with the fruits of modest levels of corruption, and created opportunities for many of them to become fully-fledged capitalists. Although this was to be capitalism in the raw at both local and national level, the CCP's strategy has been to manage the situation in such a way that newly minted millionaires would be brought down if they stole too much or defied the current leadership – avoiding the Russian dilemma of over-mighty oligarchs.

Two cases illustrate the scale of this: Zheng Xiaoyu, one-time director of the State Food and Drug Administration; and Chen Liangyu, one-time CCP Secretary in Shanghai. Zheng Xiaoyu was a once conscientious staff member of the national pharmaceutical regulatory administration who argued for some years for the creation of a State Food and Drug Administration (SFDA), which would be more competent and efficient than a government department. The new SFDA was established in 1998, and the 'amiable' Zheng became its director,[30] apparently committed to the strategy of reducing the number of pharmaceutical companies – many created from recently privatized companies established by local governments – and increasing their efficiency. He succeeded in reducing the number of companies from 6,700 to 4,500, but this figure was still so high that there was a constant downward pressure on quality, and a majority of the companies survived in the 'grey market' of supplies to hospitals and medical agencies where backhanders to medical staff were the norm. In fact, totally false drugs were also common, many of which reached the export market after being traded by criminal gangs to destinations such as south east Asia and Nigeria.

Nonetheless, during his eight-year tenure the SFDA approved more than 150,000 applications for new drugs, and Zheng fell for the opportunities for corruption that were offered by this volume of business. From 1998 to 2006 he received US$850,000 in bribes, a significant chunk channelled through a consulting company in Shanghai formed by his wife Naixue and son Hairong. In 2005, through a process of whistleblowing by another SFDA member, Zheng's behaviour was reported to prosecutors. In June 2005 his post was suspended for a year, and was eventually investigated by the State Council, China's most senior governing body, where a hostile witness commented that Zheng had 'neglected his duty to supervise the drug market, abused the administration's drug approval authority, took bribes, and turned a blind eye to bad practices by relatives and subordinate officials'. Eventually he was found guilty of accepting bribes from a range of drug companies, and finally executed on 10 July 2006.

In the subsequent years little has been done to change the structure of the industry, and its systemic susceptibility to corruption has continued to be recognized by the China Pharmaceutical Industry Association (CPIA). One analysis from that source[31] has commented that the problems arise from several interlocking factors: the undercapitalization of drug companies; the acute competition between them; the potential for reducing costs by faking ingredients; and the opaque nature of the market. Nonetheless, in his 'confession' Zheng did not blame the system but personal failings:

> Some money wasn't given to me directly, but through Naixue and Hairong. Naixue was retired and stayed at home. Hairong was just a student. So their target was still me. Indirect ways were easier for me to accept. So I agreed, consented. This was bribery.

Corruption at the local level, and within a government-sponsored agency, is a manageable though embarrassing phenomenon for the CCP. When it is addressed at the level of the party secretary for the City of Shanghai it is much more than an embarrassment and has the potential to trigger a struggle for power within the Politburo. Struggles of this kind have occurred several times. The CCP chairman in the 1990s, Jiang Zemin – whose original power base was Shanghai – succeeded in purging the Beijing party chief, Chen Xitong, on corruption charges in 1995. In 2006 his successor, Chairman Hu Jintao, ensured that relatively junior officials and well-connected businessmen were arrested on corruption charges in Shanghai. Eventually, the chain of investigation, conducted by no less than 100 central government investigators, led to the arrest of the party secretary, Chen Liangyu. He was charged with appropriating about a third (or US$1 billion) of Shanghai's social security fund, and allocating it to his network to purchase stakes in the gigantic building bonanza, which has characterized the city over the last 20 years.

The rate of accumulation by his network caused Chen to defy policy guidance from the central government on issues such as the environment, planning guidelines, industrial safety, and the need to cool the rate of growth of the economy from a national perspective. This political concern was certainly a factor in Hu Jintao's move against Chen, as reflected in the statement by Xinhua News Agency: 'Comrade Chen Liangyu has created malign political effects. Whoever it is, no matter how high their position, anyone who violates party rules or national law will be severely investigated and punished.' In fact, Chen was detained for some time and lost his post, never to recover his position in the CCP. The fact that the arrest of Chen was preceded by the arrest of smaller fry with good party connections, and that the case involved a huge social security fund, confirms that corrupt networks can originate within the party as well as privatized enterprises.

Additional light was thrown on this by the case of Lai Changxing, who developed a very large international smuggling ring from Fujian in the 1990s. According to the Chinese prosecuting authorities, Lai's empire achieved an annual turnover of US$10 billion, trading everything from crude oil to cigarettes. He succeeded in buying off local party officials with 'money, expensive gifts and prostitutes'.[32] Since Lai's smuggling operations transported goods to Vancouver he was arrested there in 1999, but was returned to China to face prosecution in July 2011. His original arrest coincided with an anti-corruption crusade in the party led by then Premier Zhu Rongji, who said it would not be enough for Lai to die 'three times over'. But the targets of Lai's gifts identified by the prosecutors indicate that there had been significant co-operation from within the CCP.

In spite of these hazards of life at the top, there is a buoyant market in the award of posts in the gift of the party's Organization Department. Richard McGregor, a close observer of the CCP,[33] reports that publicly reported 'bribes for office' in 2009 included the party secretary and head of the local real estate company in Chengdu, who took US$2.5 million; the police chief of the poorest town in Guandong Province, who was discovered to have US$4.4 million in cash in his house; the head of the huge development zone in Chongqing, who was found guilty of misappropriating US$32.1 million and taking bribes of US$1.4 million (shared with 30 others); and the vice mayor of Suzhou, who was sentenced for taking US$12 million in bribes. The fruits of corruption are definitely not an all-male business: Zhang Peili, the wife of Premier Wen Jiabao, attended the Beijing Diamond Fair in 2007 in a very ornate diamond necklace, valued by one trader in a quote to the press at US$300,000 – an assessment for which the diamond traders' association had to apologize.

It is clear that the CCP has not succeeded in slaying the dragon of corruption as envisaged by its leadership in the 1949 revolution. Rather, it has struggled with the contradictions involved in a privatization programme that sees the state retain important shareholdings in privatized enterprises, where these are often controlled by individuals with senior positions in the party. Thus 'networks' in China extend across business, government and party, and are replicated at national and regional level. The regularity of 'clean-up' campaigns shows how deeply these systems are embedded. The response evident from China's very active social media, such as Sina Weibo (see p.210) shows just how resentful and angry many members of the public are about this.

Mexico: arms, drugs and cartels

Networks of a different kind, devoted to drug smuggling, have plunged Mexico into a state of violence and tension since 2005. The 50,000 murders and executions that have occurred since President Felipe Calderón declared a frontal assault on organized crime in 2006 have been a huge blow to the country's prestige and international image. A cocktail of national trafficking networks, uncontrolled 'security' services and an army on the defensive have served to penetrate local and national political systems so that organized crime has the capacity to affect not only the award of contracts but also political outcomes. This is a case where organized crime has reversed the gains made in tackling corruption in the political sphere.

Mexico had been a *de facto* one-party state since the PRI[34] and its predecessor the NRP were elected to government in 1929. Under successive PRI governments, corruption was a recurring issue, with some advance in rolling it back made by the government of Miguel de la Madrid from 1982 to 1988 through the establishment of an anti-corruption agency, the *Contraloría*. The emergence of a long-standing minority party, the Partido Acción Nacional (PAN), as an effective opposition in the 1990s, also served as a partial check to the corruption which was inspired or tolerated by the government. Under President Ernesto Zedillo, Mexico had considerable success in economic terms with annual growth rates of close to 7 per cent and an investment grade rating. The election of the ex-Coca Cola boss, Vicente Fox, as president in 2000 was widely thought, at least outside Mexico, to herald an era in which corruption would be brought under much more effective control. One means towards this was supposed to be privatization, and a principal target was Pemex, the prestigious state-owned oil company. In fact, vested interests succeeded in blocking this process and Pemex, along with many other publicly owned bodies, remained in the state sector.

Existing networks, profiting from corruption, had retained their power over institutions such as the judiciary. Commenting on this in 2010, a foreign minister under Fox, Jorge Castañeda Gutman, said: 'Everyone just thought, probably implicitly and without thinking about it much back in 1999 and 2000 (*before taking office*) that you didn't have to change the institutions because they would work perfectly well in a democracy. Obviously that was false.'[35]

The PAN finally took power from the PRI in 2006 as Felipe Calderón became president. In principle, he was committed to launching effective anti-corruption measures but took the view that a government run by his party, which had in opposition made the control of corruption an issue, would operate with integrity, and accordingly abolished the *Contraloría*. Lacking other instruments to fight corruption, and with a weak drugs control agency, he was largely unprepared for the huge upsurge in violence generated by new forms of organized crime in drugs trafficking. While a fairly modest level of poppy and opium production had existed in the state of Sinaloa for many years, the success of the war on drug cartels in Colombia opened up a vast market for Mexican traffickers and producers in the US$60 billion[36] per year US drugs market. Roughly half of this market is accounted for by cocaine, of which 90 per cent originates in or transits through Mexico. The internal Mexican market is estimated to be valued at US$17 billion.

The two principal drug cartels have been Sinaloa (led by Joaquín 'Shorty' Guzmán) and La Línea of Juarez (led by 'Tony Tormenta' Guillén and Jorge 'El Coss' Sánchez[37]). These were originally focused mainly on organizing the transit of drugs through Mexico to the USA, and were incentivized to scale up their operations by a change in the commission system. Once restricted to a flat rate of US$1,500–2,000 per kg of cocaine, they were now rewarded with a percentage of the value of the product, and became increasingly closely linked to US-based networks with a greater capacity to control final prices. At the same time, they became active pushers of cocaine within Mexico, and promoters of other drugs supplied by their associates in the USA. The barter arrangements between the Mexican cartels and their US networks are partly accounted for by physical trade-offs rather than cash transfers: the Mexican cartels sell US-manufactured drugs as part of the deal. They can also buy weapons over the counter in the USA with the proceeds of the trade – a position which in some situations enables them to outgun the Mexican army.

The potential to extract higher levels of profit out of the US market heightened the competition from 2006 between Sinaloa and La Línea, drawing in various 'private security' operators such as Los Zetas (able to command a fighting force of more than 1,000 men and women, mainly recruited from the anti-narcotics forces), which themselves have expanded beyond security operations into the drugs trade itself, and into promoting the US-sourced drugs which are now integral to their operations. It is these conflicts, including the fight for domestic distribution systems, which have forced up the death rate in Mexico's cities – particularly those close to transit routes to the USA, and others such as Aguascalientes, which, although situated to the north of Mexico City, had appeared to be havens of peace as late as 2004. Even in Michoacán, a state capital in the south, the syndicate 'La Familia' controls the municipal authority of Michoacán, and has been held responsible for the murder of 20 municipal officials including two mayors. Seven ex-mayors have been charged with links to the syndicate; the step-brother of the state governor, elected to Congress in 2009, was charged with corruption and went into hiding. In contexts such as this it becomes almost impossible to disentangle the interface between organized crime and the corruption of political authorities.

The overall social and economic costs of these 'wars' has been huge. More than one-quarter of the Mexican army, or 45,000 troops, are committed to the drugs war. Some actions emanating from US drug-control agencies make matters worse. In 2011 the US Department of Justice, working with a drugs control bureau,[38] unleashed hundreds of weapons into Mexico, under the strategic title 'Fast and Furious', with the intention of tracking their ultimate owners. In fact, the operation was unsuccessful in its objective, and has been the object of Congressional review in the USA and extreme resentment in Mexico.

Visits by President Calderón to cities on the US border hit heavily by the war, such as Ciudad Juarez, are dominated by appeals for the restoration of order. On one such visit in January 2010 Luisa Maria Davila, a mother who had lost both her sons, beseeched him: 'Nothing gets resolved here, it just gets worse … do something for Juarez.'[39] But the government's capacity to control this 'war' is limited by the ability of the syndicates to penetrate the political system. By 2010, Guzmán could be described as 'the most powerful trafficker on earth' with 'influence at the highest level of the Mexican government'. This is not unique: 'every trafficker has a great many appointed officials and elected politicians on his payroll but Guzmán has more than the rest'.[40]

The conflict has had a direct impact on electoral politics in that the PRI is now a serious contender both in gubernatorial elections and in the presidential election scheduled for 2012. In August 2010 President Calderón proposed that since the US Government was unable to make major strides in controlling the scale of the drugs market, it should re-visit the case for liberalization – a proposition previously considered outrageous. But the underlying issue is whether, however intense the rivalry between them, the drug producers and traffickers have achieved such deep penetration of the political system that they will continue to operate in parallel with Mexico's successful formal economy for many years.

* * * * *

In these six cases there are both constant and divergent themes. In Nigeria, Indonesia and Peru, corruption has been driven by a network surrounding a head of state which has extended its support system on a wide enough basis to secure its own survival, at least for a number of years. In these cases the process has been driven by both political survival and personal enrichment. In the case of Russia and China, corruption has exploded as a result of privatization processes which have in reality been only partial and have retained a high degree of state involvement. In the case of Mexico, a long history of political corruption has survived to be matched to a new force in the form of drug cartels that have been able to buy political support.

In all of these cases there is a unifying thread of collaboration between international and domestic partners. A further common thread is the existence of a dual system in which corruption is planned and executed within an alternative channel to the formal institutions of the economy. Thus in Peru, Montesinos funded his subversion of Congress through arms and drugs deals well outside the formal government budget; in Nigeria, oil 'bunkering' generates huge returns for the defence forces never recorded by governments or the oil companies; in Russia, the manipulative pricing of gas and oil exports enabled billions of dollars to be expatriated to offshore centres in ways which escaped formal audit processes; in Indonesia, a deliberate strategy of the falsification of reforestation data enabled Bob Hasan and his associates to collect huge subsidies before selling timber at a contrived price to importing companies which they controlled in Japan and Korea.

Thus the common characteristics of corruption in today's world include the close relationship between personal enrichment and political survival, the willingness of international partners to participate in corrupt stratagems, and the extent to which dual systems facilitate this and make it very difficult for formal institutions to control the corruption at the heart of the process.

3

Secret Trades

The accelerated globalization of the world economy in the last 30 years has stepped up corruption in different ways, and has facilitated secret and unrecorded flows just as it has facilitated increased and recorded flows. Secret and hidden corners of the world trading system have experienced a massive flow of funds, much of which is ultimately 'washed' into formal trading and banking channels. Organized piracy, which has developed since 2005 off Somalia, the mining of coltan (columbite–tantalum) in the eastern DRC, and a much broader spectrum of global trading in drugs, humans and counterfeit goods all fall into this category, and feed the corruption in a range of countries.

Organized piracy: rocketing ransoms

The rise of the Somali pirates is an extraordinary story with several unusual characteristics – particularly the ability of ex-fishermen to use the west's legal and banking systems to extract colossal ransoms from world shipping companies, and defy the navies of NATO and other powers in the process.

How did this arise? Relatively stable government broke down in Somalia in 1991 after President Siad Barre was expelled in a coup. Since that time, the country has been at the mercy of various factions vying for power – some more secular, some more aligned with radical Islam – none of which has been able to establish a stable government, even when propped up by generous western aid and peace-keeping forces from the African Union. In the course of the 1990s, villagers and fishermen along Somalia's 2,000-mile coastline were the victim of both environmental 'dumping', including in some cases nuclear waste, as well as an infestation of international commercial trawlers, notably from Indonesia, Japan and Korea, operating well within Somalia's 200-mile economic zone and often within its ten-mile exclusion zone. Local leaders began to realize that whereas in normal countries international trawlers paid a fee for their fishing rights, no such fee was being collected in their waters. Accordingly they redefined themselves as 'coast guards' and began to demand fees from international vessels fishing off their shores.

From this successful collection of fees from trawlers, they went on to collect fees under duress from larger cargo boats sailing from the Red Sea and the Arabian Gulf to Mombasa and further down the east African coast. Funds collected in this way were invested in larger and faster vessels capable of taking the crews much further out and eventually as far as 1,300 km from the Somali coast. Once these were acquired, it was a consistent next step to hold such large cargo boats, carrying hundreds of containers or oil tankers, to ransom. Armed with machine guns, shoulder-carried rocket launchers and their own courage, the pirates were able to capture vessels of this kind and hold them until handsome ransoms were paid. From about 2005 they were able to use intermediaries to contact the owners of captured vessels and introduce them to London-based lawyers who could act as negotiators, and arrange delivery of the ransom in cash. In 2009, the average payment per vessel was US$2 million, delivered in notes – often to the captured boat – by professional security companies. By the end of 2010, about US$250 million had been collected in this way. At the same time 30 ships and 620 sailors were being held pending payment of further ransom.[1]

The ability of the pirates to track individual boats in 2012 is as great as that of major shipping companies, since they have access to sophisticated equipment known as long-range information tracking equipment (LRITE), which details the location of cargo vessels at any point in time, and identifies the nature of the cargo. In some cases they have even obtained access to passenger manifests before storming the ship. Of the total funds collected by the pirates, perhaps only 10 per cent is retained within Somalia, with much of the remainder being invested in property in Nairobi and Mombasa.

This extraordinary level of activity has built up in spite of naval vessels from countries ranging from China to the UK being active in 'patrolling' – with the use of sophisticated satellite technology – much of the Indian Ocean through which the pirates now roam. However, with the exception of the Indian Navy, none of the navies concerned is empowered to kill the pirates. Many have been arrested and taken for trial in Kenya, which signed an agreement with several EU countries to prosecute pirates handed to them. However, several of those convicted have won a reprieve on appeal because a Kenyan High Court judge threw doubt on the legality of Kenya's right to prosecute piracy outside Kenyan waters. Trials in Denmark and Germany have collapsed for similar reasons. As a result, apart from a small number still in jail in Kenya in 2012, most captured pirates have been returned to the high seas or the Somali coast as free men.

The Somali pirate saga represents a very unusual form of organized crime created by the collapse of a community's economy, is very lucrative, is largely immune to prosecution, and can prey on the huge resource of Indian Ocean shipping. At the same time its effectiveness depends on very sophisticated

modern communications, and on the good offices of international lawyers and security companies to negotiate and deliver
ransoms. Once laundered into the Nairobi property market, the
proceeds are secure, and in principle could be reinvested
anywhere. While shipping companies are aggrieved, and
frightened by a huge increase in insurance premiums, the pirates
legitimately claim that they were the victims of the arrogant
behaviour of commercial fishermen and environmental
dumping. In his study of contemporary piracy, *Pirates of the 21st
Century*,[2] Nigel Crawthorne quotes one as saying: 'Our fish were
all eradicated, so we can't eat fish now, so we're going to fish
whatever passes through our sea because we need to eat.' Such
organized piracy might be described as redistributive organized
crime, with a small cut for London lawyers. It is made possible
only by the complete failure of the Somali state, but as elsewhere
when such failures occur could repeat itself. In other cases, illegal
trade – in products such as coltan and timber – generates
unrecorded income for a regime, and sustains its political base.

DRC and coltan: militias to mobiles

The mining of coltan – short for columbite–tantalum – in the
north and south Kivu provinces of the eastern DRC is an
extraordinary example of the conversion of a corruptly mined
product into the ubiquitous must-have emblem of global care-
free consumerism – the mobile phone. Products derived from
coltan are used as capacitors in a range of electronic devices to
facilitate conductivity. Since the requirement per device is very
small, total annual production is about 1,000 tonnes, of which
two of the largest producers are Australia and the DRC. However,
the DRC has by far the world's largest reserves – estimated at
about 450,000 metric tonnes, of which 80 per cent are in the Kivu
provinces. Over the decade since 2000, prices have fluctuated
widely but have been as high as US$600,000 per tonne.

Not surprisingly, coltan and other key metals such as cassiterite have attracted international mining companies for many years. Long-established Belgian mining companies continued to operate after Congolese independence in 1960, and merged their interests after 1976 in the eastern DRC into a new company, Société Minière du Kivu, or Sominki SA, which conducted its own formal mining operations. However, the subsequent political and economic crises of the 1980s obliged Sominki to withdraw from formal mining and to allow individual artisan miners to operate on a freelance basis within its concessions. Mobutu's fading government attempted to wrest at least nominal control of these mining assets from Sominki and its successor companies (dominated by Canadian and American investors) from 1995 to 1997. By May of 1997 Rwandese armed forces had placed Laurent Kabila in power in Kinshasa, but his writ in the eastern DRC was challenged within a year by rebel forces, and the Kinshasa government, subsequently led by his son Joseph Kabila, never regained full control of the Kivu mines (although its armed forces periodically took short-term possession).

In the ensuing decade, the mines became the subject of a grim and tragic battle between contending forces in the region. The forces of the Rwanda Patriotic Front were fighting the Hutu *interahamwe*, who had been responsible for the genocide in Rwanda, and who had fled to the forests of the DRC. The Ugandan army was initially supporting them in this campaign but later adopted its own objectives, dominated by the personal financial interests of its commanders. The tension between these two military forces ultimately led to a shoot-out in the city of Kivu, but not before it had drawn into the conflict the armed forces of no less than six other neighbouring states – a conflict dubbed Africa's 'first world war'. Coltan, together with gold, diamonds and timber, were at the heart of this struggle. The individual miners at the centre of the process, the majority of whom were youths under 20, were the victims of whichever armed group controlled the concession and who could ruthlessly manipulate the price and enforce a 'tax' on the miners.

By 2000, international pressure succeeded in ending the major war and in securing the nominal retreat of Rwandese forces. The government of Paul Kagame developed a successful strategy of supporting other local militias against the continuing threat of the Hutu *interahamwe*. In the course of this he allowed his commanders to work through *comptoirs* to purchase coltan and other minerals. They washed, separated, graded, consolidated and packaged ore for shipment, and the majority of this material then passed through Rwanda and Uganda: in 2008 half of Rwanda's mineral exports were re-exports from the DRC. But the ownership of *comptoirs* was not restricted to local commanders. For example, Eagle Wings International (EWI), a subsidiary of Trinitech International from Ohio, operated a *comptoir* and exported through Rwanda. A UN report (hotly contested by the Rwandese government) commented that EWI had close ties to the Rwandese government and so was able to avoid customs and 'received privileged access to coltan sites and captive labour'. The ultimate customer was EWI's own parent company in the USA, and other owners of smelters in Kazakhstan, China and Germany, whose refined products were sold to chip manufacturers around the world. Other intermediate customers – selling on to the chip manufacturers – included the UK-listed Amalgamated Metals Corporation and Afrimex, an independent London trader.

The cumulative impact of this form of mining, and the *intarahamwe* and other Congolese and Rwandese militias, have been the extensive destruction of the agricultural base of the area:

> the massive destruction of former grazing land is catastrophic. Soil which has been used for unplanned prospection and artisanal coltan mining is no longer suitable for agriculture. Entire hills and valleys have been turned into giant craters,

turning the landscape of the region into an expanse of naked earth, at the bottom of which flow rivers and streams which were diverted for the requirements of mining coltan.[3]

There has been a huge human and natural resource cost as a result of the militia-dominated exploitation of thousands of youths in the Kivu mining industry. A key observer of this conflict has been the UK-based advocacy body Global Witness, which commented in 2011: 'The trade substantially exacerbates existing sources of conflict and blocks efforts to break the cycle of violence in the eastern Kivu provinces, where human rights, including gender based violence such as rape and sexual slavery, have reached catastrophic proportions.'[4]

The militias themselves have been partly the pawns of the governments in Kigale, Kinshasha and their proxies in the region who in turn seek access to these resources at the lowest possible price. The chip manufacturers who supply products partly based on coltan to electronic device manufacturers are intermediaries in a trade whose products are generally considered to be liberating. In the corrupt and violent conditions of the eastern DRC, this liberation is a tragic irony. A new chapter in attempts to redress the ignominies involved in this trade has begun as a result of provisions in the Dodd–Frank Wall Street Reform and Consumer Protection Act passed by the US Congress in mid-2010. A section of this Act requires companies to disclose to the Securities Exchange Commission of the USA any use of 'conflict minerals' including coltan, although it does not impose a penalty on them for doing so. In 2011 the output of coltan from the eastern DRC severely diminished as a result of the suspension of all mining activities there by the government. This is not a long-term ban, and in fact the DRC has publicly supported the Dodd–Frank Act's reporting requirements on the assumption that trade will resume. In late 2012 it remains to be seen whether the DRC army, which has played an important role in the conflict minerals trade, will find it more difficult to market coltan in the face of this reporting requirement. A critical factor will be whether the European Union ensures that its member states adopt comparable provisions. Attempts to address the same issue through the Electronic Industries Citizenship Coalition (EICC) and the Global e-sustainability initiative have so far made little substantive progress[5] – though such potential certainly exists, as has been reflected in Apple's report on its own supplier chain.[6]

Organized crime: circling the globe

The ransoms collected by the Somali pirates through successful ship boarding, and the transformation of coltan into the world's mobile phones, are a reflection of the much larger-scale processes facilitated by the networks of organized crime[7] which have expanded to almost all parts of the globe in the last 20 years. These have been able to take advantage both of a global market in goods and of the revolutions in communications which have benefited the rest of the global economy. However, the weight of current evidence is that organized crime is not run by organizations integrated across national boundaries but rather by a series of independent organizations, generally with a national base but with excellent linkages to similar organizations in other countries. The flexibility implied by this structure also facilitates changing product lines as new opportunities – such as counterfeit DVDs – come on stream. Not surprisingly, the best guide to new products traded by organized crime is the opportunity for increased profits. Such opportunities are increasing rather than diminishing.

The international drugs trade is the clearest example of this. Trafficking in drugs was made illegal in 1988 by all the signatories to the Vienna Convention on drug trafficking, yet imports into the USA of cocaine alone are estimated to be about US$60 billion per year (or 20 per cent of a global drugs trade estimated at US$300–400[8] billion at the retail level). This is the most irrepressible of trades: in Afghanistan production in 1999 was estimated to be 5,000 tonnes of opium, it fell to nearly zero after its banning by the Taliban government, but climbed back to about the same level by 2004 after the Taliban fell. In Bolivia a similar campaign to wipe out 12,000 hectares of coca leaf was waged in 1998 but proved equally ineffective as the president implementing the campaign – Gonzalo Sánchez de Lozada – was swept out of office by 'narco syndicalists, terrorist groups and cartels'.[9] In Colombia, both the 'leftist' FARC and the 'rightist' AUC have been and remain large-scale producers of coca leaf, with sophisticated factory-based systems for adding value – a total trade currently estimated at US$6 billion.[10] Although a significant percentage is captured by Mexican traffickers, the majority of these funds are retained by the Colombian suppliers, and are held outside Colombia.

In Central Asia, the drugs trade has expanded rapidly since the 1980s. The Soviet occupation of Afghanistan had initiated a demand for heroin from Afghan sources in Russia and central Asia, and established drug-trafficking routes which have systematically expanded since the 1980s. The International Narcotics Board reports the huge total of 140 tonnes of heroin trafficked through these countries in 2007 (with a street value in western Europe of about US$8 billion). However, the number of reported criminal charges for drugs trafficking in the central Asian republics has fallen over the previous decade.[11] In Turkmenistan, local officials, in the border guards who challenged heroin shipments crossing the border from Afghanistan, have found themselves executed on the order of senior political figures who in fact were controlling the same shipments. Since coming to power in 2003 President Gurbanguly Berdimuhamedow has shown a greater willingness to collaborate with formal international anti-corruption initiatives – such as the EITI – but there is no evidence of a reduction in the scale of drug trafficking through Turkmenistan.

In Tajikstan, where President Emomali Rahmon has been in power since 1992, the end of a long period of civil strife has enabled the government to centralize drug-trafficking routes, and to ensure that even fewer cases come to the courts. In 2008, it seized only 1.6 tonnes of heroin – three times less than in 2003, a period in which Afghanistan almost doubled production. A recent report from the International Crisis Group reports:

> While Tajikstan has a high rate of drug seizures, specialists and diplomats say that the pattern of drug operations suggests that the couriers are being caught, while large shipments slip through the net. Diplomats feel there is a high level government involvement in the drug trade.

In Kyrgystan, a revolution in 2005 threw out the corrupt president Askar Akayev, but the drugs trade did not diminish. Right to Life, a local civil society group, claimed in 2009 that 36 per cent of drug users got their supplies directly from the police.

The evidence is that drug trafficking has been appropriated by the governments of the central Asian republics as a means of bolstering their power and adding to the resources generated from natural gas and oil. In these cases organized crime and corruption feed on each other: a corrupt state is a boon for organized crime.

'Illegal trade' extends to human trafficking. For example, between 1995 and 2005 it is estimated[12] that 30 million women and children were secretly trafficked in South East Asia. A significant part of this 'trade' originated in China: in the 1990s, 25,000 Fujianese alone were entering the USA every year, at a cost to the smuggling ring which supported them of an average US$60,000 per person, implying a total 'value' of US$2.1 billion, or about 7 per cent of the estimated world annual value of human trafficking of US$32 billion.[13] The smuggling of human parts is a separate but flourishing trade in which the individual organs of both live and deceased humans can trade for very large sums. The evidence suggests that corneas traded in 2010 for about US$5,000 and livers for US$25,000, contributing to an estimated global trade of US$75 million. Since the majority of final purchasers are in high-income countries, the resultant proceeds are held outside the 'donor's' country.

The international trade in small arms has been well quantified and documented, and in 2012 is likely to lead to a new Arms Trade Treaty. The world's small wars are fed by the arms industries of a variety of countries from the UK to China. The export licences which nominally govern the trade are issued to third parties, and agents who redirect the arms from their nominal destination to the real one. The ultimate customer and user is frequently a non-governmental militia group such as the Somali pirates, the Tamil Tigers, Boko Haram in Nigeria, Hizbollah, FARC, the Taliban, the militias of the eastern DRC, and even Naxalite groups in India. Where payment is made it is likely to be through the multistage trading of natural resources such as minerals and timber. The total value of this trade originating from formal sources but destined for 'informal' purchase is US$3 billion[14] (Chart 3 on p.170), a significant part of which is channelled into secrecy jurisdictions.

Although the products traded by organized crime tend to fall within a limited spectrum, the diversity in the characteristics of groups is huge. In Mexico, in 2010 there were three dominant drug-trafficking cartels and several splinter groups operating smaller patches;[15] in China, of six long-established Triad gangs, five have their base in Hong Kong but may have a total membership of 100,000; in Nigeria, there is a series of ethnically-related gangs, originating principally from the eastern region with strong international linkages, both in drugs and financial fraud; in Albania, there are reported to be 15 dominant family-based mafias, who by 2010 were regarded as responsible for the majority of drugs imported into the EU;[16] in the USA, there are 25 dominant mafia families with good international linkages. A defining and common characteristic is a willingness to break the law and to use violence, and particularly murder, as a basis for establishing their economic power. A common strength is a willingness to use legitimate as well as illegitimate channels to hide and secure wealth: for organized crime the rise of offshore centres and other 'secrecy jurisdictions' has been a boon.

However, in many, if not the majority, of these cases, organized crime is close to individuals in government, and in some cases has effectively taken over the government. There are national contexts in which there is a long-standing history of independent criminal gangs having a heavy influence on the state. Although the Sicilian mafia is the best-known case in western Europe, a similar pattern can be seen with gangs in Shanghai and Fujian (which have their roots in the 1920s and 1930s, and were courted by both the Nationalists and Communists in that era) whose people-smuggling activities necessitate some form of support by officials of the government. In Japan the influence of the *yakuza* gangs has been recognized as crucial for many years. Although *yakuza* are independent entities which frequently break the law and use violence, they may also be co-opted into building projects with a public benefit, or investments in banks with retail outlets. In India, the connections between the 'Mumbai mafia' and state politicians were found by a government-appointed committee to be substantial. An expert on India's black economy, Dr Arun Kumar of the Jawaharlal Nehru University, has commented:

> They [the organized criminals] have established links at various levels of administration and where links do not exist directly, they use money to purchase influence, to get policies suitable to their requirements and subvert those not subject to their needs.[17]

In Russia, the long-serving mayor of Moscow, Yuri Luzhkov, was believed to be closely associated with criminal gangs until obliged to resign by President Medvedev in 2010. The US Ambassador to Russia at the time, John Beyrle, was reported by Wikileaks to have cabled Washington: 'Criminal elements enjoy [protection] that runs through the police, the federal security service, ministry of internal affairs and the prosecutor's office, as well as throughout the Moscow City government bureaucracy.'[18] In the USA the role of mafia families in the politics of New York and Chicago has been recognized over several decades, and not only in books and films. Bobby Kennedy, before the election of his brother to the presidency, was highly active in the investigation on behalf of the Senate's McClellan Committee of links between mafia interests and government, and made this a priority as attorney general.

In these examples, the links between government and organized crime are strong and resilient: formal campaigns to obliterate mafia-type organizations are unlikely to be successful. The experience of Italy, where successive governments have claimed to be fighting the Cosa Nostra in Sicily and the Camorra in Naples, indicates just how resilient mafias can be, with a hydra-like ability to regenerate themselves.

*   *   *   *   *

Somali pirates in the Indian Ocean, the miners and traders in coltan from the DRC, and the architects of wider organized crime share the need to use elements of the formal and legal international system to achieve the kinds of financial gains which they target. At some stage, this requires collaboration with lawyers, traders in the formal sector, or bankers. In the case of both Somalia and the DRC, the opportunities have been generated by the collapse or near collapse of a functioning state. In both cases, the players have been able to take the opportunities open to them by targeted violence and, in the case of the DRC, by collaboration with local political bosses. More broadly, the architects of organized crime in many cases have secured specific concessions by active collaboration with individual politicians, or by holding whole governments to ransom. Organized crime and corruption are frequently comfortable bedfellows.

In most of these cases, organized criminal networks have been able to use the profit of their operations to strengthen their commercial position by buying influence with governments. In India and Japan, organized crime has a stake in formal party politics which can determine political outcomes and can foster a corrupt environment, exactly as Bobby Kennedy feared in the USA. In others, notably Sicily, Bulgaria and Croatia, organized crime has been the driver and has successfully corrupted the state.

4

Victims of Corruption

The multiple effects of the impact of corruption can sometimes be seen from one catastrophic incidence, such as an earthquake, where the construction of buildings was the subject of corruption and their collapse led to thousands of deaths. Less obvious is the way in which multiple acts of corruption may converge on the life of one person, rendering him or her powerless to recover. The following story, which could be set in any country on the east African coast, is fictitious but captures such a tragedy.

At 5.00 a.m. Juma is awakened by the cry of 'maji' from ten-year-old boy water sellers touring the streets with large disused petrol drums full of water. By 5.15 a.m. his wife, Fatma, is standing in the street, clutching the 100 shilling note and a small tin can which she will need to bring two litres of water back to the ramshackle hut in which she tries to feed her five children, not one of whom is over 12. At 5.30 a.m. her bleary-eyed eldest daughter, Amina, just 12, empties enough charcoal from a small gunny bag to begin to light a fire. By 6.00 a.m. Fatma has a pot with 'ugali' – maize meal porridge – nearly at boiling point on the charcoal fire. But there is not enough charcoal to bring the water to boil by the time Amina and Juma must leave the house to try to cram into one of the newly-privatized buses which run a few hundred yards from their house. Packed with 100 others into space designed for 50, they cling together, hoping to avoid having their pockets picked, or, in Amina's case, her bracelet ripped off.

By 7.00 a.m. they have arrived at Amina's school, where her father hopes to beg for an interview with the headmistress to find out whether Amina stands any chance of going to secondary school. He was supposed to be at work by 7.30 a.m. but believes that his employer – a building contractor employing 50 others – won't notice his late arrival. In fact, the headmistress keeps him waiting for an hour, only to indicate that Amina might get a place in secondary school if he can provide the 10,000 shillings (or US$15) which she will need to pay the headmaster of the school in question. Despondent, he leaves by 9.00 a.m. only to reach the building site where he is working by 9.45 a.m. – his foreman notices his late arrival and says that he will recommend that he's sacked if he doesn't pay him 2,000 shillings. Juma promises to pay him when he receives his 5,000 shillings salary at the end of the month – thereby reducing the proportion he is free to spend to 3,000 shillings.

He staggers through the rest of the working day, deciding to save the 50 shillings bus fare by walking the two miles to the edge of the city where his hut stands in a township of similarly precarious construction. When he arrives back at 6 p.m. he sees a scene of desolation, as nearly every house in the square half mile in which he lives has been demolished. In tears, his wife, children and neighbours relate the arrival of the demolition squad from the city council, whose mayor has decreed that this village of illegitimate 'squatters' must be demolished to make way for a 'new development'. While directing the bulldozers, the mayor's representative has spoken of land elsewhere where people can be taken next day by truck in return for a fee of 5,000 shillings per family. Juma, who persuaded his wife to leave their village home in the hills five years earlier, doesn't know where to turn.

This story could be expanded or multiplied almost indefinitely. But it is not just a story about urban deprivation in a developing country. It is also a story about bribery and corruption, and its indirect and direct effects. The first example surrounds water supply: the shallow well and hand pump installed three years ago, intended to supply free water, is no longer in use because its construction was flawed, as the technicians building it sold a key part of the pump to a builder. The supply of charcoal is too little because Juma's family cannot afford to pay more than 100 shillings per bundle – a high price conditioned by the fact that the 'charcoal burners', who sold it to the traders who brought it to the city, had to pay off the forestry officials who were supposed to be controlling the supply of charcoal.[1] The bus fare was exorbitant because the ticket touts were demanding more than the owner of the newly-privatized bus service would ever admit asking, because he had paid a bribe to win the rights for a service on that route. The headmistress was in league with the secondary school headmaster in the business of awarding places, because the purchasing power of her salary had fallen three times in five years and she was now hardly able to feed her own children – unless propped up by under-the-table 'extra income'. Finally, the mayor and his demolition team had been moved to destroy the squatters' settlement because the Minister of Defence had recently purchased a nominal long-term lease over the area in question (which had previously been gazetted as communal land), and had paid US$50,000 to the mayor to demolish the housing on that site. He had financed this partly from a loan of US$1 million from a newly-installed international bank, with which he intended to build housing suitable for middle-class buyers, who would pay 'key money' up front. The international bank had moved into the country only this year as a result of its success in financing a 'commodity offset' deal involving the forward sale of coffee in return for the purchase by the Ministry of Defence of five military helicopters. These were sourced from a supplier willing to falsify the invoice so that 20 per cent of the US$1 million purchase went into the coffers of the party in power.

The story illustrates both the forces which cause corruption to flourish and the ways in which they reinforce each other. The key drivers in this process were: first, the small-scale corruption required by the charcoal burners to buy off the local forestry officials; second, the larger-scale bribing of district officials by the big-scale charcoal traders, who are able to ensure transit and a market in the capital city (a form of organized crime since they are in illegal control of the whole system); third, the sale by an international manufacturer of helicopters who were prepared to manipulate invoices to steer a significant sum into a secret account; and fourth, the deposit of this sum partly in the accounts of the governing party, and partly in the personal accounts of the Minister of Defence and his immediate clique. The defence contractor is making these payment arrangements because his agent has advised him that it 'is the only way to do business here', and he has a sales target to meet. It is the interaction of these forces which makes corruption so difficult to roll back.

The forces which are at work here were caught with great clarity in a report of a commission on 'the state of corruption' in Tanzania, chaired by an ex-prime minister, Joseph Warioba, and commissioned by the incoming president, Benjamin Mkapa, in 1996.[2] It placed some of its key findings on the first page and commented:

> In relation to education: 'Corruption is demanded and given during the registration of children in schools; to enable pupils to pass examinations; to enable students to obtain placement in secondary schools and colleges, transfers and opportunities to repeat a class. Moreover, teachers give bribes in order to be promoted, to be transferred and to be given placements.' In relation to health: 'Patients are forced to offer bribes at hospitals in order to be treated, x-rayed, allocated a bed in the ward or operated upon.' At the level of the leadership: 'Leaders

who are supposed to take important national decisions are bribed by businessmen in order for them to take decisions which are in the interests of those businessmen, interfering in executive decisions like the allocation of plots in areas not permitted by law.'

Perceptions of corruption by the public in Tanzania do not indicate a significant improvement since 1996. In a survey conducted in mid-2011 as part of TI's Global Corruption Barometer, 64 per cent of respondents thought that corruption had become worse over the previous three years, and nearly 50 per cent said they had paid a bribe to one of nine providers of basic services in the previous year.[3]

This chapter will show how these individual experiences undermine the possibility of an improved standard of life, negate human rights, and are part of a pattern which distorts the overall performance of the economy, and undermines the credibility of the political system.

Impact on the individual

The price of tea money

There is now considerable quantified evidence which illustrates the hardship created by this kind of corruption, sometimes known as 'tea money', on the lives of poorer individual citizens in countries where corruption is endemic. This has advanced as a result of surveys at the community, national and regional level. For instance, a survey carried out in 2010 by the chapter of TI in Pakistan reported that 43 per cent of those polled found that they faced a demand for bribes when dealing with local government, 69 per cent when dealing with the judiciary and 84 per cent when dealing with the police; 48 per cent of respondents reported that they faced corruption in order to procure medical services *after* being admitted to the hospital.[4] The average cost of a bribe was very significant for low-income families: US$7 for health services, US$18 for education and US$69 for the judiciary.

In India, one of the keys to accessing services for the very poor is to formally register as being 'below the poverty line' (BPL), and there are 60 million households who nominally qualify for this, and can accordingly acquire registration cards. In practice, nearly half of these, or 27 million, go to richer households which do not qualify, but obtain the cards through bribery. Even when registered, more than one-third of BPL households still had to bribe to get access to the services designed for them.[5]

In the five member countries of the East African Community,[6] bribery is equally rife. In Kenya, a 2002 survey found that urban citizens were paying bribes once every two weeks, which over the year accounted for 15 per cent of their income. A subsequent survey – taken after the apparently reformist government of Mwai Kibaki came to power in 2003 – found a significant improvement, but the figure had returned to the 2002 level by 2006. A survey conducted in 2010 with more than 12,000 members of the public reported that, in citizens dealing with government, bribes had been expected in nearly 40 per cent of cases, and had been paid in a majority of these instances.

In the case of access to the judiciary, in India and Sri Lanka 100 per cent of plaintiffs reported that they had to pay a bribe to the magistrate or judge to get their cases heard. Comparable figures in Latin America for rates of incidence of bribery tend to be lower, but in 2000, across Ecuador, Paraguay and Bolivia, 20 to 30 per cent of contacts, polled by TI chapters, reported that the provision of a public service had required a bribe.

In a 2004 survey by the University of Zambia's Department of Politics, over 80 per cent of the 3,000 households surveyed rated corruption in the public sector as a serious challenge, and 40 per cent said they had been asked for a bribe to obtain a public service or license. Surveys conducted by the World Bank indicate that a poor performance in corruption indices in a given country is linked to higher school dropout rates and higher levels of infant mortality.

The problem is equally serious in Latin America and the Middle East – including north Africa – as in south Asia and Africa below the Sahara. In fact, a worldwide survey – the Global Corruption Barometer – carried out in 2010 found that, in relation to most government services, including the judiciary, the population was more likely to be asked to pay a bribe in the countries of the Middle East and north Africa[7] than in sub-Saharan Africa.

Millennium Development Goals

A useful way to look at the impact of corruption on the poorest people in the globe is by reference to the Millennium Development Goals (MDGs) – a set of 18 targets adopted by the UN in 2000. These identify the most critical factors which keep at least a billion individuals on incomes of less than US$1 per day, and are regarded as a route map for improving their condition. Four of the key goals may be identified as halving the percentage of people suffering from hunger, ensuring that all children complete primary school, reducing the percentage of the population with HIV, and halving the percentage of people without access to safe drinking water and sanitation.

The achievement of each of these goals is frequently threatened by corruption. In the case of hunger, a significant part of those who are regularly hungry – and an easy majority in contexts of civil strife – are fed by emergency food programmes managed by the World Food Programme itself, by its satellite organizations and by independent NGOs such as Oxfam. These programmes are easy victims of corruption, as local government officials skim food from total supplies and divert them to the market for profit. Within a year of taking office in 2005 President Jakaya Kikwete of Tanzania had publicly castigated district commissioners for exactly this crime, specifically in relation to the distribution of rice. In highly politicized contexts, such as Zimbabwe, the dominant party regularly uses the availability of food to maintain or buy in support.

The goal of universal primary school education throughout the world is clear cut, and should be achievable. However, in 2007 a total of 72 million children of primary school age were out of school altogether, of whom half were in sub-Saharan Africa. This is partly because although primary education is supposed to be free almost everywhere, in practice the kind of payments identified in the Warioba report remain widespread. A 2009, seven-country study in Africa[8] showed that 44 per cent of parents surveyed had to pay bribes to head teachers to get their children into school. About the same time, across Asia and Africa, children from poor households were nearly two and a half times more likely to be out of school than rich ones.[9]

Access to water is becoming a scarce resource both at the level of the slums in mushrooming cities and at the level of the village where there may be strong competition from irrigation systems, and from declining reservoirs of ground water. While village water supplies can be the victim of corruption when they fall prey to the self-interest of village elites, an even more severe problem may occur in the big cities of the developing world. Civic regulations frequently prevent state or private water companies making connections to the shanty towns that have grown up on an illegal basis. The private sector water vendors who then supply these settlements through kiosks, pushcarts and yoked buckets are able to charge huge multiples of the cost of water which face families in the formal part of town. In Jakarta, Lima, Manila and Nairobi, the poor pay five to ten times more for water than their wealthy counterparts,[10] a system which is often sustained by informal connivance between vendors and city halls. These arrangements continue to militate against the target of ensuring a 50 per cent reduction in the numbers of people without adequate access to water.

The cumulative impact of corruption on achievement of the MDGs is certainly severe enough to prevent their broad fulfilment by 2015, and in the case of many countries may completely negate their realization.

Health care

The distribution of drugs crucial to public health may itself be the subject of corruption. In the case of HIV/AIDS, huge sums have been committed by donor agencies to the supply of anti-retroviral drugs (ARVs) and associated preventive care, with a major focus on Africa, where in the late 1990s the problem of HIV appeared to be catastrophic. These flows were running at about US$8 billion per year in aggregate in 2004. A significant part of the funding was earmarked to ensure the supply of ARVs at very low prices: a part of this total was diverted to meet the needs of wealthier HIV victims at a relatively attractive price. A Nigerian HIV victim, speaking at an African Union summit in 2005, said:

> The ARVs that come to the AIDS centre are not given to those of us who have come out to declare our status, but to those 'big men' who bribe their way through, and we are left to suffer and scout around for the drug.[11]

Management of the distribution programmes at national level have generally been invested in a combination of NGOs and government. In Kenya, various agents in the national AIDS programme received aid from the UK of US$48 million from 2001 to 2006 for their activities – most of this fell victim to blatant embezzlement by managers of several NGOs, and could never be accounted for. By 2006, only about 10 per cent of the target group of 200,000 were actually receiving the ARVs (out of an estimated 1.4 million Kenyans to have been infected).

In Nigeria, the director general of the National Agency for Food and Drug Administration, Dr Dorothy Akunyili, waged a heroic battle from 2001 to 2008 with both local counterfeit drug manufacturers and wholesale imports of counterfeit drugs from China. She estimated that more than half of both locally-produced drugs and imported drugs are of no value to the consumer, and are potentially harmful. Akunyili braved an assassination attempt and many attacks on her position and reputation in order to continue to clean up drug distribution in Nigeria. While she has had a major impact, many of the drugs in use in Nigeria remain ineffective, while the distribution system remains extremely profitable to those who control it.

In China itself, counterfeit and substandard drugs are a huge issue – and one which led to the execution of the chief executive of the National Drugs Agency (NDA), Zheng Xiaoyu, in 2006. The size of the counterfeit drugs sector in China results from the structure of the industry. Drugs are sourced from over 4,000 local companies whose ability to do business is linked to their access to contracts awarded by hospitals in their own Province, where doctors have a high degree of control over purchases. In this 'grey market', as it is called in China, the scope for conspiracy between the local drug companies and the hospital staff is very high. It has regularly been exposed, but the resulting racket continues to generate sub-standard drugs for the majority of the population, with serious consequences for individuals and public health, resulting in 'extra' deaths of between 200,000 and 300,000 per year.[12]

The production of counterfeit drugs, the resale of drugs targeted to the poor to higher income groups, and the embezzlement of funds deployed in distribution and health care systems, form a context in which the potential benefits to the poor of HIV and related programmes are consistently failing to achieve their goals.

Agriculture

Where forms of corruption are endemic, the impact on productivity at the level of the small farmer can make the difference between bare survival and an adequate living. This is particularly true in the case of irrigation, which is crucial to the 500 million small farmers who need some form of irrigation to secure their output, as well as to the future of food production on a global basis. On a worldwide basis, farmers participating in irrigation systems typically have yields up to three or four times higher than farmers without irrigation. However, water from irrigation schemes involving both large and small dams, with canals and furrows, is frequently sequestered by larger-scale farmers, and particularly those living upstream and closer to the source of supply. In India, managers of large-scale irrigation schemes – which deliver water to many thousands of farmers – often seek the highest potential for raising illicit revenue, and will buy positions to access this revenue. Hence 'canal managers are under pressure to behave almost exactly contrary to the ostensible objectives of their job: instead of reducing water uncertainty they artificially increase it if they wish to maximize bribe revenue'.[13]

Cost overruns in irrigation due to corruption are common. In India, the total excess cost of irrigation projects as a result of corruption has been estimated to be at least 25 per cent. The comptroller and auditor general found that over a seven-year period, under a programme to accelerate the completion of irrigation projects in the state of Orissa, about 32 per cent was lost to various forms of corruption.[14] The proceeds were 'shared between officials and then funnelled upwards through the political system, making it hard to break the collusion'. The experience of Ghana similarly shows how corruption can undermine relatively small-scale irrigation projects. In the fairly low rainfall area of the north east of the country, 29 dams were built between 1999 and 2004, but by 2006 only five were in use as a result of 'construction errors'.

This was in fact mainly due to shortcuts being taken by consultants and contractors, who had to bribe local officials to be awarded the contract, and make a contribution to the ruling political party.[15]

In both rain-fed and small-scale irrigated agriculture, small farmers face agricultural input supply and crop marketing systems which are frequently severely undermined by corruption. In Africa, distributors add margins of up to 100 per cent on fertilizers imported at the world price before delivering them to farmers. There are frequent cases of pesticides being of substandard quality, as with cotton pesticides from China delivered to thousands of two-acre cotton growers in Tanzania in 2010.[16] Crop marketing systems for small farmers – whether state controlled or private – are often rigged to deliver super margins to the marketing boards or companies, generating prices to farmers which are well below those justified by the international market. Agricultural credit should be an integral part of delivering improved inputs to farmers: many agricultural credit organizations in the poorest countries have experienced successive collapses, as lending to politically favoured customers (including co-operative organizations) has spiralled out of control. As a consequence, the world's 2 billion small farmers are severely restricted in their ability to increase output by a partially corrupt input supply, marketing and credit system.

The Warioba report in Tanzania encapsulated the ways in which citizens on very low incomes can be completely hemmed in by everyday small-scale corruption. The story of Ali Juma showed how this can be manifested in the life of one vulnerable family. Corruption impacts on the individual, and may destroy a family's livelihood, through the combined effect of the cost of small-scale bribery, the distortion of poverty relief programmes, the absence of recourse to justice, the cash cost of 'free' education, the failure of counterfeit medical drugs, and an agricultural supply system rigged against the small farmer. This is a truth which is little understood and needs far more widespread acceptance. It consists of an 'alternative reality' to that supposed by a western observer: the idea that institutions exist to serve the public is reversed. All those institutions which we might assume to operate in the service of the public, as a resource paid for by the taxation system, actually function on the opposite premise – that the user pays. However, he or she pays not to the state or to an agency which is nominally providing the service, but to an individual functionary who has real control of the service. The millions of individuals confronted with this reality find it difficult, if not impossible, to escape from it.

Wider economic impact

What are the real costs of this situation, manifested at the level of the individual, to the wider economy? There are both direct and indirect costs which vary by country, both in their overall impact and in their relative importance. In a range of countries – particularly in Africa – corruption has had a very negative effect on both the growth of income and its distribution. In others – particularly in east Asia – it has existed in parallel with high growth rates and a remarkable reduction in poverty levels (though not in the distribution of income). Not surprisingly, a number of large and important countries, such as Indonesia and Brazil, fall between these two extremes.

What explains these differences? The key question is whether the corruption by one means or another activates local resources, or leaves them idle, or erodes them (such as in the corrupt exploitation of natural resources). The related question is whether the financial gain is held outside the country in question, or 'invested', directly or indirectly, within it. In the east Asian 'Tigers',[17] whose economies leaped ahead in the 1980s and 1990s, a high level of corruption was consistent with a high level of investment in local resources. Professor Mushtaq Khan has argued persuasively that the investment strategies of those who acquired the fruits of corruption were, by and large, conducive to growth,[18] though with a large difference between countries depending on their political complexion. In most parts of Africa, of which Nigeria is a dramatic example, a much higher proportion of corruptly gained assets were held overseas. Many countries fell between these extremes, and to that extent the corruption they experienced had a mixed impact at the national level. This has been effectively captured by Dr Ha-Joon Chang of Cambridge University: 'The economic consequences of corruption depend on which decisions the corrupt act affects, how the bribes are used by the recipients and what would have been done with the money had there been no corruption.'[19] One of the major costs common across this spectrum is the presence of a 'black' or 'shadow' economy in which a large part of economic transactions are unrecorded. Even in relatively high-income economies where corruption is rife, such as Russia, the shadow economy may account for close to half of the total activity. The existence of high levels of corruption in these cases serves to reinforce the shadow economy as enterprises shy away from the formal system, where formal tax rates may be even higher than costs in the informal system. The resilience of the shadow economy and its implications for corruption are discussed further in Chapter 9.

Recognizing that the impact of corruption varies, we look first at national contexts where the consequences of corruption have clearly been disastrous – at least for those in the lowest income groups. In these cases, the national costs of corruption are not difficult to identify. They include, first, inflated costs for large-scale projects commissioned by governments, which result in both a poorly performing asset (such as a road, or drainage system) or an unjustified expenditure of scarce foreign exchange (where governments have chosen a foreign supplier over a domestic one because the associated bribes outweighed local bribes). This is a cost to the exchequer, and to the public through the increase in taxes required to finance these extra charges.

The benefits of attacking these forms of grand corruption in large-scale contracts became clear as a result of a relatively successful anti-corruption campaign in Milan in the mid-1990s. In this campaign, Antonio Di Pietro, a senior investigating magistrate in Milan, and his colleagues elsewhere sought and obtained the right to interrogate more than 4,000 civil servants, many of whom were prosecuted and found guilty. The impact of this campaign was a reduction of more than 50 per cent in the capital cost of city rail links under construction, of 57 per cent in the cost of 1 km of subway and of 60 per cent in the budget for a new airport.[20]

Second, the costs include a poorly functioning set of social services – most importantly including health and education – the value of which is gravely diminished and may be hardly accessible to the poor, as already described in this chapter. Third, they have included a distorted privatization process, where state-owned assets are sold to private buyers, including existing management teams, on a corrupt basis, often ensuring that the purchased assets will be managed in ways which maximize the externalization of income and even capital value.

Fourth, they include the recognition that corruption is a determining factor in economic management, and can undermine the whole basis of a competently managed tax collection system. If large- and small-scale businesses are aware that tax officials are both creaming off the system and offering arbitrary deals – often in cash – to tax payers, their reluctance to pay is magnified. A low revenue take, in relation to payments due, establishes a pattern which is very difficult to reverse. In India, in 2008 the underpriced sale of 120 new licenses for 2G mobile phone systems, on a corrupt basis, resulted in the payment of royalties of US$30 billion less than could have been achieved.[21]

In contexts such as this, the additional burden of arbitrary embezzlement can further worsen the situation. Kenya's Anglo Leasing scam, discussed in Chapter 8, had a probable cost to the exchequer of US$600 million, or more than 15 per cent[22] of government expenditure in any one year; the total sums stolen by Abacha in Nigeria amounted to about 5 per cent of GDP[23] during his four-year period as head of state, a similar figure to that attributed to Fujimori during his 11-year presidency in Peru.[24] These losses are on a sufficient scale to have a major impact on economic growth and investment in human capital.

The indirect costs to the economy can be equally, if not more, serious. There is a wide, if not uniform, consensus today that a form of the free market system is more efficient than an economy controlled by the state. The functioning of the system requires in turn that it is not distorted by corruption. However, where bribery can determine the outcome of public procurement, or a specific tariff exemption can benefit one importer at the expense of others; where a city centre site can be allocated to the most expensive bidder who has bribed the right minister; where the defence budget can be inflated by corrupt deals with international suppliers; or where organized crime can determine contract allocations, the market does not reflect supply and demand or outcomes that generate a general public benefit. Where markets are distorted in this way, decisions taken by both large- and small-scale business, will reflect this situation and compound it. The existence of a corrupt tax-collection system will cause enterprises and individuals to minimize tax payments and settle for the corruption of tax officials. At the level of very small enterprises, entrepreneurs will tend to retain a position in the informal economy where there is little regulation, or where the regulators such as city officials can be bought off for small sums in cash.

Where there are relatively high levels of corporation tax, or where tax systems are corrupt, or where there have been other arbitrary costs, companies engaged in international trade – whether local or foreign – engage in 'mispricing' in order to recapture some of the income they consider they have lost to corruption, or simply to take the opportunity to achieve super profits. The essential objective of mispricing is to transfer profits from a sale in one country where tax rates are deemed too high, or deposits too risky, or the exchange risk too unfavourable, to another location where tax rates are low or non-existent, even if these are ultimately to be transferred over time to a higher tax rate regime. This is achieved by either inflating the cost of imported inputs, or deflating the value of exports so that taxable revenues in the host country are minimized. Mispricing may be legitimately classified as a form of corruption, since it undermines the public interest on the basis of pricing strategy which can never be publicly defended and which withdraws resources from the host economy. Its effects are further discussed in Chapter 7. In China and Russia, outflows attributable to forms of mispricing have proved to be sufficiently serious to be damaging even to these huge economies. The Centre for Global Financial Integrity estimates that illicit outflows from China due to mispricing from 2000 to 2008 averaged US$240 billion per year (on a total official export trade valued at US$1.428 trillion).[25] In the case of Russia, it estimates an average annual outflow of illicit funds of US$47 billion for the same period.

In all these cases, the costs of corruption to the state are grave. They can be illustrated clearly in the extreme case of Nigeria. From 1980 to 2000, Nigeria's gross oil revenue exceeded US$600 billion, representing about US$300 per head of the population per year. Yet between 1975 and the year 2003, Nigeria experienced per capita GDP growth of –0.5 per cent per year. Today, over 70 per cent of Nigeria's population – or about 80 million people – live below the poverty line of US$1 per day. Outside the majestic buildings of the capital city of Abuja, there is very little to show for Nigeria's oil wealth.

Is there a cost to corruption for those countries which have grown rapidly in spite of it? South Korea, China and India are cases in point. In South Korea, in its most rapid phase of growth from the 1960s to the 1980s, the government of General Park Chung-hee used the already established *chaebols* and smaller companies to develop specific products using international technology and carefully targeted tariff policy. Park Chung-hee died in 1979 but his legacy was a GDP growth rate of 9.4 per cent from 1980 to 1990. However, as the economy became more complex, his successors, Generals Chun Doo-hwan and Roh Tae-woo, were increasingly unable to control the flows of corrupt payments between officials and Korea's leading companies, to which they were a party. From 2000 to 2008 Korea's annual growth rate slowed to 4.5 per cent per year. Corruption remained a major issue in public life and a cause of immense disquiet.

China's phenomenal growth rate since the early 1990s has been based on a pattern of growth which has in some cases enhanced resources, and in others undermined them. However, value added in manufacturing has clearly outweighed, for the time being, the depletion of resources such as land and water, while forms of corruption, mainly informally licensed by the CCP, have so far held the political system together. The Party's control system has operated at both regional and central level, and so, in spite of China's size and its huge population, corruption has served as a means of securing loyalty, a factor which may change in the second decade of the twenty-first century. Even in this context, one of the key weaknesses in the system has been the extent of uncontrolled, private capital flight, estimated by the Central Bank itself at US$124 billion from 1993 to 2001[26] quite apart from illicit flows due to mispricing, most of which has corrupt origins. These funds could have been much more effectively invested inside China.

India's rapid growth of more than 8 per cent in the first decade of this century is almost double that from 1980 to 1995, yet corruption is an even more serious problem today than in

1995. Growth has been driven by private corporate investment with an important contribution from new foreign direct investment. But this growth has not led to a smaller 'shadow economy' which is now estimated to account for close to more than 50 per cent of real GDP[27] and is both a principal channel for corruption and a driver in the process, facilitating corruption at many different levels. Growth of this kind has done little to offset the corruption experienced by many at the local and individual level, as discussed earlier in this chapter, which in some states led to violent opposition by Naxalite or Maoist groups.

The cases of high-growth Asian countries, which have lived with high levels of corruption, do not suggest that corruption is a phenomenon which is irrelevant to economic development, or that it will diminish as economic growth steps up. Rather, they suggest that 'growth with corruption' generates a range of tensions, many triggered by increasing inequality, which feed into political systems with outcomes ranging from violent resistance from the marginalized poor (as in India), to the defensive dominance of a single political party (as in China), to very rapid regime turnover (as in South Korea). This is a high and unnecessary price to pay. The consequences of corruption for economic growth are discussed in more detail in Chapter 9.

Environmental dimension

Ashok Khosla, a delegate to an international anti-corruption conference in 2010, commented: 'The bounty of nature is limited, greed is unlimited.' Corruption is a key factor undermining some of the critical determinants in reversing environmental degradation, and hence accentuating global warming. This is at its most dramatic in the forestry sector. The public benefits of forestry are derived from its role as standing timber: the protection of watersheds, the sequestration of carbon, and protection of biodiversity. Once logged, timber becomes a purely private gain, and worldwide experience shows that it is in the interests of many private loggers, public companies and political elites to accelerate the logging process regardless of regulation. There is a remarkable range of countries of which this is true: in Canada, violations of logging regulations have been detected in 55 per cent of areas scheduled for protection; in Brazil, a recent Presidential Commission concluded that more than 70 per cent of forestry management plans did not comply with the law; and in Cameroon, at least one-third of timber cut is 'undeclared'.[28] These figures exclude the creeping deforestation which is characteristic of savannah woodland in much of Africa, where freelance charcoal burners cut back light woodland more or less without hindrance, or after having bought off forest guards. Deforestation of this kind may account for as much as 3 per cent per year of existing forest resources in east Africa, a fatally high figure.

However, larger-scale deforestation is the domain of big local and foreign corporations. Indonesia is one of the countries with a huge forest resource which is prey to the impact of corruption. The total annual value of output from its forestry sector is about US$6.6 billion, of which only about US$1.5 billion[29] is the subject of legally gained permits, even after the fall of Suharto. It is safe to say that the whole industry is controlled by corrupt deals, which are orchestrated primarily by collaboration between local and foreign timber companies and individuals close to government.

As traded timber moves into the international markets, its illegal origins become more obscure and are finally eliminated. The American Forest and Paper Association commissioned a study in 2005 which found that 17 per cent of all uncut timber traded internationally was from illegal sources. There have been partially successful moves to promote the adoption of systems of certification which would confirm that timber felled has been balanced by new plantings (but not that is necessarily untainted by corruption). The industry in the developed world has not been keen to see an anti-corruption criterion integrated into certification. In fact, in the USA, the timber and timber-processing industry is the third largest contributor amongst public affairs committees to party political campaigns.

In some cases the conjunction of factors described here can lead to the total degradation of a state. Thus, a combination of highly corrupt procurement procedures, the diversion of budgetary funds from social expenditure, irresponsible foreign investment, and the accelerated degradation of natural resources can create the circumstances for a 'failed state'. Examples of this in the recent past include Sierra Leone, Liberia and the Democratic Republic of the Congo (DRC). As a result of a huge domestic and international effort, the first two are beginning to climb out of this status, but at a time when other candidates (such as Sudan) are being described in this way. While corruption plays only a part in these extreme outcomes, it is a very significant factor, and is typically addressed too late by the outside world.

Overall impact

On a worldwide basis, the prime victims of corruption are the poor, whose prospect of social, educational and economic advance are directly impacted by the corruption of both local and national elite groups. While corruption remains a major force it is inconceivable that targets such as the Millennium Development Goals in low-income countries will be achieved on a universal basis. In a broader sense countries in which corruption is endemic will fail to achieve the kinds of economic growth which generate recognizable public and private progress for its citizens in a context of political stability.

Similarly, public goals embodied in environmental targets will continue to be undermined as long as corporate and state interests connive at the dismantling of the 'global commons' both on sea and land in ways which fatally undermine 'Kyoto' and 'Copenhagen' targets. The impact of corruption is profound at the level of livelihoods, national economic progress, the environment, and the credibility of the political system. Its potential – in different forms – to undermine the global progress is immense, and is achievable, but remains elusive.

5

Constant Values, Changing Standards

Although the last 20 years have seen a big and increased recognition of corruption as a world problem, it is hardly a new phenomenon. This chapter shows how each of the major religious traditions has recognized corruption as an issue, and how resistance to corruption is recognized as an ethical goal on a constant basis, though one which is only seldom incorporated into the political and social standards of the day.

Bobby Kennedy made his name as a young advocate who successfully identified, through Senate hearings, the mafia links of two of the most powerful union bosses in American history: Dave Beck and Jimmy Hoffa of the Teamsters' Union, which in the 1950s had a membership of 1.5 million and dominated the trucking and related industries. Having cut his teeth working for Senator Joe McCarthy in 1953 at the age of 27, Kennedy's first real success came as Chief Counsel to Senator McClellan's Committee on Improper Activities in the Labour and Management Fields. Investigating the Teamsters on behalf of this Committee, Kennedy became convinced that the Union was infiltrated by organized crime and that both Dave Beck and his successor, Jimmy Hoffa, used collaboration with the mafia to expand the Union's reach and to acquire property and income for themselves.

Kennedy was instrumental in securing a jail sentence for Beck in 1957 and then turned his attention to Hoffa. He believed that

> *Hoffa had shifted democratic procedures within the Union, had ordered the beating and very possibly the murder of union rebels, had misused union funds to the amount of at least $95 million, had taken money and other favours from employers to promote personal business deals, had bought gangsters to consolidate his control and had tampered with the judicial process in order to escape prosecution.[1]*

But for Kennedy the issues went beyond this. As a believer in the American system, Kennedy despised Hoffa for his conviction that American society was irredeemably corrupt. He feared that organized crime was spreading its tentacles from the underworld into labour relations, business and politics and that this reflected the 'moral sickness of a greedy society'.[2]

But Hoffa and his close associates were tough nuts to crack and by 1959 Kennedy resigned from the position of Counsel to the McClellan Committee but took the time to write a book explaining his case: 'The Enemy Within'. Appointed Attorney General in 1962 in his brother John Kennedy's cabinet he acted on the conviction that organized crime was a bigger threat to the American political system than Communism and returned to the issue of organized crime and its political tentacles.

Hoffa was convicted in 1964 on both bribery and fraud charges and sentenced to 13 years in jail in 1967.[3] Kennedy's campaign was a courageous attempt to show how the political system had become infiltrated by corrupt Union barons and how they could be confronted. But in essence it was a vindication of the justice system, which had since the 1920s for the most part side-stepped the issue of organized crime and its political influence. The fact that although the mafia in the USA is alive, its

power is much less than 50 years ago is a tribute to Kennedy and
the effect that one catalyst can have in seeing that a judicial system
is effective – a true alignment of standards with ethics.

There is no ethical tradition which would have countenanced
Hoffa's use of the mafia to enforce control of his Union, given
its association with both violence and bribery. Yet, in a country
which considered itself to have a fair and ethical judicial system,
actual standards had fallen well behind public ethics. This
contradiction between ethics and standards runs through the
history of corruption, with ethics sometimes breaking through
to repair or disrupt the standards of the day. The intrusion
of ethics has certainly not always led to an improvement in
standards, but has served as a reference point, the content
of which is seldom disputed.

The basis of ethics has always been primarily religious, and
the religious traditions have been remarkably clear on the issue
of corruption, and especially on the use of bribery to distort
justice. No prophet or philosopher has argued that the
distortion of justice by the bribing of judges is legitimate. In
fact, there is religious consensus in the opposite direction:
corruption always implies a betrayal of trust by its beneficiaries
at the expense of others. In the Judaic tradition, after God had
given Moses the Ten Commandments he went on to prescribe
how those who were to rule Israel should govern. In relation to
judges God decreed: 'You must not distort justice; you must not
show partiality; and you must not accept bribes, for a bribe
blinds the eyes of the wise and subverts the cause of those who
are in the right.'[4]

The teaching of Confucius in about 500 BC was concerned
with establishing the equivalence between the family and the
state – arguing that the same morality which governed the rules
of a paternalistic family should also guide the state. The
position of Confucius was determined by the fact that he had
resigned as the most senior official at the court of the Duke of

Lu on an issue arising from the corruption of the Prince (his acceptance of a gift of 'dancing girls'). Confucius asserted: 'When the ruler's personal conduct is correct his government is effective without the issuing of orders. If his personal conduct is not correct, he may issue orders but they will not be followed.' He always acknowledged that governments could become corrupt: at this point the moral obligation of the public to support their leaders could fall away, and they would have a right to overthrow it. The Confucian tradition clearly indicated that the contract between citizen and state can legitimately be ended if the Prince behaves corruptly.

Hindu scriptures have an explicit view on corruption, derived both from the 3,000-year-old *Vedas*, akin to the Biblical psalms, and from the later epic legends of the Ramayana and Mahabharata. Corruption is a major subject of the *Vedas*. One such verse refers to corruption in the following way:

> Knowing the secret of possessing wealth, the demon of vagrancy earns riches and carries it off to himself. Let both his wives – greed and luxury – bathe in the deep sea. O resplendent Lord, may he with his wives be drowned in the depth of that river of luxury.[5]

The *Sam Veda* mentions 99 sources of corruption and evil, and calls the former a disease which feeds on itself and makes the power of the human soul weaker and weaker.

In the Indian epic of the Ramayana, the demon King Ravana has ten heads, of which nine represent 'evil and corruption' and only the tenth represents soul, spirit and divine nature. Only when the nine are cut off by Lord Rama can virtue be restored. The Mahabharata depicts a great war for control of the state in which the 100 dissolute sons of the blind king Dhritarashtra are pitted against the five noble Pandava princes, led by Arjun, who triumph as a result of a bloody battle. On the eve of the battle, Arjun, the leading Pandava prince, has a dialogue (as recorded in the Bhagavad Gita) with the god

Krishna as to whether the forthcoming slaughter on both sides can justify the destruction of a dissolute and corrupt kingdom – and concludes that the elimination of so much evil does justify it.

The Islamic attitude to corruption is heavily influenced by the fact that within 100 years of the death of Muhammad his followers were ruling a huge land mass stretching from Spain to Afghanistan. Morality was not only a question of ethics but also a basis for government. For this purpose, the Muslims sought to draw on the *hadith*, or the sayings of Muhammad recorded after his death. One of the key leaders of this early expansion of Islam, the second Caliph, Umar ibn al-Khattab (634–44), used to record the assets of officials at the time of their appointment, and confiscate partly or wholly whatever they added while in office on suspicion of benefiting from a public appointment.[6] One of his successors, Caliph Umar ibn Abd al-Aziz (717–20), ruled:

> I am of the view that the ruler should not trade. It is also not lawful for the officer to trade in the area of his office because when he involves himself in trade he inadvertently misuses his office in his interest and to the detriment of others, even if he does not like to do so.[7]

In the Islamic tradition, corruption is clearly understood as the opposite of 'truth' or 'honesty'; the words used to describe it are very negative and imply a specifically immoral act which will ultimately attract God's retribution. Many of the 'reformation' movements which have taken place within Islam have had the objective of 'purifying' government of all forms of corruption and building or re-building a 'moral society'.

In summary, the Judaic tradition interprets corruption as the subversion of justice, the Confucian tradition emphasizes the need to preserve the personal morality of the prince, Hindu teachings stress the constant battle between corruption as a danger to the state and the creation of a virtuous society, and the focus of Islam is on corruption as a threat to a disinterested leadership. As societies have struggled with corruption – especially the corruption of justice – these ethical values have served as an unchanging reference point, however abused by the standards of the day. Five cases in history demonstrate this consistency.

Marcus Tullius Cicero

In the last two centuries of the Roman republic, when a Senate elected by an Italy-wide franchise was a reality, there was a long-running battle lasting more than 120 years over how to ensure that elections were not influenced by bribery. Legislation passed in 181 BC and toughened in 151 BC was designed to clamp down on expensive dinners and gifts by wealthy candidates, and even set specific spending limits. In 139 BC, a secret ballot was introduced to eliminate the link between bribery and the vote. It was not enough: by 81 BC the penalty of a ten-year exclusion from politics for electoral bribery was carried.

It was this Senate which heard the case that Cicero brought against Verres, the highly corrupt Governor of Sicily in 70 BC, who had seized a range of valuable statues, paintings and floor mosaics from public places and private houses. However, the charge that Cicero used to prosecute Verres was that he had subverted the course of justice. In the build-up to the case, Verres had attempted to preclude Cicero's right to prosecute, for which he had to be elected an *aedile*, by paying out 'ten chests of Sicilian money' to the representatives of voters. This was the background to Cicero's later move as Consul in 63 BC to introduce even tougher electoral reform laws, designed to curb the three evils of exaggerating a candidate's popularity by greeting and following him from his house to the Forum, reserving blocks of seats for public games, and sponsoring private games and large-scale public dinners. The following year the penalty of a ten-year exclusion from politics was extended to exile.

But the fine line between fighting corruption and the priority of politics was soon in evidence, as standards triumphed over ethics. In 62 BC, Cicero defended his political ally, the consul elect Murena, against infringing the new legislation. Cicero's arguments reflect those subsequently used to defend corrupt electoral practice in many contexts: Murena had not himself reserved the blocks of seats at the games; the crowd which accompanied him from his house to the Senate had not been hired but was spontaneous; and payments made to the voting colleges should be seen as an integral part of the system. The legal arguments proved strong enough for Murena to be acquitted. Cicero's career had shown that the corruption issue in Roman electoral politics remained very much alive, that there was an ethical system to which citizens could respond, and that it could be used to promote a career but was easily compromised in the defence of a political ally.

Martin Luther

The career of Martin Luther, who challenged the power of the Vatican – the centre of the Roman Catholic Church – laying the basis for the Protestant Church, was an epic struggle between standards and ethics. Luther had intended to qualify as a lawyer but was diverted by a near death experience in a lightning storm. He became a monk and went on a pilgrimage to Rome, but was shocked by the pomp and splendour and emptiness of the faith, recognizing its financial origins. Equally importantly, he could see that Pope Leo X was himself at the centre of the system of indulgences since this was critical to funding the continued building of the Basilica of St Peter in the Vatican. Returning to Germany, he became a lecturer in theology at the University of Wittenberg, teaching Paul's epistles to the Romans – a text which sets out Christian teaching in its most basic form.

By 1517, Luther had identified 95 propositions which together constituted a grand indictment of the whole system of indulgences. Proposition 27 states: 'They preach only human doctrines who say that as soon as the money clinks into the money chest, the soul flies out of purgatory.' Proposition 28 says: 'It is certain that when money clinks in the money chest, greed and avarice can be increased; but when the Church intercedes, the result is in the hands of God alone.' After posting the 95 propositions in Latin on the door of the church in Wittenberg, Luther wrote three more pamphlets arguing for the restructuring of the Church on a more egalitarian basis. In the pamphlet of August 1520 he concluded: 'It seems as though canon law were instituted solely for the purpose of making a great deal of money.'

Luther's claims were cleverly phrased as matters for debate, and in themselves echoed criticisms of the Church which had been alive for well over a century. Their novelty lay not only in their comprehensiveness but also in the rapid speed of their dissemination all over Europe, now facilitated by the printing press. Within two weeks of the translation of the original Propositions into German in January 1518, they were available in printed form throughout the German-speaking states and further abroad. This constituted a major blow to the Church, describing it as a corrupt institution culminating in Luther's excommunication at the Diet of Worms in 1521. This was a spark which triggered the founding and accelerated growth of Protestant churches in Denmark, Sweden and Germany, and set the context for the establishment of a Protestant Church in England. Luther's appeal to an ethical tradition which rejected both hypocrisy and embezzlement at the expense of the public triggered a major change in standards – at least for the time being.

Francis Bacon

In the England of James I, in the opening years of the sixteenth century, the Lord Chancellor himself, Francis Bacon, pleaded guilty to taking bribes on a huge scale, though only after months of continuous denial. King James himself had been adamant that judges must be kept 'free from corruption'. On being appointed Lord Chancellor in 1618, Bacon declared that 'justice is a sacred thing', a reaffirmation of ethical values. But three years later he was involved in a series of controversial cases, pressed with great effect by Edward Coke (his rival at the Bar), which aroused the scrutiny and eventually the condemnation of parliament.

In 1621, John Churchill, who ran the Court of Chancery, submitted a report to the House of Lords entitled 'Bribes and Abuses in Chancery', which fingered Bacon as the recipient of bribes. The Commons, thoroughly encouraged by Coke, were in no doubt that bribery was a criminal act under common law and commissioned their own report. As other cases were raised by offending litigants – who had no problem in admitting that they had been bribe payers – the House of Lords established no less than three committees to hear each case, and to examine whether the unquestioned payments constituted a bribe or a 'gratuity' (a payment which did not influence the outcome of the case but speeded up the verdict).

Bacon's response was ingenious: in 11 out of 12 cases he did not dispute the payment but claimed that they had either not influenced his judgment or – if that were not true – they did not involve the interests of the Crown. This was a feeble attempt to build a case based on ethics, but which acknowledged that the interests of the political power of the day were the first consideration. However, within a few weeks, by 24 April 1621, he had made a modest confession, admitting all wrong-doing but justifying his behaviour as typical of 'the vices of the day'. In response, Coke uncovered three cases where judges had been executed for accepting bribes, and parliamentary opinion remained unsatisfied. On 25 April Bacon submitted a full confession to the Lords, which began 'I do plainly and ingenuously confess that I am guilty of corruption', and went on to confess guilt in relation to 28 charges, derived from 21 cases, and begged for mercy – though continuing to plead extenuating circumstances. Here there was no question that ethics had triumphed.

The 'guilty' verdict of the Lords was clear, but the punishment less severe than might have been expected: Bacon was fined £40,000, imprisoned at the King's Leisure, and banned from holding office again and from parliamentary election. But in the eye of the King this was too severe for a faithful servant: he restricted the prison sentence to five days in the Tower, the other specific penalties were rescinded and, incredibly enough, he was not only assisted in the payment of the fine[8] by the King but allowed to pay it out to individuals of his own choice.

The Bacon case, and the close involvement of King James I, shows how important it was for a king (accessing the English throne from Scotland and 13 years later still uneasy on it) to promise to run a corruption-free judiciary. Bacon, as the newly-appointed Lord Chancellor, could see how important it was to be seen to mirror this, but in practice subverted the ideal of justice on a spectacular scale. The King's favourite, George Villiers, estimated that Bacon had taken £25,000 a year in gifts, or ten times his annual salary.[9] The conclusion of the Commons report was that Bacon's Chancery was 'an inextricable labyrinth wherein resideth such a Minotaur, as gormandiseth the liberty of all subjects whatsoever'.

Although many witnesses in the cases investigated admitted paying a bribe, and complained that it had been unproductive, the key outcome of the process was to re-assert that an uncorrupt judiciary was essential to a stable state. It also showed how this ethical value can easily be compromised by standards: in this case, the extent to which a publicly held anti-corruption stance can disguise corruption, the extent to which participants in the system (in this case the staff of chancery) can be co-opted, that systemic bribe payers can rapidly flip to becoming critics of the system in which they have participated, and that the establishment of the day will be deeply reluctant to bring down its leading servants.

Juan and Ulloa: corruption in Spanish America

In 1749 a remarkable report was presented to the Bourbon King Fernando VI of Spain, who was seeking a reform of the Spanish imperial system. Although entitled 'Discourse and Political reflections upon the Kingdoms of Peru', it was in fact a devastating analysis of a state of endemic corruption in the colonial states of Peru and Ecuador. Authored by Jorge Juan and Antonio de Ulloa, who had just completed a sojourn of more than ten years in these states, it was written in parallel with a more positive travelogue. However, unlike the travelogue published in 1748, the 'Discourse' was published only 78 years later in 1826, partly as an explanation of the dazzling speed with which Spain's colonial empire had turned into a set of independent countries. The legacy of the state of affairs described by Juan and Ulloa was to set the stage for the unrelenting persistence of corruption in South America's new dawn.

The Discourse is not only remarkable in describing the different forms of corruption at work, but also in exploring their origin. It argues that the spiritual mandate which, it was frequently argued, upheld the Spanish imperial regime had collapsed. Relevant forms of corruption included illicit trade (in economies where the state sought a high degree of control over commerce), the tyrannical government of local officials (*corregidores*) and the Church hierarchy over the Indian communities whose interests they were supposed to safeguard, the evasion of laws by the white 'settler' population, and the widespread misuse of powers by more senior government officials up to and including the level of viceroy. Anthony McFarlane, a historian of hispanic Latin America, has commented: 'The catalogue of corrupt practices listed in the Discourse is so unremitting that it seems to embrace every simple abuse of public office for private gain that was possible within the administrative system of ancien regime monarchy.'[10]

At the apex of the system were viceroys whose activities reflected the interests of their own extended families and their interest in accumulating large personal fortunes while holding office. Juan and Ulloa commented:

> Those governing Peru are presented with the pleasant prospect of absolute authority growing ever larger and more ostentatious, of precious metals to satisfy their lust and greed, and of people who ingratiate, enrich, and shower praise on one least deserving. These three factors are the poison which chokes and destroys good government in these kingdoms.[11]

A large part of Spain's rationale for holding her South American colonies was the supply of gold, and commissions derived from this easily found their way to vice-regal hands. Further, the sale of office by viceroys for personal enrichment created a classic multiplication effect: following the purchase of office it was essential for the incumbents to both recoup their outlay and capitalize on it. This was a system which fed on itself, reinforced by the law and effectively blessed by the Church.

The proposals for change of Juan and Ulloa had a modest short-term impact: the Spanish King Carlos III initiated reforms which were based on them in 1759, though he was ultimately unsuccessful in bringing most of the recommended reforms into place. However, the Discourse had described a regime that was highly inefficient, and of decreasing value to the Spanish crown, but based its central case on the collapse of an ethical mandate in the colonies.

* * * * *

In each of these cases – from Rome to Peru – a common factor has been a context of 'distress', if not crisis, in which individuals have taken action in the courts (Cicero), challenged a deeply entrenched institution such as the Church (Luther), exposed a powerful Lord Chancellor (as Coke did with Bacon), or laid bare a crippling gap in governance (Juan and Ulloa). In these cases the individuals who were a catalyst to the process were able to secure support from some members of a small but powerful elite, close to those with real power. Cicero spoke to his fellow senators, but used the mob outside the Senate building to pressure those inside. Luther and his supporters ensured that his Propositions were circulated in printed form with extraordinary speed. Coke played to both the Lords and the Commons in the English Parliament, creating a crescendo of opposition to Bacon. Juan and Ulloa succeeded in co-opting the support of King Carlos III but had only limited impact because the crisis in the Spanish colonies was so grave. But the nineteenth century was to see a new dimension in fighting corruption: the modern newspaper.

Boss Tweed and the 'ring'

The contradiction between ethics and standards became a subject of increased debate as the suffrage was extended in most European countries and the USA in the nineteenth century. The career of 'Boss' Tweed in the politics of New York in the 1860s captures this conflict. William Marcy Tweed was the son of Scottish immigrants. By the time he was 20, New York was entering one of its most dynamic phases: the population tripled to a million between 1840 and 1870. All political parties fought hard for the support of the immigrants who poured off the ships from Europe. Tweed hitched his political star to Tammany Hall, a political club competing with other clubs for the support of immigrant communities on behalf of the Democratic Party.

Tweed was elected to the US House of Representatives in 1852, aged 29, but served for only two years and was not reselected by his Party. In spite of this setback, in the course of the 1860s he became the dominant figure in New York's Democratic politics. His dominance of Tammany Hall enabled him to implement a strategy with two key components: first, building a co-ordinated and highly effective political machine; and second, embarking on the redesign of the city and a public works programme which still defines the layout of New York. Both of these success stories depended on the accumulation of large 'war chests' through forms of corruption – which became the standard by which Tweed operated.

This successful political manipulation was financed through a bold programme of public works, masterminded by Tweed's 'ring': including the mayor, the comptroller and the county treasurer. Tweed himself was Commissioner for Public Works. Their projects included a huge network of mid-town drains and gas pipes, and the Brooklyn Bridge. The ring regularly bought land on which public works were scheduled to be constructed, on the basis of insider information, and sold it at a massive profit to the City. In addition, the ring established a commission rate of 15 per cent, to be paid by contractors to themselves as individuals.

Ultimately, it was the sheer scale of the consequent personal enrichment which brought down Tweed. A whistleblower, who was a former co-conspirator, leaked incriminating records to George Jones of New York's *Times* newspaper, which declined a bribe of US$5 million to suppress the story. A hard-hitting exposure and series of editorials followed which ensured that a prosecution was inevitable. But it proved difficult to pin a straight corruption charge on Tweed.

In 1873 he was found guilty of neglect and dishonesty in examining the accounts of the City – a breach of statutory duty in his role as a member of the City audit committee. In this case the crime of bribery escaped prosecution, but Tweed was sent to jail for 12 years. He managed to bribe the prison authorities to the extent of escaping to Cuba – and taking a ship to Spain where he was promptly arrested and returned to the USA. He died in jail in 1878, just after his 55th birthday.

At his trial, Tweed offered the classic corruptor's defence:

> The fact is New York politics were always dishonest – long before my time. There never was a time when you couldn't buy the Board Aldermen. A politician coming forward takes things as they are. This population is too hopelessly split up into races and factions to be governed by universal suffrage, except by bribery of patronage or corruption.[12]

In fact, Tweed and his associates had enriched themselves on a very large scale, initially with the intention of both buying political support and acquiring personal enrichment. Their activities coincided with the rise of a media prepared to tackle corruption head on and to call for prosecution, and a judiciary prepared to tackle corruption even if it was conducted by key elements of the governing political party. In this case ethics eventually triumphed over the argument that corruption is just another way of getting things done.

* * * * *

In the UK in the first part of the nineteenth century, there was a similar conjunction of reaction against established standards of electoral practice, but which was also driven by a new reading public, as novelists and newspapers began to draw attention to the corruption of political life. In the *Pickwick Papers*, Charles Dickens, writing in 1836, four years after the English franchise had been substantially widened, depicted an election in the fictitious constituency of Eatanswill in which the contest was determined mainly by the very cheap food and drink supplied by the rival candidates. The extravaganza of the poll left many voters exhausted and drunk on the pavement. Other 'swing' voters had been prevented from voting by the bribing of a driver to drive his stagecoach to an off-road crash.

But reaction against this situation was building up. Seven years later the British social commentator Thomas Carlyle wrote: 'Have we reflected what bribery is? Bribery means dishonesty, and even impudent dishonesty, brazen insensibility to lying and to making others lie; total oblivion, and flinging overboard...of any real thing you can call veracity, morality.'[13]

The subsequent 60 years saw a sea change in British practice relating to corruption, with reforms governing elections in 1854, public procurement in 1889, and commercial bribery (of one company by another) in 1906. The arguments advanced in favour of each of these measures reflected a concern that the nominal ethics of Victorian society were fundamentally at odds with both electoral and business practice. Oscar Wilde's play, *An Ideal Husband*, opening in 1895, perfectly reflected this. It depicted the near downfall of Sir Robert Chiltern, a British Foreign Office minister whose wealth was built entirely on the sale of a Cabinet secret 25 years earlier, an issue which would have hardly registered in the first part of the nineteenth century.[14] The 1906 Act resulted from pressure from a range of businessmen and lawyers, organized in the Secret Commissions and Bribery Prevention League, who urged the case for a new Act to address commercial bribery. The supporters of the League considered that it would only be effective if a significant number of cases were brought to the courts: in the following seven years they supported the prosecution of more than 100 cases in different parts of the country.[15] Only in 1913 did they conclude that there was sufficient momentum to have ensured a real change in practice. A similar organization in Germany, the Society against the

Abuse of Bribery,[16] financed by professionals, was equally successful in taking cases to court and securing prosecutions. By 1913 it had 30 actions pending in the courts, and survived as an organization until 1935.

However, a good deal of the new-found energy for combating corruption was also driven by concerns with 'efficiency' as industrial economies began to mature. In nineteenth-century Europe and the USA, corruption came to be seen by some as a source of inefficiency – anathema to a part of the entrepreneurial class, though not to those with monopoly interests. Procurement for the armed forces was a major factor in this. In the American Civil War commencing in 1863, fraudulent tendering and overpricing came to be recognized as a major problem for the Union army. The 'Lincoln Act', passed during the war, promised any whistleblower who could identify fraudulent tendering a commission of 10 per cent of the value of contracts repaid to the Federal Government. By the end of the century in the USA the 'Progressive' movement had coalesced around the objective of dismantling the closed shop political machines which allocated many municipal contracts, often at a premium of 30 per cent. Efficiency yielding dividends to taxpayers was often at the heart of these initiatives: Seth Low, a New York mayor, re-assessed property values upwards, lowered tax rates and increased revenues, contributing to a US$1.5 million cut in the city's budget.[17] In Germany, after the unification of 1871, the government streamlined the military procurement process to eliminate the corruption which had characterized procurement at the level of individual states. The criterion of efficiency extended to the civil service: in 1854, Britain introduced competitive civil service entrance systems, largely doing away with an entry based on privilege. In the USA, the Pendleton Act,[18] passed in 1883, had a similar objective: eliminating the political connections which had determined administrative appointments up to that time.

Thus the drive towards a higher level of public ethics was matched to a drive for efficiency in industrial economies which together contributed to forming a new standard, however tentative. Its fragility was frequently apparent. In the UK, there were recurrent scandals around political finance in the 1920s, of which Prime Minister Lloyd George's sale of seats in the House of Lords was the most conspicuous. The press played a key role in exposing this and Lloyd George's intermediary, Major Gregory, met an untimely death in the River Thames. By the early 1970s bribes paid by an architect, John Poulson, to the chairman of a large regional development authority alerted the public to the dangers of bribery at the level of regional government, displayed through the report of a public commission of inquiry. These values seldom extended to export markets, where the armament manufacturer Vickers Armstrong was able to offer a steady commission of 10 per cent to the buyer's intermediary. But by and large, the standard set in the UK in the late nineteenth century held for about 100 years until the 1990s, when major cases in the domain of politics – trading in influence in the 1990s,[19] a further round of 'cash for honours', an MPs' expenses claim racket, and several scandals in the world of sports in the first decade of the new century – undermined the public's belief that any 'standard' existed.

In the USA, the standard was in principle upheld by the courts and parts of the media. Several attorneys at Federal, State and City level have been responsible for this, though nearly always controversially, and since the position of public attorney at State level is elected there are always political consequences. Eliot Spitzer, as New York State Attorney General from 1998 to 2007, held the financial community to account in a range of cases focused on fraud and stock price fixing, but extending to organized crime as he successfully exposed Joseph and Thomas Gambino, mafia controllers of much of New York's sweatshop business. But Spitzer was ultimately undermined by political opposition, focused on his personal life, following his election to the Governorship of New York. Robert Morgenthau, as Manhattan District Attorney from 1975 to 2009, ran a series of prosecutions against powerful corporate interests ranging from BCCI[20] to Credit Suisse in 2009. Patrick Fitzgerald, elected US Attorney for the Northern District of Illinois in 2001, has prosecuted State Governor George Ryan for the corrupt leasing of vehicles with kickbacks to City Hall, and his successor, Governor Rod Blagojevich, for the attempted sale to the highest bidder of the Senate seat previously occupied by President Barack Obama. As Fitzgerald said: 'Governor Blagojevich put a "for sale" sign on the naming of a US Senator.'[21] Both Governors were arrested and convicted.

However, the major flaw in the consistent application of standards in the USA is a system of party political finance that gives extraordinary leverage over congressmen and senators to those who bankroll them. Funding from a corporate source can easily translate into pressure for tariff reform or preferential status in a bidding process at state level. When President Eisenhower left office in 1960, he spoke of the power of the 'military industrial complex' to capture government policy. The agricultural sector has provided some of the most blatant examples of corporate finance, with southern Senators continuously ramping up subsidies to the highly mechanized and already profitable cotton sector. Decisions taken by the US Supreme Court in 2010, in response to lobbying by Citizens United, have lifted restrictions on the scale of corporate and private donations to political campaigns, which further increases the political leverage of corporate donors. Senator Edward Kaufman commented at the time:

> Despite nearly one hundred years of statutes and precedent that establish the authority of Congress to limit the corrupting influence of corporate money in Federal elections, the Court today ruled that corporations are absolutely free to spend shareholder money with the intent to promote the election or defeat of a candidate for political office.[22]

If standards and ethics have been in the balance in the USA it has been a fine one, tilting in different directions at different times, but never allowing the lasting triumph of either.

*   *   *   *   *

If there is an underlying agreement across religious beliefs on the ethics of corruption which is sometimes successfully translated into standards, what causes a major identifiable decline in personal and public ethics? The most telling conclusion is that people in a position of power – whether at a local level or at a national or international level – will suppress broader principles for personal enrichment, if and when opportunities allow, and when regulatory systems make it possible. Although not inevitably corrupt, they are 'inherently corruptible'.[23] This objective of self-enrichment may be linked to the objectives of a group – such as a political party or a mafia network – but the principal goal is personal income or wealth. The opportunities to achieve this come in many different forms which influence the speed with which corrupt gains can be captured.

In the USA, the executives of Enron, who stole several hundred million dollars from the company, saw an opportunity to enrich themselves through 'special purpose vehicles', and did so very successfully, until the law caught up with them. In the UK, in 2009, members of parliament inflated their expenses because the regulatory regime was lax. In France, Roland Dumas, already wealthy, accepted an indulgent and expensive lifestyle from Christine Deviers-Joncour, funded by the energy company Elf, because it was on offer. In Russia, the new generation of oligarchs saw the potential for immense gains through the voucher system at the time of privatization and took them. In Peru, Montesinos saw the potential of funding for the war on drugs to yield huge personal gains, and did not hesitate to capitalize on it. In Tanzania, businessmen and politicians took advantage of the acute shortages of the 1980s to build significant fortunes from the black market. In South Africa in 1998, Joe Modise, Defence Minister in Nelson Mandela's government, was tempted by bribes from European arms manufacturers, available for the first time to ANC politicians after majority rule, and he took them. In China, Zheng Xiayou, originally committed to 'efficiency' in the State Food and Drug Administration, saw a golden opportunity to link regulation to family wealth and seized the opportunity. As he said at his trial: 'So I agreed and consented. This was bribery.'

The exploitation of these opportunities by individuals, even when part of a syndicate, and before the law has caught up with them, has the effect of triggering similar activity by others which can escalate within only a few years to create a context in which corruption is endemic. In Russia, the enrichment of the oligarchs within a very brief period reinforced corruption at lower levels, where both business executives and government officials could see that regulation scarcely existed, and could identify a way forward to personal wealth undreamed of in the Soviet era. In South Africa, where there had been moderate government-based corruption during the apartheid era, the successful seizure of new opportunities by a few individual ANC leaders in the mid-1990s rapidly spread throughout the system, and especially to provincial government. Those found guilty in relation to the arms deal were either never jailed (such as Tony Yengeni, ANC Chief Whip), or released after a very short sentence (such as Schabir Shaik, Joe Modise's intermediary). By 2010 corruption in and around the government in South Africa had escalated and received daily coverage in the national press. In China in 2005, the acceptance of bribes by Zheng Xiaoyu of the Drug Administration triggered similar behaviour by his immediate colleagues – eight of whom were subsequently charged with corruption which occurred under his leadership.

It was the opportunity to exploit weak standards which enabled these individuals to walk away from ethics and initiate or expand corruption on a large scale. There were, of course, major contextual factors which reinforced this behaviour and accelerated the diffusion of corruption, and which have made it so difficult to roll back where it is endemic. In the book titled *The Lucifer Effect: Understanding how Good People turn Evil*, Philip Zimbardo examined the processes by which a particular context can degrade the values of those who participate in it. His studies embrace both the extreme cases of jails where warders turn on their prisoners, and the Rwanda genocide of 1984. He concludes that it is extremely difficult for individuals to resist a predominant pattern of community values, which can erode their original sense of morality in a surprisingly short time-frame, as exemplified by US army warders at the Abu Ghraib jail in Baghdad after the invasion of Iraq. In a less dramatic way this might be applied to members of a cabinet who sense that all their fellow members are hooked into various forms of corruption. One former cabinet minister in Latvia described it in this way:

> I have seen it from inside and I do not think that I will ever go back there. There is only one set of rules for playing that game. If you cannot play by these rules, you are out. It is not possible to describe all [the absurdities] and sharing that takes place within the government. And what is the sense to get them to the Prosecutor's Office? There are no institutions to control the Prosecutor's Office. They go hand in hand, after the principle scratch my back and I'll scratch yours – I see that [the] system works that way. And if I rise up against it I'll lose everything, both job and bread. I am forced to obey the system, otherwise I cannot pull through.[24]

Public perceptions of corruption reflect this split between a recognition that corruption is an evil for society as a whole, but may be essential for personal survival, or even simply a useful and productive strategy for the individual. In the many contexts where the state is despised, corruption can become an expression of hostility to government altogether. However, conversely, where specific contexts are very supportive of standards, individual behaviour can change.

In Singapore, Lee Kuan Yew, soon after taking full control in 1965, resolved to create a context in which corruption was minimized. By creating an attractive salary structure for civil servants, and greatly strengthening the investigative powers of the Corrupt Practices Investigation Bureau,[25] he pushed Singapore to the forefront of 'clean regimes'. Although critics argue that this has been achieved at the expense of human rights,[26] the outcome is remarkable. The country has sustained a score of 9.2 on TI's Corruption Perception Index between 2000 and 2011, and ranks together with Finland and New Zealand in the least corrupt trio. A comparable story exists for Hong Kong, where the then colonial government established in 1973 the Independent Anti-Corruption Commission (IACC) which has likewise created a context in which domestic corruption has been minimized. So far this position has not been undermined by Hong Kong's integration into China, but it has always rested on the creation of a very high level of public awareness of the nature of the threat from corruption. Educational and public awareness campaigns were an integral part of the IACC's strategy from its inception. In both cases a context has been created in which standards have been aligned with ethics.

Elsewhere, this conjunction has been elusive, and other factors – the 'drivers' of corruption – have overwhelmed the quest for standards, where it existed. This is explored in the next chapter.

6

Why Now?

Globalization over the last 20 years has both exposed and accelerated corruption, in contrast to the period of the Cold War (from 1950 onwards) in which the west was only too happy to ignore the corruption prevalent in many low-income countries, the majority of which in Asia and Africa had been colonies in the recent past. Although by 1950 the majority of Latin American countries had more than 130 years of independence, patterns of corruption which had been established during the previous 400 years of colonial rule had been reinforced during the nineteenth century and the first part of the twentieth century. Dean Acheson, US Secretary of State from 1949 to 1953, described Latin America as seething with 'an explosive population, stagnant economy, archaic society, primitive politics, massive ignorance, illiteracy and poverty'.[1] He could see that this situation was an invitation to Communist takeovers, and he and subsequent Secretaries of State chose to welcome the right-wing nationalist governments that held power in the 1950s, disregarding the corruption that went with them.

In this context, national leaders such as Fernando Belaúnde in Peru, François Duvalier in Haiti, Sukarno in Indonesia and

Mobutu in the DRC were sustained, provided they maintained an anti-Soviet position. At the same time, the use of bribery by multinational companies – especially in the defence and construction sectors – was considered by both companies and governments to be a valid means of expanding market share (challenged for the first time in the USA by the Foreign Corrupt Practices Act of 1977). Within the Soviet system, political and financial trade-offs between individuals were common but hardly ever exposed; in China, forms of corruption were rife but had few international ramifications. The collapse of the Soviet system, and the privatization of its huge state-owned assets, the integration of China in the world economy, the rapid expansion of 'offshore financial centres', and global media coverage of corruption, have all contributed to both raising its profile and initiating moves to control it.

By the 1950s in Asia, both Indonesia and India were recognized, at least domestically, to have major corruption problems at both an elite and a grass-roots level. One Indonesian statesman, Mohammad Hatta, wrote in 1957:

> Corruption runs riot through our society; corruption has also infected a great many of our government departments…Workers and government employees, whose wages and salaries are no longer adequate for their daily needs, are being exploited by enterprising adventurers who want to get rich quickly … This is why all businessmen who remain faithful to economic morality are constantly being pushed backward. Bribery and graft have become increasingly common, to the detriment of our community and our country.[2]

Under Sukarno, President from 1945 to 1967, Indonesia was regarded as an important pivot in East–West relations, and early Western aid programmes from both the World Bank and the US Government chose to be oblivious to these issues.

But it was not only international diplomats and development financiers who chose to turn away from the question of corruption. In India, by the 1950s, there was extensive debate about it reflected in parliament and the media. However, Prime Minister Nehru was concerned that the existence of this sometimes high-pitched debate was itself an incentive to corruption. He commented:

> Merely shouting from the house-tops that everybody is corrupt creates an atmosphere of corruption. People feel they live in a climate of corruption and they get corrupted themselves. The man in the street says to himself: '*Well if everybody seems corrupt, why shouldn't I be corrupt?*'. That is the climate sought to be created which must be discouraged.[3]

However, the underlying reality was indeed serious, and was revealed with particular clarity by the Santhanam Committee, at the instigation of future Prime Minister Lal Bahadur Shastri in 1963, which both described corruption and made a series of recommendations for its suppression. The Committee searched for the origins of corruption in its contemporary form, arguing that it had been prevalent before World War II at fairly low levels of the civil service and construction departments, but that the huge war effort had 'created unprecedented opportunities for acquisition of wealth by doubtful means'. The report went on to say: 'It would not be far wrong to say that the high watermark of corruption was reached in India during the period of the Second World War.'[4]

Its thesis was that this was sustained in the years after independence in 1947, and manifested itself throughout the government and the judiciary: 'We were informed ... that corruption exists in the lower ranks of the judiciary all over India and that in some places it has spread to the higher ranks also. We were deeply distressed at this information.'[5]

The Home Affairs Minister at the time of the publication – Gulzarilal Nanda – described eliminating corruption as his 'main occupation', and convened daily public sessions at his house to engage with the public on their individual corruption-related complaints. The recommendations made by the Santhanam Committee are thorough and almost identical to those made by civil society and development agencies in the much more recent past.[6] The report even led to the release of a Code for the conduct of ministers, requiring them to disclose their assets and liabilities, and to divest themselves of any business interest. But it also recognized that the problem and recommendations went well beyond specifics, referring to the need to change 'the entire system of moral values and the socio-economic structure'.[7]

In commenting on the report and its message, the Swedish economist Gunnar Myrdal pointed out that western business was itself a source of corruption in the 1960s. He wrote: 'In private conversation they ... admit that it is necessary to bribe officials and politicians in order to get a business deal through and to bribe officials both high and low in order to run their businesses without too many obstacles.'[8]

Thus, a pattern of corruption was well established in India by the early 1960s and was part of a national debate. However, western governments and the World Bank turned a blind eye to it as the danger of famine and relations between India and Pakistan became the dominant questions. President Kennedy's ambassador to India in the early 1960s was the famous economist John Galbraith, whose diary, *Ambassador's Journey*, contains scarcely a reference to corruption.

In Peru, Fernando Belaúnde was elected president in 1963, succeeding a military junta. Initially considered clean, he was shortly suborned by corrupt interests in the military, whose involvement in contraband rackets led to a huge deficit in government revenues, estimated to have reached at least US$400 million a year by 1967,[9] or 14–15 per cent of government revenue. Left-leaning elements under Juan Velasco in the military ousted Belaúnde in a coup in 1968: their platform included strong anti-corruption objectives, which were not to be fulfilled. At this time, the drugs trade was recognized as a growing issue with production centres in the Andes, but this coincided with the growth of the Shining Path guerrilla group whose grievances reflected the neglect of rural infrastructure and services by all previous governments. Collaboration with the drug producers was considered to be a necessary strategy to win the support necessary to control the Shining Path, leading to a continuing collaboration between the armed forces and the drug producers and traffickers. Corruption in Peru has been a continuous business, which escalated under Fujimori but was far from novel.

But the greatest symbol of the west's indifference to corruption in Cold War times is the extraordinary saga of Mobutu and his Zaire, now the Democratic Republic of the Congo (DRC). Abandoned as a colony by the government of Belgium in a dramatic reversal of policy in 1960, the DRC experienced a unique baptism of fire. The regime, which had won an eve-of-independence election, rapidly fell prey to three bids for secession from the warring regions of Kasai, Katanga and Kivu, and to a major conflict between its new prime minister, Patrice Lumumba, and its president, Joseph Kasavubu. Lumumba had been marked as a dangerous leftist and Soviet sympathizer by the USA and the UK, and he had no external support as an individual. The young ex-army sergeant, Mobutu, now Army Chief, was able to neutralize both of them in the course of one day on 14 September 1960 as he implemented a coup (in the course of which Lumumba was murdered) which put him in power for the next 37 years.

Far from earning the disapproval of western powers for aborting the DRC's first shot at democracy, Mobutu was effectively acclaimed as the only possible saviour of his country, and had in fact (as army Chief of Staff) already visited Washington. One of his first moves was to expel the cadre of Soviet advisers who had been invited to the country by Lumumba.

These moves raised the curtain on a very successful and corrupt strategy of manipulating the resources of the state to sustain his regime in power – and accumulate a string of homes and buildings in France, Switzerland and Belgium. The basis of Mobutu's power was his talent for assessing the propensity for greed in all who might work for his regime, including those who once were his most bitter enemies. In her masterly account of his reign and his demise, Michela Wrong comments: 'Once the members of an emerging elite had ceded to temptation, once their dirty secrets were logged in the intelligence service's files and stored in his gargantuan memory, they were effectively neutered.'[10]

Mobutu's ability to sustain this political largesse was largely facilitated by his access to the revenues of Gécamines (formerly Union Minière), the huge mining company whose main base was Katanga, and which mined cobalt, zinc and copper. Having nationalized the company in 1967, Mobutu ensured that a share of its revenue stream reached his own account, and from 1978 to 1980 arranged that all of it should do so. Even when this arrangement was modified in 1980, his income stream from the company was close to US$250 million per year.

Yet this personalization of the assets of the country did not prevent the DRC becoming an important client of western donors, and especially of the World Bank and the IMF. From 1975 to 1984 the country received an average US$330 million per year in aid and development finance, and US$540 million per year from 1985 to 1994 – or nearly US$10 billion in all. From 1976 to 1989 the country's external debt (particularly to the World Bank and the IMF) was rescheduled nine times, nearly a record for the normally tough-minded Washington institutions. Yet, during this period, the reality of the DRC's financial management was exposed by Erwin Blumenthal, a high-level German central banker (and sometime World Bank staff member), who served as the director of the DRC's Central Bank from 1978 to 1979. Resigning from the post after a year in the job, he presented a detailed report to the IMF laying bare the mechanisms by which Mobutu pre-empted revenues due to the state, and the behaviour of civil servants and army chiefs in pursuing their own claims in a more direct way. Nonetheless, the World Bank was reviewing plans for economic 'reform' through the 1980s – at the behest of the USA and some European governments, and to the almost continuous discomfort of its own staff.

Mobutu represents the extreme case of a thoroughly corrupt regime propped up by the west during the Cold War years, through a supply of development finance which was only a third greater in scale to the sums which he himself extracted for the manipulation of his political supporters and his personal wealth. Speaking to a conference in the DRC he is recorded as having said: 'Everything is for sale everything can be bought in this country. And in this trade, the slightest access to power constitutes a veritable instrument of change.'[11]

It was only in 1990, the year of the fall of the Berlin Wall, that development assistance from the Bank and the Fund were suspended for the remainder of his presidency. Mobutu had served his purpose.

But in the course of the early 1990s, with the USA and Europe freed from the inhibitions of the Cold War, a new view of corruption as an impediment to growth emerged, though mainly in 'development finance' circles. Earlier 'aid strategies', which linked a country's aid programme to its own exports (requiring aid recipients to use at least part of the funds to buy the donor's exports), were increasingly under challenge. In 1989 during the premiership of Margaret Thatcher, the UK government had put through a complex deal with Malaysia in which aid for the Pergau Dam of £234 million was linked to an arms purchase from British defence companies of close to £1 billion.[12] Five years later, this was the subject of an intense inquiry by parliament's Foreign Affairs Committee, which followed very full coverage of the affair by the *Sunday Times* newspaper, opposing the deal and alleging a high level of corruption at the heart of the Malaysian Government.[13]

Although the dam was built and the arms deal was executed, the whole story brought out the political dangers of linking export sales to arms, and the inherent dangers of mixing business and aid in a corrupt environment. Partly as a by-product, Douglas Hurd, the Foreign Secretary with ultimate responsibility for overseas aid, made a speech at the OECD in 1990 calling for corruption prevention measures to be factored into all aid-funded projects. Subsequently the UK department responsible for aid – initially ODA[14] and later DFID[15] – became one of the international standard bearers in the promotion of 'good governance' in relation to aid.

These arguments were soon reinforced by authoritative statements from Jim Wolfensohn, the President of the World Bank from 1995 to 2005, who in a major address at the organization's Annual General Meeting in 1996[16] recognized that corruption was a basic impediment to economic growth, saying:

> We also need to address transparency, accountability, and institutional capacity. And let's face it: we need to deal with the cancer of corruption.
>
> Let me emphasise that the Bank group will not tolerate corruption in the programmes that we support and we are taking steps to ensure that our own activities continue to meet the highest steps of probity.

This new paradigm was taken up with enthusiasm by the international development finance community, and very large sums to support governance reforms – much of which focused on corruption – were given in the form of grants by both national and international donor agencies in the next ten years. Some of this grant-making reflected a broad view of 'governance' and included funding for judicial systems, for an improvement in national audit reports to parliaments and for the reform of police forces. Some of it was more narrowly focused on Anti-Corruption Commissions with powers to investigate, and sometimes prosecute, corruption cases, often based on the successful example of the Hong Kong Anti-Corruption Commission.

The ultimate expression of this new concern amongst aid donors with the issue of corruption was a 'Declaration', made in Paris at the OECD in 2005, in which it was recognized by both donors and recipients that the reform of governance and an assault on corruption should be a condition of all aid programmes from OECD member states. Wolfensohn's successor at the World Bank, the former Deputy Secretary of Defence Paul Wolfowitz, took an even harsher view of corruption and identified it as the single largest obstacle to development, further strengthening the bank's internal investigations unit and holding up high-profile loans on the grounds of the risks of corruption. These positions represented a major shift of policy in development aid circles from the decades of the Cold War. But, as Chapter 9 will show, the strategies of the aid-givers were still not consistent with those of the makers of foreign policy. This was especially true in the context of reconstruction in Iraq and Afghanistan, where the aid-disbursement strategy contravened the new 'donor' strategies of containing corruption and promoting 'good governance'.

A separate strand in the recognition of corruption as a significant threat to basic ethics in business practice had come from the USA at an earlier period in the mid-1970s, under the presidency of Jimmy Carter. The Foreign Corrupt Practices Act (FCPA) was the first legislation anywhere in the world to outlaw a bribe paid in another country. It arose both from Congressional investigations originating in the Watergate scandal, which led to President Nixon's resignation in 1974, and from parallel investigations by the Securities and Exchange Commission, which focused on bribes paid overseas by more than 400 companies. These payments totalled more than US$300 million, and had been paid to civil servants, politicians and businessmen. The investigation extended to bribes paid by the CEO of Chiquita bananas to the President of Honduras in order to lower corporate taxes. Bribes paid by Lockheed Martin included those to Prime Ministers Tanaka of Japan and Andreotti of Italy and Prince Bernhard of the Netherlands. The Congressional investigation also established that political 'slush funds' held overseas for the purpose of the payment of bribes were also used to be recycled back into party political funding in the USA. In contrite mood Congress accepted the case, as a way of establishing basic business ethics, for outlawing such payments.

From the moment of its introduction, the US government was under pressure from its own business community to see similar legislation passed elsewhere. The International Chamber of Commerce was helpful, issuing in the same year the first version of its own anti-corruption rules. But no other government was prepared to follow suit with legislation. Prime Minister Callaghan of the UK was reported to have said that his country, with an eye on arms sales to the Middle East, 'could not afford it'. Later, Congress required the Administration to persuade other OECD states to adopt similar legislation, and to report back to Congress annually on its progress.

The Clinton administration, coming to power in 1994, sought to use the OECD – an industrial country group designed to foster more liberal trade and economic efficiency – to promote the cause of introducing an international legal anti-bribery framework. Between 1994 and 1997, the OECD's 'Working Group' was the fulcrum of this process, which was chaired skilfully by Professor Mark Pieth, a Swiss lawyer who had been the chief investigator of white collar crime at the Ministry of Justice. The US Government continued to push hard for the outcome of the Group's work to be an international Convention which committed all 31 member states[17] to pass legislation criminalizing offshore bribery, which was finally achieved in 1997.

There were other comparable international initiatives in process at this time. The Council of Europe introduced its own Anti-Corruption Convention in 1998, and by 2003 a UN Agency, the United Nations Office to Combat Drugs and Crime (UNODC), had succeeded in launching a UN Convention Against Corruption (UNCAC), which has subsequently become the lodestar of international anti-corruption initiatives. It is in principle the most important international rallying point for the fight against corruption, and the most important benchmark of progress. The Convention, which came into effect in 2005, placed a major emphasis on combating foreign bribery; facilitating the extradition of individuals with corruptly gained wealth from a host country to a 'victim' country (for example, from France to Gabon); mutual legal assistance (enabling one country to glean information on corrupt cases from another); and the recovery and return of stolen assets (held in 'secrecy jurisdictions' and elsewhere). It extended these principles to denying entry to, for instance, the EU to individuals with a recognized record of corruption. In a constructive vein, and looking to the future, it promised more action at the sector level, such as the Extractive Industries Transparency Initiative (EITI).

The Convention has provided the most important tool for the G20 as a key forum for international decision-making, and has created a new opportunity for international action in relation to corruption. Meeting twice a year since 2008, the G20 have recognized corruption as a global issue, have developed an 'Action Plan' to address it, and have promised to report against the Plan. Nearly all of this activity builds on the UN and OECD conventions, and the work of the Financial Action Task Force (FATF) originally set up by the G8. Ultimately, the success of the Convention will depend on effective monitoring of progress by member states: the first stages of this were in place by the end of 2011 with 'peer review' reports on 13 countries, although the first full cycle involving all countries will take ten years.

These measures certainly reflected a change of perspective on the impact of corruption across the world, inducing changes of legislation in relation to corruption and bribery in a large number of states. In 2011, India,[18] Russia, Indonesia and China passed acts criminalizing foreign bribery, partly in response to pressure from the G20 Working Group on Bribery for both countries to live up to their commitments under UNCAC. By the end of 2011, the institutional framework at international level for addressing corruption was very different from that of 1990 and preceding decades.

7

What Drives Corruption Forward?

Given the contexts in which corruption can accelerate – as well as sometimes diminish – what are the main factors which drive this forward? At the level of small-scale or petty corruption, individuals are confronted with major pressures in a context which may prove to be overwhelming. Once they succumb to these, corruption proves to be contagious. At a national level, the key drivers are: political funding as identified in Chapter 3; the interplay between organized crime and governments; and the role which local and multinational companies can play in using corruption to increase market share.

'Tea money' and big shots

Small-scale corruption often involves the exploitation of poor and very poor people by those who are often only two or three notches higher on the income scale than those they are exploiting. The outcomes can be disastrous for victims of the system, crippling lives and the opportunities of children as well as adults. What are the pressures that confront individuals?

There are perhaps four answers: first, survival; second, greed; third, orchestration from above; and fourth, some form of *guanxi* or reciprocal payment. In the first case, there is no doubt that employees in the lower echelons of government service in low-income countries, who may have several children to support, are paid less than a living wage. As policemen, nurses or junior local government employees, they will have opportunities to levy 'tolls' on those applying for services at a rate that has some impact on their net income, or may even double it. In the face of the on-going domestic crisis which is typical of life in the sprawling shanty towns of big cities, it is easy to see how bribes of this kind become acceptable practice to those demanding them. From the perspective of the bribe payer, debate about the moral justification for this is clearly a cul de sac: few parents anywhere in the world would turn down the opportunity to rescue a child from sickness or possible death if it could be achieved by a swingeing payment to a hospital nurse on the wards. Thus both the demander of the bribe and the payee can have recourse to a doctrine of necessity.

The second driver of the process is 'greed', a state which may emerge simply from the efficacy of the 'survival' bribe, as the possibilities emerge of doing much more than doubling income, and on a continuous basis. Once an individual has established that 'fees' of this kind can be levied, it is safe to say that many will take the opportunity to do so. This is the reciprocal face of the fact that many surveys in low-income countries show that bribes were solicited by between 15 and 45 per cent of public service providers. While the driver here is 'greed', the unregulated context is also the culprit.

The fact that the context is 'unregulated' – that public service standards are not regulated by supervision – is mainly explained by the fact that a significant part of 'petty' bribery is either orchestrated from above, or takes place in a context where much bigger deals are being conducted on a frequent basis. This is the third driver of the process. 'Orchestration from above' leads to the organization of scams in which, say, every policeman on the street is required to bring back a predictable sum to his chief on a daily basis – a process that may reach up in pyramid style to the Chief of Police in a town and even further up the system. A comparable system may be organized by Port Authorities, who levy arbitrary clearing charges on cargo at the docks. In some national contexts, such systems are recognized as valuable both by the high-level organizer and by the lower-level implementer. Thus TI-Kenya[1] discovered in 2000 that potential police officers were taking middle-level positions by preference, since this enabled them to earn far more 'from the streets' than from the higher salary payable to a more senior officer.

The final and fourth driver is the system of reciprocity built into the *guanxi*, the informal system typical of China, but certainly prevalent in the clan loyalties characteristic of many parts of Africa. This context is governed by mutual support: the senior member of a family network secures a position for a junior relative on the assumption that he or she will be rewarded by the 'extra income' earned by the new appointee.

Taken together, these factors account for much of the petty corruption which degrades the lives of so many in low-income countries. Insofar as they are linked to poverty, the behaviour of big players in government systems, and clan and group loyalties, they are at the heart of the corruption problem. The convergence of personal need with the interests of those running organized rackets has a capacity to sustain a system which may well be impervious to changes of political regime at the top, and has a force for continuity that is as strong as those of networks geared to the acquisition of much larger capital sums.

Political funding: keeping the party going

The need for 'political finance', broadly defined, is probably the largest single driver of large-scale corruption. Deals which appear to be straightforward examples of grand corruption, apparently tailor-made for the pockets of an individual or small team, are in fact designed partly to secure the interests of a political faction or party – or simply a well-embedded governing elite. These interests may include bribing unsympathetic members of a Congress or parliament to ensure the passing of specific legislation.

Several of the most high-profile corruption cases of the last 20 years – from the case of Watergate in the USA, to Bofors in India, to the Elf-related cases in France – have had the ultimate objective of raising funding for a political party. But political funding, in the sense of money needed to sustain a regime in power, is wider than party funding. Michela Wrong, searching for the reported mega fortune of President Mobutu of Zaire,[2] concluded that it had nearly all been dissipated in the need to retain the loyalty of the regional potentates who supported his regime over more than 30 years. President Suharto of Indonesia survived a similar period in power through comparable tactics, as Michael Johnston has described:

> Corruption from the top down was not only a temptation, but also the essence of political strategy: the loyalties of local elites, bureaucrats, military leaders, and would be politicians and businessmen could not be compelled in such a large and far-flung nation, but they could be bought.[3]

Although this model hardly characterizes the funding of political parties in much of Western Europe or the USA, the leaders of those parties have frequently found it necessary to resort to forms of corruption to fund local and national election campaigns. This has occurred in the party funding systems established in France, Germany and Italy, in which a standard backhander on public sector contracts has been levied for the benefit either of the governing party, or (in the case of Italy) for a consortium of parties.

The end of the Cold War, and the birth or rebirth of multiparty politics in many ex-Soviet and developing countries, has raised additional and acute problems in the field of party political funding, since in only very few cases do such parties have extensive membership, and in even fewer cases are members able to contribute sufficient funding to finance electoral activities. Those 'investors' who put up party finance expect to be rewarded, but a return can only be achieved by the allocation of contracts to financial backers once a party has achieved or retained power. The need to build very large   sometimes exaggerated – financial reserves for this purpose means that this form of corruption can come to dominate the award of tenders and budgetary processes – with a serious 'knock-on' effect well outside party funding. In this context, embedded networks – often able to pre-finance electoral costs – become potential allies of government rather than a force to be resisted, and may in turn ratchet up their financial ambitions. Military procurement is a sector which particularly lends itself to be manipulated in this way.

Some of the different mechanisms which contribute are indicated by Chart 1, showing the interface which may occur between different sources of party funding.

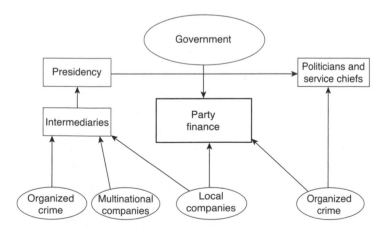

Chart 1   Political finance: Mechanisms

Once funds are directed from these various sources to a party that achieves power, its obligations to local and multinational companies, and perhaps to organized crime, constitute a cocktail which will tend to stimulate rather than enable it to constrain corruption.

National experiences: close to the wind

Amongst the founding member states of the EU, Italy is undoubtedly the country in which the use of corrupt techniques to fund political parties has been most intense. This is at least partly the outcome of the artificiality of party funding after World War II, in which the USA indirectly became a major funder of the Christian Democrats, and the Soviet Union funded the powerful Communist Party – an arrangement which had become fully discredited by the early 1970s. In 1974, the National Assembly approved legislation which banned financial contributions from state-owned corporations, and obliged parties to rethink their fundraising strategy. The solutions that emerged included a nominal increase in funding from the government budget, but in fact the main outcome was a system of levies on most contracts tendered by the public sector that ultimately led to the arrest of more than 4,000 civil servants and politicians in the 'clean hands'[4] campaign of 1994–7. Although, as already discussed, this campaign led to dramatic reductions in the average price of some public investments, it did not change the basic nature of political funding in Italy, or the ability of political leaders to escape corruption-related criminal charges. Thus three-times Prime Minister Giulio Andreotti only escaped conviction by successfully appealing, on four occasions, mafia-related charges of corruption, and Prime Minister Silvio Berlusconi was acquitted in 2004 on two charges of bribery in the 1980s,[5] mainly by reference to the elapse of time under 'the statute of limitations'. In late 2011 he continued to face three court cases, two of which embraced false accounting charges. Corruption originating in party funding has created a deep problem of credibility in the Italian political system.

The marriage between finance and politics has been characteristic of Japanese politics for an even longer period. The Liberal Democratic Party (LDP), when in power, spent more than US$10 billion in an electoral cycle to fight local and national elections, and the opposition parties about a fifth of this in total. The money is raised from corporate sources and through supporters' clubs (*koenkai*), which are a source of entertainment for their members. One of the principal origins of this system was the partial adoption of a primary electoral system by the LDP in 1955, which created strong competition between prospective candidates who developed their own *koenkai*. Parallel funding initiatives included the issue of underpriced stock to politicians and civil servants (as in the Recruit scandal of the 1980s), and payments to politicians and organized crime bosses for the expansion of 'trucking companies' rights (as in the Sagawa Kyubin case in 1991–3). In 1991, out of total donations to the LDP of ¥900 billion, only ¥356 billion were registered. Much of the difference was gleaned from *koenkai* and from commissions on public works averaging about 3 per cent, and from the mafia-like *yakuza* syndicates.[6]

The system has ensured that political posts were handed out to those who could raise the most for the party, who in turn could then use a highly centralized but efficient bureaucracy to allocate resources in ways which benefited specific elements of the private sector, including both large companies and *yakuza* (who had raised some of the funds in the first place). Similarly, the need for individual members of the Diet to recoup their outlays on *koenkai* has led to a well-recognized trail of elaborate and overpriced projects in rural areas, and to the use of construction techniques in large-scale infrastructure which were clearly inadequate for their purpose. Professor Minoru O'uchi, an analyst of corruption in Japan, has written: 'Almost all political corruption cases are directly or indirectly related to political donations, which can give rise to the arbitrary or unfair use of political power or influence the disposal of rights and interests in return for these donations.'[7]

This has created a situation where the world's third largest economy finds it difficult to initiate major change – as Prime Minister Koizumi found when he sought to semi-privatize the Post Office Bank, a process requiring two years of parliamentary time. Japanese voters finally rejected the whole system associated with the LDP in 2009, and elected the Democratic Party of Japan (DPJ) to government, although financial scandals have continued to dog the DPJ. It remains to be seen whether Japan will escape from a political funding system that has sapped the roots of its success, and is partly fed by the corrupt activities of the *yakuza*.

Indian election campaigns provide a striking example of 'investment' in politics as a way of securing business objectives. Although India has established limits on electoral spending at constituency level, these stood in 2010 at only US$1000 for a parliamentary candidate (and there was no limit on total expenditure by the same candidate's party). In fact, an authoritative former Chief Election Commissioner of India, Shri R.K. Trivedi, has said: 'The huge expenditures incurred by candidates and political parties have no relationship to the ceiling prescribed by the law.' In 1999, Arun Kumar estimated that expenditure per candidate[8] was closer to US$40,000; in 2011, an Indian anti-corruption watchdog estimated the cost at more than US$1 million for a state level constituency, and up to US$10 million for a federal constituency.[9] Expenditure on this scale is an investment, as Tarun Das, a former Director General of the Confederation of Indian Industry, has asserted: 'When an individual businessman donates to politicians, he expects some quid pro quo for his enterprise. Nobody makes political contributions in the interest of policies that benefit the entire nation.'

Indian parliamentary politics are further complicated by the fact that known criminals frequently run successfully in elections, having been able to apply the proceeds of white-collar crime to their campaign. A Parliamentary Committee meeting in 2007 found that:

> There have been several instances of persons charged with serious and heinous crimes, like murder, rape, dacoity (*armed robbery*) etc. contesting elections during pendency of their trial … Once an accused is elected during the trial period, he allegedly gets the advantage of twisting the arms of police/prosecution to dilute the case, or pressurising the government to withdraw the prosecution against him. This is the chief reason why political office is very attractive to persons with criminal antecedents.[10]

In fact, in the elections to the Indian Parliament in 2009, there were 275 serious criminal cases pending against 76 of the elected candidates,[11] representing an increase of one-third over the comparable figure for the previous parliament. Civil society in India has continued to press for reform of legislation to ban candidates with criminal records from being eligible to run in elections. In a petition to the Supreme Court made in November 2011, an alliance of three NGOs requested the court to rule in line with this objective:[12]

> Little has been done (*in recent years*) to weed out the criminal elements and their influence in politics. Rather, if anything, their influence has grown manifold over the years and their participation has become more and more active. From having a nexus with politicians, criminals today have themselves taken on the role of becoming politicians themselves.[13]

This is an unusually explicit statement of the problem and of action taken by civil society to combat it.

In Tanzania, the funding of the dominant party, the CCM,[14] blended with the personal enrichment of some of its leaders, has created a series of scandals and political crises. The country's first President, Julius Nyerere, the protagonist of a relatively austere form of one-party Socialism, ultimately created an economy characterized by chronic shortages. By the time he left office in 1985, corruption was widely recognized as a big problem. The introduction of multiparty politics for the election of 1990 created the need for party finance on an unprecedented scale. Raising funds for the CCM came to be a route which included the personal enrichment of party leaders.

By the time of his election for a second term in 2000, President Mkapa had facilitated the development of an 'embedded network' for this purpose, with antennae in the Bank of Tanzania, the Ministry of Finance and the rapidly developing gold mining sector. The chief enabler of this network was Daudi Ballali, the Governor of the Bank of Tanzania (who was reported to have died in the USA in 2007), who colluded in deals of which the primary architects were a small network of businessmen. Ballali presided over gross overruns in the construction of a new building for the Bank – for which the final bill was close to US$357 million. The Governor was also at the centre of the extraordinary misdirection of US$130 million of funds held in the Bank's 'Foreign Debt Service Account'. These funds were due to be paid over time to international commercial creditors, mainly from Japan, and had been rescheduled in recognition of Tanzania's foreign exchange constraints. In fact, in 2005 the Bank assigned these funds, through fraudulent means, to 28 shell companies registered in Tanzania, most of which had close connections to this network. The funds were laundered through a newly established bank – Bank M – in which a majority of shares were owned by members of the network.

The network also had strong links into the sale of an aerial surveillance system by BAE Systems of the UK in (2002) for a total of US$54 million.[15] The key, and self-identified, middle man for this deal was Shailesh Vithlani. The details of this case were explored by the US Department of Justice and the UK Serious Fraud Office in 2009, culminating in a plea bargaining process in which BAE Systems admitted its 'guilt' to producing 'misleading accounts', although Vithlani himself has admitted orchestrating the deal.

The successful operations of this syndicate in the second period of President Mkapa's government and in the first term of his successor, Jakaya Kikwete, have created very serious political problems for Tanzania. In the national elections held in November 2010, the electoral damage to the governing party reflected public condemnation of the corruption linked to party funding.

In Brazil, the presidency of Fernando Collor de Mello set a high watermark for the blending of politics with corruption. But his two successors were not to escape using political finance to pay off Congressmen as controversial legislation came before them, a syndrome made worse by the fact that Brazilian governments have to rely on multiparty support. Collor's immediate successor, Fernando Henrique Cardoso, served out his two-term limit, and a period of successful economic consolidation, which was nonetheless characterized by reported bribery scandals, not least in relation to the award to the American company Raytheon of a US$1 billion contract for the surveillance of the Amazon. His successor, Lula da Silva, was dogged in his first term by the *mensalão* scandal, in which members of both Houses of Congress were shown to have been bribed by Lula's inner circle to deliver crucial votes on a series of Bills.

On 6 May 2005, a member of the Chamber of Deputies, Roberto Jefferson, also a member of the Brazilian Labour Party which was a part of Lula's coalition, publicly revealed a scheme in which members of Lula's private office had used illegal payments to win votes in Congress. In fact, Jefferson had been caught on camera participating in one such deal, and exposed the process as part of a defensive strategy. The two committees established by Congress to investigate these payments both concluded that these 'had been synchronised with important roll call votes over the previous two years'.[16] The final report delivered a year later named 18 deputies who had received *mensalão* (or monthly payments) during this period. It described this as a form of vote-buying conducted by the President's aides, but did not attribute responsibility directly to him. By the end of the year, Congress had expelled Jefferson and his colleague José Dirceu, a former Chief of Staff to Lula, and withdrawn their right to stand in an election for eight years.

Matters were to escalate. At the request of Lula, the Federal Public Prosecutor, Antonio Fernando de Souza, launched an independent investigation, and eventually recommended that the Supreme Court launch criminal proceedings against 40 individuals linked to the affair. In a dramatic reversal to his personal strategy, Roberto Jefferson himself was accused of money laundering. The head of Lula's own Workers Party,[17] José Genoíno, and his Party Treasurer, Delúbio Soares, were both accused of racketeering and intent to corrupt others. Dubbed the 'Gang of Forty' by the colourful Brazilian press, all the individuals identified by Prosecutor de Souza were brought to Court – though verdicts had still not been handed down in late 2011. The impact on Lula's support in the 2006 presidential election was severe. The broad-based popularity he had achieved in the first half of his first term, and the fact of a booming economy, was diminished. In 2005 a national opinion poll showed confidence in politicians to be only 8 per cent, and of political parties to be only 9 per cent.[18] A year later, 30 per cent of voters regarded corruption scandals as the 'key' to the presidential campaign – far ahead of the economy at 10 per cent. Lula had to go to the second round of the presidential election in 2006, achieving only a narrow majority over Gerald Ackmin. Although Lula left the presidency in 2010 after a successful second term, his successor, Dilma Rousseff, has had to contend with a complex legacy of political corruption, and by the end of 2011 had to fire five Cabinet ministers[19] and Antonio Palocci, her own Chief of Staff, for their involvement in deals which dated back to Lula's presidency. The spectre of politics, finance and corruption has not yet deserted Brazil, as opinion polls continually affirm.

These cases indicate that the interface between political finance and corruption is strong – either because funds which have been corruptly gained are channelled into political finance or because politicians are bribed to achieve specific outcomes. This in itself may not be surprising but the capacity of corrupt interests to reassert themselves after attempted reform is striking, and is one of the most powerful indicators of the impact of corruption in a majority of political systems.

Organized crime as a driver

Organized crime is an important driver in many countries in fostering a corrupt relationship with politicians to protect criminal interests, and once such a nexus is established it is always difficult to break. The experience of Italy, where successive governments have claimed to be fighting the Cosa Nostra in Sicily and the Camorra in Naples, indicates just how resilient mafias can be, with a hydra-like ability to rebuild themselves. In southern Italy between 1991 and 2008, 177 local councils were dissolved due to mafia infiltration[20] in spite of Sicily's 'maxi trial' of 1986.

The problem is clearly reflected in the contemporary Balkans. The Balkan wars of the 1990s initiated a complex pattern of interdependent organized crime and corruption that has proved sufficiently enduring to challenge the wisdom of the EU in admitting Bulgaria, and nearly derailed the entry of Croatia in December 2011. An EU assessment in 2009 concluded that organized crime groups originating in the Balkans controlled 70 per cent of the heroin trade, and were rapidly gaining a dominant position in human smuggling and prostitution throughout the EU.[21] The legacy of the wars following the dissolution of Yugoslavia reflected a pattern that has characterized many other post-civil war 'recovery' situations, in which patterns of undercover trade survived the peace and morphed into established but grey and illegal post-war channels.

Croatia, under Franjo Tudjman, was the first of the Balkan republics to receive international recognition in 1991. Senior members of Tudjman's HDZ party quickly reaped personal benefits from the regime of rapid economic liberalization which was ushered in following independence. These included former arms dealers such as ex-General Zagorac, who had stolen US$5 million of diamonds that had been earmarked to buy weapons during the civil war, but who later was able to borrow millions of Euros from an Austrian bank (Hypo Alpe-Adria) for property investment purposes. After Tudjman's death in 1999, the HDZ lost power, only to regain it in 2003, ostensibly with the intention of combating both organized crime and corruption, and setting up a new joint police and judicial task force – *Uskok* – to do so. But the networks which had flourished under the HDZ's previous term in office proved resilient and particularly effective in assassinating individuals who may have challenged their power – such as Ivo Pukanić, publisher of a weekly news magazine, *Nacional*, which exposed organized crime. Reaction against this brought a new generation of leaders to the HDZ in 2009 and 2010. Jadranka Kosor, who became Prime Minister in 2009, and Ivo Josipović, who became President in 2010, have prioritized the fight against corruption as 'the basis for everything'.[22] However, observers point out that this is an enormous challenge given the depth of complicity in corruption by members of the current government. Joel Anand Samy, at the Adriatic Institute for Public Policy, has commented: 'Over twenty past and present HDZ cabinet officials have accumulated vast amounts of unexplained wealth. Yet they and several thousand of their partners remain free, without any investigations or charges.'[23]

The role of organized crime is even more explicit in the case of Bulgaria, where some of the survivors of the dismemberment of the Soviet Union, and of the Balkan civil wars, are pre-eminent. Bulgaria's richest tycoons are a trio of ex-naval officers: Tihomir Mitev, Martin Mitev and Ivo Kamenov jointly control the TIM Group – a diversified conglomerate with holdings in chemicals, property and finance. Other tycoons such as Ilya Pavlov, Emil Kyulev and Barislav Georgiev, owners of a trading company, a bank and a nuclear power repair company respectively, were assassinated between 2003 and 2010, adding to the list of more than 80 contract killings identified in official Bulgarian figures, but believed by other sources to be significantly higher. The key role played by corporate leaders with this kind of background ensures that the money generated in the grey or untaxed economy account for 20–30 per cent of GDP – and about half of that of the construction industry. The significance of these circuits is that public procurement processes are seldom clean. In fact, in 2010 the Interior Minister, Rumen Petkov, was accused of leaking information to criminals and engaging in face-to-face meetings with organized crime chiefs. The synergy between organized crime and corruption in Bulgaria is a powerful example of the ways in which their entanglement can drive the political process – so much so that Bulgaria's score on TI's Corruption Perception Index[24] fell from 4.0 in 2005 to 3.3 in 2009.

In the case of Brazil the synergy between organized crime and politicians is particularly manifested at the level of some of the 26 states in the Federation. Here, a complex chequerboard of relationships between organized crime, the police and politicians continues to determine many political decisions. In 1995, in the state of Espírito Santo federal prosecutors began a long journey to eliminate a crime ring and death squad, known as *Scuderie Detetive le Cocq*, which originated in a police mutual insurance society but by the 1990s had morphed into an organization focused on killing human rights activists and street children. The corpses of those killed were displayed to increase the leverage power of the police in negotiating pay rises. Once in a federal court, under the senior federal judge, Antonio Ivan Athié, the case proceeded over five years, at which point Athié and associated legal officers were themselves removed from office on charges of racketeering and extortion. The *Scuderie* was closed down in 2004, but not before another state level judge, Alexandre Martins de Castro Filho, involved in the case, had been gunned down by some of its members for exposing a colleague on the bench, Judge Antônio Leopoldo Teixeira (a former military police officer), for his role in selling his influence to the *Scuderie*. Teixeira was put on trial for the crime, but by the end of 2011 the case had not been resolved.[25]

The targets for political influence which organized crime may define change over time. In 2005, Guinea-Bissau and Guinea-Conakry in west Africa became recognized entrepots in the export of drugs from Latin America to Europe, a situation created particularly by the Colombian cartels as their relationship with their Mexican intermediaries deteriorated. In this case, very senior politicians were bought at the cost of a few million dollars to ensure that drugs could be moved from the west African coast to the Mediterranean coast, and into the drug trafficking networks of Europe.[26] The trade in human organs from China is a further example. In this case, the traffickers involved are believed to work with the prison service, and in a documented instance offered an undercover investigator the organs of 50 prisoners over a year – ranging from US$5,000 for a pair of corneas to US$25,000 for a liver. This revenue accrues to the prison authorities.[27]

A further example is the shipment of counterfeit medical products, particularly into markets in south east Asia and Africa, a trade controlled by organized crime groups who not only source products in China but also manufacture drugs within Cambodia with rogue ingredients. In 2009 officials seized 20 million doses of illegal medicines, and closed more than 100 retail outlets in six countries of south east Asia – but every seizure reflected the previous compliance of an influential figure in government.[28] The organizers of the global trade in arms also have proximity to government: in Ghana, 2,500 small enterprises manufacture guns and pistols for distribution in west Africa, many of them counterfeits of recognized brands,[29] an arrangement which would not be possible without a pay-off to government. In 2005, the incoming government of Viktor Yushchenko in Ukraine found that intermediaries close to the previous government of Viktor Yanukovych had sold 55 Kh-55 nuclear capable missiles to Iran and China.[30]

A third context in which organized crime can come close to governments, and be interdependent with it, is in the context of terrorist groups, or networks trading in the elements of nuclear weapons. Al Qaeda, as it existed under Osama bin Laden's leadership in Afghanistan in the 1990s, had a close relationship with the Taliban government led by Mullah Omar. The nuclear scientist A.Q. Khan put together a network designed to smuggle inputs into nuclear weapons systems initially for Pakistan itself, but later to meet the needs of other would-be nuclear powers such as Libya and North Korea. As Moisés Naím has commented:

> It is … A tale of politics in which the national interest of a sovereign state becomes inextricably entwined with the criminal motives of a clique that captures and redirects important parts of the government to support a long term illicit enterprise. It also illustrates how stealthy and resourceful criminal organisations can play larger geo-political interests to their advantage.[31]

These instances of varying levels of the penetration or co-option of government by organized crime, in some cases over many decades and in others in the last decade or less, form part of the aggregate picture of corruption. Organized crime, either to achieve a very specific objective, or to ensure broad immunity for its operations, needs compliant governments, and will use corruption to achieve these ends. In this sense it is a principal driver of corruption in many countries.

In most of these cases, organized crime networks have been able to use the profit of their operations to strengthen their commercial position by buying influence with governments. In India and Japan, organized crime has a stake in formal party politics which can determine political outcomes, and can foster a corrupt environment, exactly as Bobby Kennedy feared in the USA. In others, notably Sicily, Bulgaria and Croatia, organized crime has been the driver, and has successfully corrupted the state. There is no more apt description of the situation in these countries than the description by Kennedy of the situation in the USA in the late 1950s:

> The gangsters of today work in a highly organised fashion and are far more powerful now than at any time in the history of our country. They control political figures and threaten whole communities. They have stretched their tentacles of corruption and fear into industries both large and small. They grow stronger every day.[32]

Multinational corporations: bribing for market share

To what extent are multinationals drivers of corruption, as opposed to reluctant victims of a process? Four types of corporate behaviour indicate the areas in which some companies clearly have been, or still are, drivers of the process of corruption.

The first may be most appropriately described as simply 'market development'. In several sectors – notably construction, defence and power generation – bribery as a means to secure orders of huge value has been commonplace, and a recognized means of corporate marketing strategy. This may now be changing, but it has certainly characterized the recent past. Perhaps the most dramatic single relevant case has been that of Siemens, which faced several prosecutions in Germany for bribery from 2006 to 2007, culminating in a prosecution by the Securities Exchange Commission (SEC) in the USA in 2008. In the course of the investigations surrounding these cases, the Chairman and CEO both resigned. The CEO appointed in 2008, Peter Löscher, has said that the total identifiable funds paid in bribes in 20 countries by Siemens in the recent past may have been as much as US$1.5 billion. In fact, in a plea bargaining process Siemens agreed a fine of the same amount with the SEC in 2008. The Siemens case is remarkable because of the light it threw on the market-winning tactics of a highly respected international business, which had continued to adopt a strategy laced with bribery well after the OECD Anti-Bribery Convention of 1997, and in spite of claims to be a leader in business ethics.[33]

However, Siemens' tactics were typical of many respected companies in the global arena. ABB is a major power-generating company with roots in both Sweden and Switzerland. Yet, in 2007, two subsidiaries of ABB, VetcoGray of Houston and VetcoGray of the UK, pleaded guilty to paying bribes of more than US$1 million to win contracts in Nigeria – leading to fines of US$25 million imposed by the US Department of Justice. The defence sector is replete with examples of bribery as a means to widen markets, as the settlement reached by the US Department of Justice and BAE Systems in 2010 confirmed.[34] The construction sector is a crucial exemplar of the large-scale bribery process, as is regularly demonstrated by the TI's Bribe Payers' Index, which in three bi-annual surveys has found the sector to be more prone to bribery than any other. The UK construction industry issued its own report on corruption in 2007, and found that 'one-third' of companies had been asked for a bribe in the previous ten years.

A key illustration of this in Africa was the Lesotho Highlands Water project, involving the construction of a dam in Lesotho to serve South Africa, in which several members of the consortium of 15 mainly European (and one Canadian) companies were found guilty between 2003 and 2006 of bribing the Chief Executive Officer of the Authority, Masupha Sole. They had been operating on the assumption that a bribe was required to secure the contract – an assumption which was turned on its head by the decision of the Attorney General of Lesotho, Lebohang Fine Maema, to prosecute the companies concerned. The strength of the assumptions lying behind the corporate position is confirmed by several international surveys, such as that of the Control Risks Group in 2006, which found that 44 per cent of US companies, 36 per cent of German companies and 26 per cent of British companies considered that they had lost a contract through the bribery of a competitor in the previous five years.

The ultimate outcome of corruption as a tool for market development is a situation in which a multinational company becomes a very close partner of a government which both invites corrupt payments and whose own position is made even more corrupt by the relationship. Cases of this kind are particularly common in the natural resources sector. Key examples include Liberia under President Tubman, where the Firestone Tyre company was the dominant corporate investor for many years; Angola during the 30 years of civil war after independence when Chevron was the leading oil production company in the oil-rich enclave of Cabinda; and Gabon, whose oil industry was and is dominated by the French company Total (historically with complex payment loops back to France). The companies concerned have maintained a series of corrupt and clandestine payments in order to preserve their monopoly of the market. Recent trends in liberalization, and in international mechanisms which promote transparency, have succeeded in undermining the strength of such relationships in some parts of the world (see Chapter 8), but they have resurfaced in post-Socialist economies where privatization has created the opportunity for 'state capture' by nominally privatized businesses such as Gazprom in Russia.

The second context in which multinational companies may act as the drivers of corruption is one in which the financial interests of management and perhaps the Board become divorced from those of shareholders. The scandals attached to Enron in the USA in 2006, to Parmalat in the Netherlands in 2004 and to Satyam in India in 2009 all illustrate contexts in which the management of huge businesses were able to manipulate them for their personal benefit. By generating false but audited statements Enron was able to attract joint venture partners into deals outside the USA which later fell apart and the Indian company Satyam was able to overstate its assets in 2008 by US$1.7 billion[35] or nearly 200 per cent, attracting investments from a wide variety of shareholders. The ultimate outcome of wilful deception in reporting by management is a culture in which all audited reports become so suspect as to be totally unreliable. This is a recognized problem in the Nigerian audit profession, which led to legislation being passed in 1990 requiring the countersignature of audited accounts by a legal firm – but only after the murder of three auditors of the accounts of Guinness plc (a thriving company in Nigeria) in 1989.[36] In 2009, the international auditor PWC was obliged to formally withdraw its audit report on Lukoil in Russia when the inaccuracies it contained became indefensible.

Privatization in ex-Communist countries has frequently introduced serious divisions of interest between manager-shareholders and majority shareholders who have been unable to protect their interests. Thus in Russia, as state-owned companies were privatized, private banks (also newly privatized) made loans to the new businesses taking shares as collateral, were never repaid and took over the companies for a token sum, enabling the banks and corporate managers to become the dominant shareholders. In the Czech Republic, the distribution of vouchers to a majority of the public to enable them to buy shares in privatized businesses was intended to be an imaginative approach to a new form of public ownership. In fact, the management of many such enterprises deprived other voucher holders of the real value of the enterprise by channelling the valuable assets of the business to subsidiary companies which they had set up and of which they were the principal owners. Established in this way management teams were able to quickly dominate the market for government tenders and consumer distribution systems. Thus the consequences of these mechanisms had an impact that went well beyond the companies concerned, and had a major influence on corporate practice in general, mainstreaming new forms of corruption.

No case can do more to illustrate the divorce between the short-term interests of management and Board members from shareholders, and the potential of this divorce for corruption, than the financial crisis of 2008. In this case the construction of ultra-sophisticated financial products – ranging from Credit Default Swaps to Collaterized Debt Obligations – was driven by a reckless disregard for the potential collapse in the value of underlying assets (such as sub-prime mortgages), which were theoretically the point of valuation for these financial instruments. In fact, over time these products represented no more than a series of claims and counterclaims on different issuers, regardless of the potential for income generation. The US courts have found that banks originating mortgages with a face value of US$200 billion sold them on to the home lenders Fannie Mae and Freddie Mac, misrepresenting the credit worthiness of the borrowers.[37] This was a series of trades which ultimately placed the public at an unacceptable level of risk and one which ultimately exploded.

These examples of situations in which corporate management is in practice responsible only to itself, and is able to either hoodwink shareholders or ride roughshod over them, creates huge opportunities for personal enrichment, and opens the doors to corruption on a large scale.

The third area in which multinationals can legitimately be seen as 'drivers' of corruption lies in the mechanisms for transfer pricing (also referred to as 'mispricing') of products traded internationally. This is a system by which goods are undervalued in an exporting country when invoiced to a buyer in either an importing country or a tax haven. Since well over half of global commerce is accounted for by sales between subsidiaries of the same corporation, a high proportion of this figure is attributable to these companies. The prices used for pro forma purposes in such invoicing may be less than 50 per cent of the real market price, with the consequent difference in value being profit which can be externalized. This gives the purchasing company the opportunity to hold its inflated profits in a very low or zero tax environment, bringing them into its country of domicile over time or not at all. American companies have established 'foreign sales corporations' for this purpose, with a large proportion in the Cayman Islands. UK-based companies have used the tax havens in the Channel Islands and other offshore havens for similar purposes.

This phenomenon has been explored in depth by Raymond Baker[38] of Global Financial Integrity (GFI). GFI estimates that total illicit flows from developing countries to Western banks amount to at least US$1 trillion per year. Mispricing accounts for about two-thirds of this total (with organized crime accounting for 25 per cent and 'conventional' bribery perhaps only 5 per cent). A figure on this scale ties in with intuitive estimates derived from world trade figures: total global imports and exports were valued by the World Trade Organization at about US$35 trillion in 2008. If only 5 per cent of these sums were accounted for by mispricing the total would be about US$1.7 trillion – a vast sum which far exceeds aid flows at US$100 billion. The offensive against tax havens announced by the Obama Administration in May 2009 – though it is primarily a means of raising tax revenue – is also a recognition of the scale of this problem, one in which multinationals from all over the world are effectively denying the citizens of low-income countries the tax revenues due to them.

The fourth route by which multinationals can act as a driver of corruption is in the 'legitimizing' of illegally traded products, as discussed in Chapter 3. This relates primarily to natural resources, and particularly to minerals and timber. It is best illustrated by the case of coltan,[39] a mineral which is mined mainly in the eastern Democratic Republic of the Congo (DRC) on an artisanal basis. Similar systems exist for precious stones such as tanzanite, for timber such as teak, and for oil which is tapped from export pipelines and eventually resold to wholesale distributors. In these cases, multinational companies are part of a murky process which is built on a faultline of corruption disguised in the complexity of their sourcing strategy – but of which they are ultimately the driving force.

These four areas in which multinational companies are a driver of the corruption process are a crucial means of sustaining corruption at a dangerously high level – especially in countries where it may be regarded as endemic. This behaviour is not constant, and is changing over time, at least partly for the better.

This chapter has identified four key drivers of corruption: small-scale bribery that is often part of a 'network'; political funding to keep parties and elites in power; syndicates of organized crime that can deal with governments; and large corporations who use corruption to expand market share, disguise mispricing and access illegally traded products. These factors play out in different ways in different countries and across national boundaries. However, they are to a significant extent interlinked, sometimes in ways of which the players are unaware, but which accelerate corruption in a wide range of countries.

8

The Long March: Is There Progress?

There are three important sources of change in the fight to control corruption: first, individual prosecutors and heads of anti-corruption agencies; second, civil society organizations; and third, those company chairmen who have embraced the anti-corruption goal and pledged themselves to see it adopted both within their company and more broadly. How much progress have they made?

The courage of investigators

Eva Joly: avenging angel

When Eva Joly, whose maiden name was Gro Farseth, left Norway for France, the country where she was to prosecute the President of the Council of State, she was an 18-year-old au pair to a Parisian family. Within a year she was independent, and by the time she was in her mid-20s Joly had qualified at the French bar. Aged 38, she became a *juge d'instruction* in the High Court in Paris, with the power to investigate and, where justified, prosecute on criminal charges law breakers at any level. This power was subject to veto by the Minister of Justice, a right which was seldom exercised – and which was not initially exercised against her heroic decision to prosecute Roland Dumas for his role in the Elf affair which unfolded in the courts in 1991.

The Elf affair, involving a complex sale of frigates to Taiwan, facilitated by Elf through its agent Andrew Yang, represented a major challenge to the French government. In this case, although Joly and her co-magistrate, Laurence Vichnievsky, were able to achieve convictions against the three prime defendants – Dumas; his lover, Christine Deviers-Joncour; and the CEO of Elf, Loïk Le Floch-Prigent – the sentence against Dumas was reversed and the other two served only one year in prison. Subsequently, Joly has written about the role of the 'deep state' and its secrets which beyond a point, both in western democracies and elsewhere, are impenetrable. The investigation itself took three years, involved police raids on several business premises, and incurred the wrath of many in business and corporate circles in France. Her courage in the face of the power of the State, and of Dumas himself, was formidable. It has subsequently been manifested in her continuing work in both exposing corporate corruption as a global phenomenon, and forming the Corruption Hunters Network, a group designed to strengthen the position of prosecutors of corruption in contexts where the political weight of the state makes this difficult. Her original work in France, however controversial, had a big impact on French attitudes to corporate corruption, reinforced by the OECD Anti-Bribery Convention, which came into effect at about the same time, so that the investigation and prosecution of French companies for international bribery became relatively commonplace in the subsequent decade (with 24 cases being introduced between 2000 and 2010).[1]

John Githongo: Kenya unmasked

John Githongo is an unlikely recruit to the anti-corruption cause. As the eldest son of a successful business family in Kenya, he could easily have gravitated into his father's accountancy business. In fact, after graduating from the University of Swansea in Wales in 1983 he chose to launch himself as a journalist and commentator on the Kenyan political scene. At a time when Daniel arap Moi was President, the fruits of very high-level corruption were shifting from the Kikuyu elite which had prospered under Kenya's first President – Jomo Kenyatta – to members of Moi's own Kalenjin group, and the political debate increasingly centred on the corruption issue. Githongo became known as one of the most outspoken critics of the corruption originating in Moi's government. At this point his stance was best known through a weekly column in the regional newspaper *The East African*, but he was also adept at promoting his position in international fora. At an International Anti-Corruption Conference in Peru in 1998, he made a major speech showing how Moi's State House machine controlled more than 400 Kenyan companies.

Within two years of this conference he was working as the Chief Executive of Transparency International's Kenyan chapter, bringing to bear his combination of analytical power, fluent journalism and impeccable sources to expose the corruption that beset Kenya at all levels, never forgetting that the true victims of corruption were those at the bottom of society. Githongo shared a widespread view in Kenyan and international circles that the electoral defeat of President Moi by the opposition candidate Mwai Kibaki in 2002 would herald an effective anti-corruption campaign. He did not expect that, following his election to the presidency, Kibaki would invite him to become his anti-corruption 'czar'. After much heart-searching, Githongo decided to accept the post – officially designated as Permanent Secretary for Governance and Ethics. It was to prove a poisoned chalice.

Once in office, Githongo set in train a process to implement almost every component of an anti-corruption programme as defined by what appeared to be international best practice. This included both new legislation, which *inter alia* set up a Kenyan Anti-Corruption Commission, and a body of regulatory advice which was designed to control the excesses of senior and junior civil servants. But Githongo's major targets were to clean up procurement processes at the highest level, and to retrieve the financial assets corruptly transmitted to 'offshore centres' (notably the UK and its dependencies) by senior figures in the previous regime. The latter initiative identified, through the services of Kroll Associates, approximately US$1 billion of funds which could and should have remained within the domestic economy of Kenya, all of it generated by various forms of corruption. The former initiative targeted in particular a scam unleashed by a network of politicians, civil servants and lawyers in the last years of Moi, but perpetuated in the first two years of President Kibaki. This was the Anglo Leasing scandal, under which the government of Kenya paid more than US$600 million for goods provided by phoney suppliers (Anglo Leasing itself was a spurious 'corporate' entity in the UK) into overseas accounts, all of which were dramatically overpriced. The payments were made in tranches over time, mainly through promissory notes, and were very difficult to detect in the government budget. One of the largest of these payments was made to Euromarine Industries, for the purchase of a Spanish naval frigate, which set back the government of Kenya a projected total of US$100 million.[2]

Githongo believed that his investigation of these cases had the full backing of President Kibaki and his cabinet. In fact, as his investigation intensified, key cabinet members including the vice president, Moody Awori; the Minister of Finance, David Mwiraria; and the Attorney General, Amos Wako, called him into a lunchtime meeting to inform him that 'John, we are Anglo Leasing' and to warn him off further pursuit of the case.

1. *Alberto Fujimori* (right) and *Vladimiro Montesinos* were effective partners from 1990 to 2000 in building Peru's corrupt network of politicians, organized crime and arms trading.

2. *Tweed's 'Ring'* controlled key positions in the government of New York City in the 1860s, using the system to allocate huge contracts from which they drew cuts of up to 30 per cent before media exposure landed Tweed in jail, where he died in 1878.

3. *Bobby Kennedy*: key investigator of corruption in the Teamsters' Union for the Senate's McClellan Committee in 1957–9 and as Attorney General from 1961 to 1964 continued to believe that organized crime was a bigger threat to the US political system than communism.

4. *Suharto* as President of Indonesia from 1965 to 1998 funded his Golkar Party through numerous corrupt deals, accumulating an estimated US$15 billion for his family in the process.

5. *Bob Hasan* had a close personal relationship with Suharto from the 1950s. Acquired huge forestry interests but in 2001 was convicted of defrauding the Government of Indonesia of $244 million through 'erroneous mapping'.

6. *Chen Liangyu* was Shanghai's powerful Party Secretary but was convicted in 2008 of appropriating a third of the city's Social Security Fund, or US$1 billion, for private purposes, and sentenced to 18 years in jail.

7. *Zheng Xiaoyu* started as a promising head of China's State Food and Drug Administration, but was ultimately executed in 2006 for receiving bribes on a large scale.

8. *Eva Joly* is the courageous independent magistrate who successfully prosecuted former French Foreign Minister, Roland Dumas; founded the Corruption Hunters' Network in 1991; and is a member of the European Parliament.

9. *Dora Akunyili* was Director General of Nigeria's National Agency for Food and Drug Policy Administration from 2001 to 2008 and survived several assassination attempts in challenging the country's massive reliance on imported counterfeit drugs.

10. *Giovanni Falcone* and *Paolo Borsellino*: twin heroes of the fight against the mafia in Sicily and chief Prosecutors in the 'maxi-trial' of 474 mafia suspects in 1986; both were tragically assassinated in 1992.

11. *Anna Hazare*: a crusader over many years for the rights of villagers in Maharashtra State whose hunger strike for a new Anti Corruption Law and independent monitor accelerated their debate by Parliament in mid-2011.

12. *Mobutu Sese Seko*: kleptocratic President of Zaire from 1960 to 1997; used corruption as a prime means of keeping the country together.

Reporting this to the president, Githongo found him fully aware of the facts, and anxious to use the funds to secure future election victories. However, in extraordinary cloak-and-dagger fashion Githongo had secretly recorded these and many other relevant conversations – invaluable data for the exposé he was to craft in self-imposed exile in the UK, culminating in his openly published 'Letter to the President', in which these facts were revealed. His exile in Oxford was a risky business as the Kenyan intelligence services kept watch on his every movement, and since contract killing is a regular occurrence in Kenya, he had every reason to fear for his life.

While this threat receded over the three years of exile, and Githongo risked a return to Kenya in 2008, he was able to use the time to speak very widely in the USA and Europe about corruption and the role of western countries in sustaining it. For at least a year after his exile, swathes of Kenyan public opinion voiced its support for his action – excluding those who had been the major beneficiaries of previous rounds of corrupt practice. Although the drama of the case diminished over time, Githongo's actions, and the violent election of 2007 which was itself fought over the spoils of corruption, had a lasting impact on Kenyan opinion. The approval of a new constitution in 2010, which specified a ban on ministers holding office while being prosecuted for corruption, proved to be the precursor of four ministerial resignations. Githongo himself has taken a different line, believing that real change can only come from active grass-roots support for the anti-corruption movement, and so has established a new civil society group operating at that level in some of the poorest parts of Kenya. But his actions set a new context which provided an important context to the referendum on a new constitution held in 2010 and a significant boost to future reform efforts.

Giovanni Falcone: the maximum penalty

The most stunning blow against the mafia in contemporary Sicily was wielded by Giovanni Falcone and Paolo Borsellino in the maxi trial held in Palermo in 1986, in which 474 suspected mafia members were prosecuted. The political consequences of the mafia's strength have already been discussed. The maxi trial held in 1986 was the culmination of more than 20 years of work by Falcone and Borsellino as magistrates in Sicily's court system. In fact, their careers were intertwined as they had both been brought up in La Kalsa, part of old Palermo, and both had been born into professional families – Falcone's father was a chemist and Borsellino's a pharmacist. Although La Kalsa was far from immune to the role of the mafia, Falcone in particular was brought up under a code of duty, church and patriotism which never left him.

Falcone graduated from Law School in 1961, and had a successful early career in bankruptcy cases where he developed a particular skill in hunting down information from obscure financial records, which was to prove invaluable later in his career. In 1980, he joined the Criminal Investigating Office in Palermo, making his name in two very successful and complex cases: the first against two cousins (Nino and Ignazio Salvi) who collected 40 per cent of Sicily's taxes, for an exploitative commission; and the second against a heroin smuggling gang. The latter case resulted in 74 convictions and was the first court case in which this had been achieved.

The talent and courage which Falcone displayed in these cases were recognized by Antonio Caponnetto, a senior magistrate from Florence who quixotically accepted the task of bringing the Sicilian mafia to book – a process which led to the maxi trial. Caponnetto appointed a small team of four, which included both Falcone and Borsellino. The first stage of this investigation was dominated by the 'confession' of Tommaso Buscetta, the mafia 'boss of two worlds', who was forced out of a leadership post and chose to deliver to Falcone the most complete description of the organization of the Sicilian mafia yet available, confirming that it had an interlocking structure and an overall council which could solve disputes and assign roles to the families who constituted 'Cosa Nostra'.

The trial itself, held in 1986, and criticized as being a deliberate political showcase, was on a massive scale, the prosecutors going to work each day in a speeding convoy of bullet-proof cars, some of which carried agents with machine guns. The trial itself was carried out in a specially constructed underground bunker, close to the Ucciardone prison where the 474 defendants were held, 208 of them in 30 cages placed around the outside of the bunker. Eventually, 360 were convicted, which was a huge triumph for Falcone and Borsellino and a tribute to their extraordinary commitment and courage.

The facts revealed at the trial, and the emergence of the Northern League as a new force in Italian politics, created a new opportunity to challenge the mafia on a broader front, recognizing that there were (and are) several different mafias, capable of working both alone and jointly. In recognition of this, in 1991 Falcone was invited to become Director of Penal Affairs for all Italy, with the responsibility to fight organized crime at national level. To address this, he set up two new national bodies (one investigative and one prosecutorial) which for the first time linked anti-mafia prosecutors in 26 districts. The anti-mafia campaign appeared to receive a further boost when the higher Court of Cassation confirmed in January 1992 the verdicts which had been handed out at the Sicilian trial. However, this was a short-lived triumph: within days, Salvatore 'Shorty' Riina, *capo di capo* of the Sicilian mafia, had confirmed death sentences on Falcone and Borsellino.

On 23 May, Falcone, his wife and security guards in a follow-up vehicle were blown up in a dramatic attack on a country road. Riina's men had stuffed 400 kilograms of explosives into a drain running under the road which blew Falcone's vehicle 70 metres away. He and his wife, and the security guards, were killed instantly. Within a month Borsellino had also been assassinated in the streets of Palermo. It was a huge setback to the most serious attempt since the time of Mussolini to deprive the mafia of its overriding powers in Sicily, which linked so effectively into regional and national politics. Falcone and Borsellino, and all of Caponnetto's team, knew the risks they were running, but chose to make a heroic stand, coming close to a striking success. But many subsequent appeals and re-appeals to the courts by the defendants at the maxi trial were upheld, and the courage of the prosecutors was poorly rewarded by history.

Nuhu Ribadu: governors on trial

The tragic and overwhelming contribution of corruption to Nigeria's history was explored in Chapter 2. Almost every political attempt, such as that of General Buhari, to roll back the tide of corruption has been overwhelmed by more powerful forces. However, the apparent commitment of President Obasanjo to address the issue when coming to office in 1999 created the opportunity for a renewed approach, deepening the capacity of the criminal law to address corruption through the creation of two new prosecutorial bodies. To one of these, the Economic and Financial Crimes Commission (EFCC), he appointed in 2004 the youthful Nuhu Ribadu. Ribadu is a lawyer and former police officer, and he took the helm of the EFCC in a mood to have no compunction in investigating and prosecuting 'big fish' – a stance which was initially strongly encouraged by Obasanjo.

In the years from 2004 to 2007 Ribadu conducted a whirlwind campaign by which many of Nigeria's senior political figures, particularly at both national and State level, found charges brought against them. The EFCC's targets included two ministers (S. Afolabi and Mohamad Shata) and their Permanent Secretary (Hussaini Akwanga), who had jointly accepted a total of US$214 million in bribes from the French company Sagem SA in connection with the award of the contract for National Identity Cards. In the Halliburton case, involving contracts for the Liquefied Natural Gas Plant, the targets were Petroleum Minister Don Eitiebt, Oil Minister Dan Etete and the Head of the Federal Police Force Mohamad Yusufu. Governors at the level of Nigeria's 30 states, traditionally all powerful – and a majority of them key contributors to the coffers of Obasanjo's People's Democratic Party – were also in the EFCC's sights.

One of Ribadu's most illustrious and flamboyant targets was Diepreye Alamieyeseigha, Governor of Bayelsa State, who defrauded state coffers of about US$400 million, acquiring in the process 11 properties in Nigeria and South Africa, and managing to flee bail in the UK dressed as a woman and with US$1 million on his person.

The investigation of Governor James Ibori of Delta State 'uncovered several questionable payments to companies, associates, and aides of Ibori, running into billions of naira … the most brazen and monumental case of looting of a state Treasury by any chief executive'. Furthermore, among the 103 counts that the EFCC levelled against Ibori was his attempted US$15 million bribe for EFCC officials to drop the case against him.[3]

In a similar vein the EFCC also brought charges against Governor Chimaroke Nnamani of Enugu State who 'illegally maintained 20 secret bank accounts in the US and abused his office by diverting public funds worth about N4.5 bn to acquire no fewer than 172 assets which include radio stations and higher educational institutions in Nigeria'.[4]

In all, from 1999 to 2007, 31 Governors were indicted or investigated for criminal acts by the ICPC or EFCC. Between 2004 and 2006 Ribadu's team 'investigated two thousand cases, made a similar number of arrests, prosecuted more than two hundred cases, achieved eighty eight convictions and recovered more than $5bn in stolen assets'.[5]

But as the issue of Obasanjo standing for a third term in 2008 came closer, Ribadu found that he was under increasing pressure to lay off cases which might jeopardize the President's successful nomination and re-election. Although he survived the transition from Obasanjo to his successor Yar'Adua, he was shortly thereafter relieved of his post and asked to proceed on a training course for senior police officers; subsequently, he was dismissed from the police for insubordination, and many of his effective and close associates were purged from the EFCC. Like John Githongo, he too found a base for self-imposed exile at St Anthony's College in the University of Oxford. Like Githongo, he also concluded that political reform is crucial to the reform of corruption, and stood as a candidate for the Nigerian presidency in 2011.

Ribadu's courageous use of the law showed how much could be done with the right political commitment. But his removal and persecution caused the Nigerian Nobel laureate, Wole Soyinka, to write:

> Instead of reinforcing the autonomy of an organisation that is clearly dedicated to probity and political integrity, notice has been given to all four corners of the nation and to the international community that, at the slightest threat to the hegemony of corrupt rule, the credibility of even the most laudable institutions will be eroded.[6]

*   *   *   *   *

In each of these cases the extraordinary courage of the prosecutors such as Joly and Ribadu, or directors of anti-corruption programmes such as Githongo, has yielded only very limited long-term dividends. This is true even of Falcone and Borsellino, where the impact of the maxi trial was eroded by the numerous state pardons which were issued subsequent to the trial. Eva Joly has not surprisingly identified the political pressure on individual prosecutors as being a key inhibitor of their ability to bring the corrupt to jail (and to keep them there), and accordingly founded in 2005 the Corruption Hunters Network to provide moral support to prosecutors all over the world in this situation.

Can civil society fight corruption?

Civil society organizations have been active in the anti-corruption fight. Some, such as Global Witness, have both exposed corruption and sought its redress through the formation of international alliances devoted to curbing it. Others, such as the chapter of Transparency International (together with the NGO Sherpa) in France, have sought to force the courts to freeze the assets of corrupt leaders, and ultimately to return them to their country of origin. The TI chapter in Colombia has succeeded in bargaining with the government to introduce a dramatic change in procurement systems designed to minimize or eliminate corruption. In the UK, Corner House, working through the courts together with the Campaign Against Arms Trade, was nearly successful in 2008 in getting the country's Serious Fraud Office to re-open its investigation of the Al Yamamah arms deal. In Sicily, civil society groups such as Addiopizzo and Libera have had some success in building an anti-mafia constituency. How deep have these successful initiatives been?

Global Witness: righting the resource curse

Global Witness was established by three pioneering individuals – Patrick Alley, Simon Taylor and Charmian Gooch. Each of them had previously worked in environmental NGOs with little sensitivity to the corruption issue. In 1993, they sought to redress this with a commitment to exposing the ways in which natural resources were being corruptly ransacked to the benefit of small elites close to governments. They succeeded in demonstrating this decisively in Cambodia, and slightly later in Angola, using information-gathering techniques which were innovative and technically 'smart'. In 1993 in Cambodia, they showed how the Khmer Rouge and government forces loyal to King Norodom, son of Prince Sihanouk, had financed themselves by smuggling timber into Thailand. In 2007, they showed how individuals in the government of Hun Sen (including his brother-in-law Hun Neng, a provincial governor) continued to practise large-scale and 'illegal' logging through their ability to manipulate government. Although Global Witness was threatened with annihilation by Hun Neng if they returned to Cambodia, they had by 2010 produced two further reports on corruption in the allocation of the country's natural resource base.

In relation to Angola, Global Witness mounted a brilliant campaign, based on research carried out in 1995–6, to demonstrate how both sides in the Angolan war had drawn on oil and diamonds to fund their military campaigns. The war originated in the election to power of the left-leaning MPLA government in 1974, contested by the opposition party UNITA (backed by South Africa and the USA). Although UNITA won a significant minority of seats in the 1991 election, it refused to take them up, and returned to a bush war. While the capital Luanda and much of the west of the country was occupied by the MPLA, large parts of the east and north were occupied by UNITA. In defining the role of diamonds in funding UNITA, Global Witness successfully coined the term 'blood diamonds', which was to be the basis of a campaign to certify the origin of all traded diamonds as 'conflict-free'. A more or less comparable situation had arisen in Sierra Leone, where rebels in the civil war which broke out in 1991 were also funded by diamond sales, in a process actively facilitated by Charles Taylor, then president of neighbouring Liberia. Global Witness began to try to persuade companies operating in the trade that they should initiate a process by which diamonds could be certified as 'conflict free'. In fact, these negotiations involved only a very small number of companies since De Beers controlled 80 per cent of the world market, and when confronted with their own technical material indicating that such sourcing was possible, and a possible total boycott of Valentine's Day sales, the companies eventually agreed to sign up to the Kimberley Process – an arrangement by which all traded diamonds would be certified as originating only from legally recognized sources.

In contrast to UNITA, the MPLA government drew its funding from the sale of oil, principally drilled by Chevron in the enclave of Cabinda, but these oil sales were highly opaque, and a huge percentage of them were paid into a special account outside the government budget, and controlled only by the presidency. In practice, this account was used to purchase arms from Europe and Russia through intermediary offshore companies. In its first publication to uncover these arrangements, Global Witness showed how such shell companies were used by President José Eduardo dos Santos to buy arms on the international market through arrangements made partly with Jean-Christophe Mitterrand,[7] the son of President Mitterrand of France, and which were sourced mainly from Russia, involving banks in Portugal and the Channel Islands with large kickbacks to Angolan officials. Although such a chain had been suspected, this was the first time that it had been publicly quantified and linked to a specific proposition for reform.

Based on these findings, Global Witness drew together a coalition of other mainly UK-based NGOs who shared a view that the destructive nexus between companies, governments and middlemen led to a huge misallocation of revenues which demanded an international response. Working with the UK chapter of Transparency International, Global Witness put together the coalition (including notably Save The Children) which became Publish What You Pay. This promoted the concept that in all cases of natural resource extraction the companies involved should be obliged to publish all fiscal and 'signature' payments made to government, and all recipient governments should be obliged to publish their receipts. Matching the figures would determine whether all corporate payments were reaching official public accounts. The campaign caught the eye and imagination of the philanthropist George Soros, who introduced it to the UK prime minister, Tony Blair. The latter saw that this could make a valuable contribution to securing stability in energy supplies – by reducing corruption in the energy chain – and gave it his full support. The ultimate outcome was a more or less unique international entity, the Extractive Industries Transparency Initiative (EITI), a 'coalition' of companies in the oil and mineral extraction business and the governments which hosted them, which was formally established in 2006. This novel concept was then taken to the stage of practical implementation through the chairmanship of Peter Eigen.

The twin achievements of originating both the Kimberley Initiative and EITI represents a huge success by Global Witness. How robust is the outcome? By 2010, the Kimberley process had attracted 49 member companies and was officially supported by 102 member states,[8] and was endorsed by the UN – thus effectively turning it into an international convention. It had succeeded in ensuring that very few jewellers in the EU or the USA would fail to emphasize that they were not selling 'blood diamonds'. In 2009 and 2010, there was a major split within the Kimberley process on the issue of diamonds mined informally in eastern Zimbabwe, which the government of Robert Mugabe claimed were the output of a formally registered company, paying its fiscal dues to the tax authorities, and in 2010 Global Witness withdrew from the initiative. However, the Kimberley Initiative has placed the issue of blood diamonds firmly on the international agenda, and has certainly changed the behaviour of mining companies and retailers, but it has not yet proved fully effective in eliminating trade in all diamonds from conflict zones, or in establishing that the certification process deals adequately with basic human rights concerns.

The EITI process received a tremendous boost from President Obasanjo of Nigeria, regardless of his other shortcomings, when he announced, shortly after EITI's formal birth, that his country would formally adopt its principles and obligations. The oil companies trading in Nigeria were obliged to comply, and the Minister of Finance, Mrs Ngozi Okonjo-Iweala,[9] and the Minister for Solid Minerals, Mrs Oby Ezekwesili, proved very effective executors. By 2008, all companies trading in Nigeria were signed up to the process and reporting in the agreed format. Nigeria's adoption of EITI set the stage for a rapid sign-up in the next four years by 50 oil and mineral companies – ranging from the Italian oil giant ENI, to Mitsubishi, to Oxus Gold (a London-listed company focused on mining in Africa). This was matched by the total of 32 countries, 11 of whom in 2012 are now fully 'compliant', and 21 of whom are 'candidate countries'. Support from 'investor' countries has been significant, and 17 of the world's aid donors contribute to funding the network which has a secretariat in Norway. Nonetheless, no Chinese companies have yet joined even the first stage of the process.

EITI is criticized as being a potential fig leaf for the companies and governments concerned. Implementing EITI for a country which is endemically corrupt may be a convenient means of staving off more fundamental reform, which is a greater challenge to vested interests. Likewise, from the companies' point of view, EITI may be a flag of convenience demonstrating their commitment to corporate social responsibility. The objective of corporate disclosure of payments to government by project has only been agreed by half of the participating companies even in the 'compliant' group, which have insisted on aggregating their payments across all projects.

On the other hand, the concept behind EITI has now been widely accepted as a means of reducing corrupt payments from companies to senior politicians. The basic principle of a company declaring all payments it makes to its host country has been adopted as a part of the Dodd–Franks Act, passed by the US Congress in 2010, and is now a requirement for companies listed on the New York Securities Exchange Commission. There is significant support for the adoption of similar measures across the EU. The work of Global Witness in establishing the principles behind EITI has raised a rich harvest, the lessons of which may be applicable in other sectors.

Transparency International: brokering integrity

Transparency International (TI) was the brainchild of Peter Eigen, a World Bank regional director in east Africa, and a small group of like-minded individuals from about ten countries (six of them in the global south) who he already knew or met in 1991 and 1992. Eigen had worked successfully in both Latin America and Africa for the World Bank for over 20 years, but by 1990 had concluded that corruption was a bigger threat to development than any of the financial and structural constraints which were the Bank's main focus. At that time, corruption was a taboo word in Bank circles, and Eigen's bid to have it taken seriously was consistently rejected. Working with a Kenyan friend, Joe Githongo (the father of John), he began to explore the possibility of establishing an international NGO which could address corruption, just as Amnesty International addressed human rights. The central insight was that large-scale corruption in the developing world almost always involved parties from more than one country – the deals were often put together between an agent acting for an international company and the representative of a senior political figure in the host country. If corruption was to be controlled, the strategy would have to embrace both the 'developed' and the 'developing' world.

Over more than a year of consultation with the range of people who took an interest in the idea of TI, and within the small group of those committed to its launch, it was agreed that TI would not be confrontational, but would seek to build an international consensus around the negative impact of corruption and what might be done about it. The key focus would be on bribery with an international dimension, and its role as one of the main drivers of domestic corruption. The consequent strategy would be to build a coalition of business, government and civil society which would work together to confront corruption.

If it was to be effective, this approach required the following: first, at least a few governments in highly corrupt countries to be interested in rolling corruption back; second, a significant number of international companies to commit themselves to rejecting bribery as part of normal business practice; and third, a recognition by 'northern' governments and their aid agencies that corruption was a critical issue in economic development, and impacted directly and negatively on many aid-funded projects, and held back or distorted economic development.

In order to preserve a balance of interests between the developed and developing world, it was agreed that TI must be represented across a range of countries, and that this would be best achieved by establishing national chapters which would be the antennae of TI in as many countries as possible. TI's start-up network of contacts was sufficiently effective to achieve the formation of 20 chapters, of varying strengths and formats, by 1995. Early members' meetings were focused not only on strategy but also on constitutional issues and notably the voting power of the national chapters in the affairs of the international body. By 2000, a majority of voting power was in the hands of the national chapters, who elected the board and the chairperson.

The foundation years of TI coincided with a big push from the Clinton administration in the USA to persuade and cajole other member states of the OECD ('rich countries club') to adopt legislation similar to the Foreign Corrupt Practices Act (FCPA), which the US Congress had passed in 1977. In fact, there was strong resistance among member states to the principle that many considered to be completely unrealistic in the light of market place realities. TI played a very important role in fostering a change of attitude within governments, and to some extent within companies, in the process of wearing down this resistance. In the UK, there was intense lobbying against the principle of legislation by the Confederation of British Industry (CBI); the Federation of German Industry was openly opposed; in France, powerful corporate interests were particularly keen to preserve their long-standing network of corrupt links with west African leaders; in Italy, the issue of domestic bribery revealed in the *manu polite* campaign far outweighed the question of foreign bribery. In each of these countries, TI chapters were able to launch debates about the question, respond to government consultation processes, and raise interest in the media. In every case, the defence industry was a particularly strong opponent of any legislative change. Nowhere was this truer than in the UK, where Mrs Thatcher, as prime minister, had signed the US$40 billion Al Yamamah arms deal with Saudi Arabia in 1985, which had built-in arrangements for pay-offs to leading Saudis and middlemen.

The fact that an international convention was ultimately agreed in 1997 proved to be the beginning of a fraught process. The issue of the effectiveness of the convention, and the willingness of governments first to pass follow-up legislation, and secondly to ensure its effective implementation, has been very mixed. In its 2011 assessment of progress, TI concluded that of 36 countries surveyed, seven were 'active enforcers', nine were 'moderate enforcers' and in 20 there was little or no enforcement. While there are a range of specific reasons for this, the key questions are the will to act, the resources available, and the level of international collaboration. The government of Tony Blair in the UK gave a huge blow to the convention when it required the Serious Fraud Office to abandon its investigation of the Al Yamamah Saudi–UK arms deal in 2006. The suspension was justified by Blair on the basis that the Saudi government had threatened to suspend intelligence swaps if the case was pursued, and that this put lives at risk on UK streets (following the bomb attacks on London tubes in the same year). However, there is no provision in the convention for national security to provide an exception, and other member states certainly concluded that the UK was not serious in its commitment to the process, a view further strengthened by the extraordinary 13-year delay in getting compliant legislation through parliament. Although Germany, Italy and Norway have a much better record, and the USA itself has stepped up its number of prosecutions, the long-term impact of the convention is open to question. Much will depend on whether China, Russia, and India implement their 'foreign bribery' legislation of 2011 effectively.

However, TI's most significant impact has been across a range of countries in which it has chapters. Here, activities have focused on the specific challenges of the national context. In Germany, the construction of the new Schönefeld Airport at Berlin in 2000 was started on a course which the media easily exposed as highly corrupt, and the initial contracts were cancelled. Michael Wiehen, then chairman of TI's German chapter, was one of the pioneers of TI's Integrity Pact system, which committed all contractors to a set of rules – based on the possibility of peer review – which minimized the possibility of corruption. Following the media exposure of the first round of bidding, the integrity pact system was adopted for Schönefeld, and was so successful that by the end of 2008 a total of 36 other projects, worth more than €1 billion, had been subject to integrity pact procedures, and by 2010 a total of 1,000 bidders had signed the pact.

TI's work at chapter level can be dangerous. TI reported that 20 national chapters had been under threat from physical attack in 2009. In Sri Lanka the chapter nominated the editor (Lasantha Wickramatunga) of a campaigning newspaper, the *Sunday Leader*, to receive the organization's integrity award. Nine years later Wickramatunga was shot dead by killers appointed to eliminate him as a threat to their operations. Fourteen other Sri Lankan journalists were killed between 2007 and 2010 for what they had written with regard to corruption-related issues, and more than a further 20 have fled the country. J.C. Weliamuna, who took over as Executive Director of the chapter in 2010, with a striking record in human rights work, found that his house suffered a grenade attack in 2008 – which his family narrowly escaped – and continues to live under this threat in his new role. In Zimbabwe, the TI chapter has been the target of regular harassment, and its former Chairman, Dr John Makumbe, has on several occasions been beaten up by the state police.

In the eyes of the public, anti-corruption bureaux are not necessarily institutions worth fighting for. However, in Indonesia in 2010, the state's main anti-corruption bureau, the KPK,[10] was under fire from President Susilo Bambang Yudhoyono for its uncompromising stand, even though it had handled an impressive list of cases in the previous six years, convicting eight ministers and 42 MPs of corruption, and recovering a large part of their assets. In 2009, the chairman (Antasari Azhar) and two deputy chairmen (Chandra Hamzan and Bibit Samad Rianto) were all arrested and successfully prosecuted in court. TI-Indonesia played a lead role in calling for the recognition of the vital role of the KPK, more than 1 million citizens registered their support on Facebook, and several thousand took to the streets to register their support for the organization. Although the trio were not restored to their jobs, the incoming chair, Busyro Muqoddas, was regarded as being as tough as his predecessors, and unlikely to bend before special interest groups. This was an important milestone for civil society.

However, these examples of TI's work at national level also illustrate the objective difficulty of real progress: courageous and well-designed initiatives are easily swamped by the sinews of a system that is endemically corrupt.

Corporate initiatives

The prospect of the adoption throughout the OECD world of legislation comparable to the FCPA has triggered several initiatives designed to assist multinational companies to adopt strategies intended to eliminate bribery throughout their operations. These have included the Business Principles for Countering Bribery, launched by TI in 2003; the Rules of Conduct, developed by the Anti-Corruption Commission of the International Chamber of Commerce (ICC) in 1996; and the Partnering Against Corruption Initiative of the World Economic Forum (WEF) in 2005. The core content of these principles is similar: first, an end to the use of agents as intermediaries for the payment of bribes; second, the full vetting of joint venture partners to ensure that they are not themselves intermediaries for corrupt payments; third, a veto on political contributions with a business objective, and the full declaration of any political contributions; fourth, an end to 'gifts' and charitable contributions with a business objective; and finally, a policy of requiring contractors and suppliers to act consistently with these values.

In each case, the development of the core content of the principles has been in association with high-recognition multi-national companies with a strong interest in reducing corruption in the market place. Jack Welch, Chairman of GE from 1981 to 2001, and Sir Mark Moody-Stuart, Chairman of Royal Dutch Shell's Committee of Managing Directors in the years from 1998 to 2001, were both very active supporters of the adoption of these sets of principles. GE had adopted an 'in principle' set of anti-bribery rules under Welch's leadership in the 1980s. However, they were not effective enough to deter corporate executives from paying bribes in relation to defence equipment sales in Israel and Egypt, reported by a whistleblower to the US Department of Justice, which led to a prosecution under the FCPA in 1993. The penalty awarded against GE included a fine of US$70 million, a requirement that it would completely revise its in-house rules, and use its best endeavours to promote the adoption of FCPA-like legislation across the OECD. Jack Welch and his senior management team were dismayed that their existing anti-bribery rules had proved completely ineffective in the Egyptian case, and lent the company's support both to the formation of TI and to the development of the corporate anti-bribery 'principles' developed by ICC, TI and the WEF.

By the time he became chairman of the Royal Dutch Shell Committee of Managing Directors (as the board of Shell was then known) in 1998, Mark Moody-Stuart had spent more than 30 years working for Shell in countries where corruption is endemic, including Nigeria, Malaysia and Turkey, and as Group Managing Director had a global view of the corruption issue. His predecessor as chairman had been Cor Herkströter, who initiated the 'management letter' system, which required the CEOs of Shell's subsidiaries in the countries for which they were responsible to confirm on an annual basis that no bribe had been paid. Moody-Stuart raised the profile of this system in the company, commissioned new and tougher in-house anti-bribery rules, and sacked any identified transgressors – publicizing the numbers of those fired as part of the company's annual reporting system. He, too, lent the company's support to the development of the TI and WEF 'principles'. When UN Secretary General Kofi Annan established the Global Compact in 2000 – an association of international companies committed to promoting human rights and environmental objectives – Moody-Stuart, as deputy chairman, played an important role in ensuring that an anti-corruption principle joined the other nine principles designed to promote sustainability. Consequently, the more than 6,000 companies who are formal members of the Compact have each made an 'in principle' commitment to fighting corruption, and have to report on it annually.[11] More than 1,000 companies have in fact been de-listed for failing to report on the principles they have formally adopted under the Compact.

What has been the impact of these and related initiatives?[12] While they have undoubtedly raised the profile of the dangers of bribery to companies trading on an international basis, there have been some conspicuous failures of bribery prevention systems. These include the Halliburton case in Nigeria discussed in Chapter 2, the case of ABB (a respected Swedish/Swiss power company) and its payments through two subsidiaries also in Nigeria, the payment by Hewlett Packard of bribes in Russia (disclosed in the German courts), payments by Mobil, Amoco, Texaco and Phillips Petroleum through an agent[13] to obtain oil and gas rights in Khazakstan, and payments made by the Franco-American company Alcatel-Lucent to individuals in the government of Costa Rica. In a plea bargain with the Department of Justice in November 2010, Shell admitted that its Nigerian subsidiary, Shell Nigeria Exploration and Production Company, had funded bribes of US$2 million paid by Panalpina, a freight forwarding company contracted by Shell Nigeria, to avoid customs duties.[14] Dwarfing these cases was the exposure of the Siemens strategy of consistent bribery in many world markets over a period of years in the cases that were prosecuted in the German courts, and by the SEC in the USA in 2007–8, discussed in Chapter 7.

Wider surveys confirm this pattern of the inadequacy of corporate guidelines unless backed up by real internal mechanisms. Reviews carried out by the consultancies Control Risks Group and PWC in 2006 and 2008, found that although 90 per cent of the large companies they surveyed had anti-bribery policies, only about a fifth of those executives questioned thought the policies significantly mitigated the risk of corruption. In a survey of 500 international companies carried out by TI in 2009, only 70 had established clear reporting and accessible systems for combating bribery and corruption.[15]

In large part, this inadequacy is due to the need for constant and clear leadership on the issue from the top of every company – at both an international and subsidiary level – and the monitoring of executives with contract signing powers. Chris Currant, a Washington-based expert on the FCPA, told the *Financial Times* in 2005: 'There are few other areas where a single employee in a multinational organization can with one instance of misjudgement create huge embarrassment and ... even criminal liability, for the whole corporation.'

But there are contextual reasons for mixed messages from the top. First, shareholder attitudes on the issue of bribery are mixed. Although an increasing number of the institutional investors who control about 40 per cent of stock market capital in the USA and the UK[16] take a position on bribery, there are many who are neutral. Further, there are many CEOs who would rather demonstrate their sense of public responsibility by focusing on environmental and community level investment issues, rather than on eliminating bribery, where this limits market share. Global stock markets appear to accept this emphasis, as indicated by the response of share prices (a slight decline followed by full recovery) to the 'guilty' verdicts imposed in the most important of the cases against Siemens (announced in October 2007), Alcatel-Lucent in February 2010 and BAE Systems in the same month. There is not yet a significant shareholder penalty for corrupt corporate behaviour.[17]

The heroic efforts of individual anti-corruption fighters epitomized by Eva Joly, John Githongo, Giovanni Falcone and Nuhu Ribadu have had a major impact in raising the profile of the fight against corruption, but have also demonstrated the limits of individual action. Of Joly's three prime targets in the

Elf case, two were given very light sentences, and the biggest catch, Dumas, had his sentence reversed. However, her work set the scene for a series of anti-corruption initiatives taken later by France's investigating magistrates. Githongo did not succeed in having the several contracts collectively known as Anglo Leasing cancelled, but his actions added to the demands for Kenya's new constitution (approved by referendum in 2010) to have an explicit anti-corruption strategy by appointing non-elected individuals as heads of ministries. Falcone and Borsellino dealt a major but not fatal blow to the Sicilian mafia, as nearly three-quarters of the defendants at the maxi trial had their sentences shortened or repealed. Nuhu Ribadu established the principle of the liability of Nigeria's State Governors for prosecution on corruption-related charges, but saw most of those cases withdrawn in Obasanjo's last months in power, and his own career as a prosecutor dramatically curtailed. He was not able to translate popular support for his actions as an investigator into electoral support in the presidential election of 2011. Individual action of this kind in an endemically corrupt environment will hardly ever achieve long-term success.

The civil society initiatives of Global Witness and TI have had a substantive impact through campaigns such as blood diamonds, sector initiatives such as EITI, and support for international conventions. But these initiatives are between five and ten years old, and it is too early to judge their real effect. Anti-corruption initiatives supported by large international companies – such as those initiated by the World Economic Forum and TI – are valuable, but can easily be reduced to window dressing, as the record of some leading corporate adopters suggests. The progress made by each of these sources of action is limited, not by the ambition behind the initiatives, but by the strength of the resistance which they face, and the three key obstacles to progress discussed in the next chapter.

9

Key Roadblocks

There are three major roadblocks to progress in fighting corruption which go beyond the strength of embedded networks, the imperative of political finance and the fact of politicized judicial systems. The first is the importance of the 'informal' or 'shadow' economy in nearly all countries where corruption is endemic. The second is the ease with which funds gained illegally can be channelled into 'black holes' which co-exist with the formal economy. This system ultimately thrives on the network of 'offshore centres' through which corruptly gained funds can be laundered, and traced only with great difficulty. The third is the ambivalence of western governments in relation to severely corrupt countries where strategic objectives outweigh concerns about the social and economic damage of domestic corruption. This chapter will examine each of these in turn.

The shadow economy: disguising reality

In 2010 the World Bank asked the question: who controls the charcoal business in Tanzania, a trade which generates 1 million tonnes of charcoal each year and provides the principal fuel for the majority of the urban population?[1] It had been living with the myth that licences and a tax structure imposed by government were the determining factors.

However, in 2006 the Ministry of Natural Resources imposed a ban on charcoal production which was completely ineffective, and was withdrawn after only two weeks – suggesting that the government's capacity to determine anything in this sector was extremely limited. The analysis commissioned by the World Bank, and based on more than 200 focus group meetings at local level, concluded that the real power in the system was wielded by dealers, transporters and wholesalers. These were often the same people, and were well able to fund activities at every level – from cutting down trees, to organizing charcoal production on controlled bonfires, to despatching produce to the huge market in the capital city of Dar es Salaam. In the course of this trade, less than 20 per cent of all taxes due were paid, a phenomenon overlooked by officials at the local level who were happy enough to receive the bribes paid to keep the system going. Since the total value of charcoal produced in Tanzania is estimated at roughly US$650 million, the value of bribes paid to individuals is high, as is the cost to the government of lost revenue (estimated at US$100 million,[2] or about 10 per cent of gross annual aid flows).

This unregulated and largely unrecorded trade is part of Tanzania's shadow economy, implying that its real economic output or GDP is much higher than official figures suggest. But this is not a phenomenon that is limited to low-income economies in the developing world. In post-Soviet Russia, a comparable unrecorded economy also flourishes. One of its keenest observers is Professor Alena Ledeneva, who has written about it extensively[3] and concludes that in its current form it is shaped by the system of *blat*, or reciprocal favours, which characterized the Soviet system. During that time many transactions designed to short-circuit both industrial and personal requirements were met by deals in kind, which also went unrecorded. These are now the subject of payments in cash, but remain unrecorded. At a grander, corporate level the shadow economy in Russia is sustained by the use of multiple books of account. There may be three of these: for management purposes (the real situation), for the Russian audit system and (for companies with foreign investors) for compliance with international accounting standards. The last two will frequently omit a part of turnover and profit, and these omissions are an integral part of the shadow economy.

Are we able to estimate the real size of these shadow economies in whatever part of the world they are found? Friedrich Schneider of Linz University in Austria[4] is one of the pioneers of these estimates. He concluded in 2007 that in Tanzania the shadow economy accounted for no less than an additional 60 per cent of GDP, and in Russia for 47 per cent. These were by no means exceptional for their regions: in Africa, the estimates for Zimbabwe and Nigeria were equally high; amongst the ex-Soviet countries Ukraine was close to Russia itself at 55 per cent. However, in the 'industrial' countries that comprise the OECD, the average size of the shadow economy is about 15 per cent. Although there is a debate about whether there is a link between corruption and the shadow economy in high-income countries, it is clear in the developing world that where the shadow economy is large corruption is nearly always high.[5] This is not surprising; it is far easier to make and receive a small-scale bribe in cash than by cheque, to deliver a payment in kind to a patron's house, or to contribute a vehicle for a month's campaigning. As long as a very significant part of economic activity continues to operate in this way, and is essentially cash based, it will be very difficult to control not only bribes paid at differing levels, but also cash contributions to electoral campaigns. Although some countries have incentivized small- and large-scale businesses to formalize, or at least to increase the proportion of their business in the formal sector, there is a huge distance to travel. If we say that the informal sector will be one of the last redoubts of corruption, that is cold comfort in economies where the informal sector accounts for a quarter or more of GDP.

'Black holes' and grand looting

A roadblock of a different kind is provided by the corrupt extraction of large sums based on scams which include the creation of completely phoney line items in budgets ('ghost projects'), to the underpricing of exported products, to claiming rebates on non-existent exports.

In Zambia, ex-President Frederick Chiluba was found guilty in a UK court in 2007 of having channelled US$46 million to an account in London in the Zambia National Commercial Bank. The transfer was defended by Chiluba on the grounds that it was to fund operations by the intelligence services, although such services were found to be fictional. The oil and gas exports which keep Russia afloat, and much of Europe warm, have been partly channelled through intermediary companies such as RosUkrEnergo (RUE), which have been allowed to buy gas at about a quarter of the world price, and sell at prices closer to the world price but still well below it.[6] RUE flourished between 2003 and 2009, and was nominally owned by Dmytro Firtash, a Russian citizen, two Austrians appointed by Bank Raffeisen, and two British executives from Denby Holdings who also sat on the Board. RUE channelled gas from both Turkmenistan and Russia to Ukraine (and further west), but it was in fact an instrument of Gazprom, designed to externalize earnings realized through this mechanism.

In Nigeria, a comparable scam, playing on the local and world price of petrol, has been orchestrated by a tiny group of traders. Nigeria's four major oil refineries are ultimately owned by the Nigerian National Petroleum Company (NNPC), which has had access to oil at a highly subsidised price, but then sold at least a third of the refined petrol to private traders for sale on the west African market. As a consequence, the 40-year-old refineries have been consistently short of supplies, and are notorious for totally failing to meet demand. However, oil traders and the 'big men' behind them have prospered greatly from this arrangement.

In some cases, such international transactions originate in the shadow economy but the product is moved into the formal economy. For example, in the case of coltan or diamonds mined in the DRC, the first stage of the product chain is based on completely unrecorded mining carried out 'illegally' in areas controlled by militias. However, the *comptoirs* that buy the product channel it to formal international processors, whose sales legitimize it on the world market. In the case of the market for small arms, the case is reversed: recorded sales from manufacturers in Europe pass through agents who sell on to other intermediaries (including those in the armed forces), who in turn may sell to militia groups.

An even larger-scale parallel system is represented by 'oil bunkering', by which pipelines in the territory of the Niger delta are tapped by local militias and the product sold out at sea to vessels capable of taking small quantities of oil – which are themselves owned or leased by senior officials (often in the armed forces) and politicians. These and related scams have probably diminished the Nigerian public revenues by at least a sixth, or about US$100 billion, over the period from 1990 to 2010.

The operation of such systems where a product is moved between formal and informal systems (and vice versa) is shown in Charts 2 and 3. Chart 2 shows how the proceeds of 'oil bunkering' in Nigeria – with an estimated value on the international market of US$1.5 billion – are partly generated on an illegal and secret market, but transit through to the formal and legal market where they are accounted for formally.

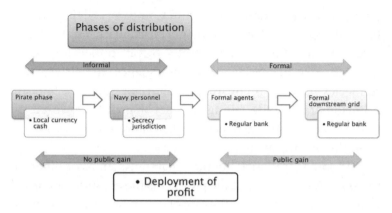

Chart 2   Informal to formal trade: Oil bunkering

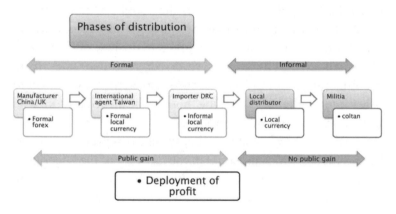

Chart 3   Formal to informal trade: Small arms

Chart 3 shows the reverse process in the small arms trade, where exports are made legally from countries ranging from the UK to China but transit into informal and illegal transactions. The scale of the resources gathered through the 'informal' parts of these systems is huge. Much of it is invested in 'secrecy jurisdictions', where banking regulations are non-existent or very light. This is even clearer in the case of tradable products in which the trade is formally illegal, and which originate from the operations of organized crime, almost always with some form of political support, procured corruptly.

An even larger contribution to funds held in 'secrecy jurisdictions' is the product of mispricing, or the over- and under-invoicing of exports and imports, particularly to emerging markets. The outcome of these several different processes of exporting funds offshore is to generate two types of pools of finance. The first, arising from trade which is itself illegal (such as drugs trafficking), is largely in the hands of local criminal syndicates who are likely to exercise considerable control over politicians, to ensure that their operations can continue. This is at its most dramatic in states such as Nicaragua and Thailand, but is an important factor elsewhere – notably west Africa. Here, the interface between organized crime and corruption is acute. The second type of financial pool is retained by multinational companies and international traders mainly in 'secrecy jurisdictions', but may be reticulated gradually, to minimize corporation tax, into a country where the company has its principal domicile. Alternatively, it may be recycled into the economy from which it was extracted, but categorized as formal foreign investment, a pattern which is particularly true of India.

'Secrecy jurisdictions': out of sight

Each of these forms of externalization have strengthened the position of many offshore centres and given them a key position in the global banking system. The misnamed 'offshore system' refers to any financial domain where the financial system is either subject to no effective regulation or to regulation which is so 'light touch' that it can host almost any type of finance house or product. Several of its hubs – such as Zug, Luxembourg, Delaware, Dublin and the City of London – are very much onshore in any normal definition.

For this reason, 'secrecy jurisdictions'[7] has been suggested as a more accurate description of these hubs. The ambition to 'host' a range of financial entities has led to zero or nominal corporate tax rates, which in turn have proved a very attractive domicile for the subsidiaries of multinational companies and banks.

The roots of the English-speaking component of this system lie in the 1960s, when sterling was an increasingly less attractive currency in which to invest in view of the constant risk of devaluation. The City of London, led by the Bank of England,[8] fostered the development of the 'Eurodollar' market in which US banks and other international investors could invest in dollars without being subject to the regulation implicit in capital reserve ratios and similar conventional banking criteria. It proved convenient to park some of these Eurodollar assets in specific jurisdictions where the tax rate on income would also be very low. The UK's Crown Dependencies of Jersey, Guernsey, Sark and the Isle of Man owed their allegiance to the Queen, but not to the Parliament at Westminster. They had also maintained a low rate of taxation as UK taxes rose remorselessly through the twentieth century, and lent themselves most fittingly to the need to park dollar denominated funds outside the USA and – as a result of tax rates – outside the UK. In the same decade as this market developed, the British islands of the Caribbean were given either independence or internal self-government, and the latter group (under a nominal British umbrella) were also an ideal repository for assets denominated in dollars – notably the Cayman Islands (now home to 600 banks and 18,000 companies) and the British Virgin Islands (now home to 800,000 international business companies). By the 1990s both the Crown Dependencies and the Caribbean Islands would prove appropriate bases for the products of the 'shadow banking system', such as credit derivative swaps, launched in the first decade of the new century, which were designed to minimize risk but actually disguised it.

But the UK-linked offshore centres were not the only players to act as a magnet to international funds from the 1960s onwards. In the USA, the state of Delaware, in league with Wall Street, developed a tax regime for company registration which was so attractive that 50 per cent of US-traded companies came to be registered there, and two-thirds of the Fortune 500. No less than 217,000 companies have registered their incorporation in one office block in the state capital of Wilmington.[9]

On the European continent, Switzerland has, until recently, reigned supreme in the domain of financial opacity, with secret accounts being legalized from 1934 onwards. While Switzerland undoubtedly offered an invaluable facility in the 1930s to Jewish refugees from Germany, its financial regime developed in ways after World War II which were to prove invaluable to international flight capital. It was only after attracting considerable international criticism for the way it maintained a veil of secrecy over the funds of holocaust victims that the banks in Zurich and Geneva began to change their whole modus operandi. In the canton of Zug in central Switzerland this was less true, and Zug remains a magnet for funds seeking 'offshore status'. Luxembourg, Lichtenstein and Monaco maintain several of the same characteristics.

The system is facilitated by the mechanics of 'correspondent banking' by which inter-bank transactions are at the discretion of international partner banks. In this way, the Bank of New York in 1999 laundered more than US$7 billion from its 160 correspondent banks in Russia to a bank in Cyprus for eventual transmission to the USA. More recently, Pacific islands such as Nauru and the Malaysian island of Labuan have become players in this system. For example, by establishing a shell bank for US$25,000 in Nauru a bank in any other part of the world can transfer funds to it and distribute them elsewhere. Nauru is home to 40,000 registered companies.

Determined money launderers can move funds around this world at their discretion. This is in spite of the fact that international pressure on 'secrecy jurisdictions' has risen considerably since the establishment by the G8 of the Financial Action Task Force (FATF) in 1995. Moreover, during this period the level of deposits in such centres has steadily increased, falling only briefly as a result of the financial crisis of 2008–9. Raymond Baker's team at Global Financial Integrity in Washington has been able to throw considerable light on the trend of deposits by companies and individuals in this system.[10] Total deposits rose from about US$900 billion in 1996 (a year after the establishment of FATF) to nearly US$10 trillion in 2009, representing a rate of growth of 9 per cent per year. This is about 4 per cent higher than the rate of growth of global wealth in the same period, clearly indicating that, on an international basis, an increasing proportion of wealth was being diverted into 'secrecy jurisdictions'. Throughout this period, the three leading hosts of such deposits have been the USA (with a cumulative US$2.6 trillion in 2007), the UK (with US$1.9 trillion) and the Cayman Islands (with US$1.3 trillion). In this league table, Switzerland is fourth (with US$540 billion in 2007) and Jersey seventh (with US$367 billion).[11] In 2009, the Bank for International Settlements estimated that total deposits in the banking system in all the British connected jurisdictions were US$3.2 trillion, accounting for 55 per cent of the global total.

For both the USA and the UK, with serious balance of payments deficits, deposits on the scale of more than US$250 billion into their banking systems is an unquestionable asset. For the UK, additional deposits of close to US$140 billion per year into the Cayman Islands, and US$35 billion per year into Jersey, much of which is recycled through the City of London, is similarly a very useful asset. Barclays Bank confirmed to a House of Commons Committee in 2009 that it had 315 subsidiaries in various tax havens.

In the Caribbean islands under nominal British jurisdiction[12] the concept of effective regulation by local government is a chimera; guidance from London is self-interested and ineffective, particularly when confronted with the complexities of local politics heavily influenced by corruption. Political leaders in the offshore centres of the Caribbean have developed a significant capacity for self-defence, lobbying the Black Caucus in the US Congress to the effect that the OECD was coercing them without justification. In 2008, members of the Foreign Affairs Committee of the British Parliament issued a report on both the Caribbean jurisdictions and the Crown Dependencies such as the Channel Islands,[13] which in turn led to a more detailed report[14] by Michael Foot, a former managing director of the UK Financial Services Authority. The report concluded that the Crown Dependencies alone had contributed 'net financing' of US$332.5 billion to UK banks in the second quarter of 2009, largely due to the 'upstreaming' of the deposits placed in the Dependencies but transferred to London. In relation to Bermuda, an island centre for insurance and re-insurance, it found that it accounted for about 30 per cent of the premiums (worth US$5.4 billion) paid into the Lloyds insurance market in London. These sums are extremely valuable to the British economy, and constitute a huge disincentive to any attempt to undermine the system. Further, the opinion of local citizens and of international investors is at one on the desirability of nominal British suzerainty: local citizens favour it as a means of offsetting the self-interest of local politicians, and international investors as offering a nominal degree of political stability.

The existence of this system of easily accessible international locations is a boon to both types of financial pools generated in this way. Pools derived from illegal 'trafficking' (and bribery) can be manipulated at will and recycled into the domestic economy when useful and necessary – such as the funding of a political campaign. This represents an important source of political leverage for those who control it, and one which may greatly exceed the resources which politicians and businessmen can put together from within the country. Pools derived from 'mispricing' are seldom repatriated to the country in which the income was earned, but remain either as a financial asset or a source of tax minimization and evasion over several years, or in a minority of cases recycled as 'new' foreign investment. However, in many contexts, local politicians and businessmen may have been a party to the mispricing, either as exporters in their own right, or as facilitators acting on behalf of corporations, and will retain some personal benefit. The first type of pool is both a 'black hole' and a roadblock to rolling back corruption; the second type of pool is more or less definable, but is a major roadblock to reform since it thrives on a corrupt environment, and its promoters have little incentive to favour change. The combination of huge dual economies in endemically corrupt countries, and the existence of 'secrecy jurisdictions', is at the heart of the problem of addressing corruption on a global basis.

Given that one of the drivers of these flows is mispricing, which deprives an exporting country of financial resources, there is every reason for international development finance institutions, such as the World Bank, to take a strong position on the issue. In practice, no such body has ever spoken out on the question, although in-house economists are more than aware of the work of Global Financial Integrity and others. Addressing the issue is to offend too many vested interest groups. The US government has never been a protagonist of change in relation to mispricing, and the Federal government has never sought to end the tax regime in Delaware, even in times of budgetary crisis.

There has certainly been a move towards international standards: all of these jurisdictions have nominally moved towards the adoption of standards of 'transparency and the exchange of information' agreed by the OECD, though Bermuda, the Cayman Islands and the British Virgin Islands have lagged behind the others. These standards envisage the reporting of 'suspicious transactions', crucial to identifying the trail of corrupt funds. However, such reporting has been minimal: in 2008, Anguilla reported 30, the Turks and Caicos reported 50, and the BVI reported 153. In fact, the Isle of Man reported a 60 per cent fall in the number of such reports from 2004 to 2008. Similarly, Guernsey and Bermuda prosecuted one individual for financial crime in 2008, and the Isle of Man prosecuted two (though Gibraltar managed 15).[15] These figures confirm how, in the world's secrecy jurisdictions, it continues to be extremely difficult to achieve significant reporting of corrupt assets, and even more so to achieve convictions.

Thus, while the regime is under challenge, particularly in relation to corporate tax evasion, it has powerful defendants. The status quo is preserved in the Caribbean by a mixture of British self-interest and indifference; in Switzerland, by a long-standing, internationally renowned tradition of banking secrecy, now enriched by measured concessions (regularly at first opposed by parliament even when recommended by government); in Delaware, by the inability of Washington to oblige states to revise their corporation tax regimes; and in the City of London, by the UK's overwhelming need to bolster its balance of payments and maximize financial assets under the management of banks domiciled there. Yet, the continued existence of this regime is an incentive to illicit traders, participants in grand corruption, and practitioners of mispricing to maintain and expand their activities.

Geopolitics and realpolitik: a cover-up

Chapter 6 showed how western powers turned a blind eye to corruption in countries such as Indonesia, Peru and the DRC in the 1960s and 1970s. A change of policy and strategy in 'development aid' circles from the 1990s has not extended to a number of countries where the objectives of 'geopolitics' have been allowed to trump concerns about corruption. The underlying concerns have been access to energy (as with Turkmenistan), the control of radical Islam (as with Afghanistan) and – as a specific case – the security of Israel (as with Egypt). In Africa, where anti-corruption standards were heavily promoted by aid donors from the mid-1990s, the very active presence of China in mining, infrastructure and general contracting is likely to undermine the governance agenda. Complex countries such as Sudan present particular policy dilemmas: divided between the Islamic and the non-Islamic world, and with a growing oil production capacity, its internal tensions are driven by corruption as well as religious and ethnic divides. These considerations are a huge but largely unspoken constraint in addressing corruption.

The republics of Central Asia are a case in point. When the five republics (Kyrgyzstan, Uzbekistan, Kazakhstan, Turkmenistan and Tajikistan) left the Soviet Union in 1991 they carried with them significant levels of corruption from the Communist era. These were dramatically inflated following independence, a process greatly assisted by the fact that, with the exception of Kyrgyzstan, they were all rich in gas reserves. Consequently, they were the target of both NATO's outreach strategy (the Partnership for Peace Alliance) and Russia's post-Soviet strategy of dominating the purchase and sale of the region's gas reserves through intermediary companies. On behalf of the USA, Strobe Talbott, a long-time Soviet specialist, outlined in 1997 a so-called 'Silk Route Strategy' for Central Asia, designed to support democracy throughout the region. However, today the positions of all five countries are close to the bottom of the table in Transparency International's Corruption Perception Index. In fact, far from contributing to rolling back corruption in these states, the USA and EU member countries have contributed to its remarkable rise. Policy towards them has been dictated by a combination of furthering the energy interests of Europe (which became an official issue for NATO), restraining radical Islam and, since 2003, servicing military supply lines to Afghanistan (often granted only under pressure).

Turkmenistan: the price of gas

Turkmenistan provides a powerful example of this situation. The gas reserves of Turkmenistan are the fourth largest in the world, and have for the last 20 years been an important target in the global struggle to control energy supplies, both into Europe and China. Turkmenistan's first president, Saparmurat Niyazov, personally controlled all contracts linked to his country's natural gas reserves – the superprofits of which were channelled to a Deutsche Bank account in Frankfurt. The murky arrangements surrounding this account caused Revenue Watch to rank Turkmenistan at the bottom of 41 countries in relation to publicly available information. However, Niyazov was determined to have a personal place in the sun, and in 1998 commissioned a rotating statue of himself which moved so that it was continuously sun-facing.

In this spirit of solar brilliance Niyazov had a set of personal philosophical principles – the *Ruknama* – which he was keen to promote, and even managed to enlist Daimler of Germany in support of this task. On 6 February 2003, Daimler presented Niyazov with a 'translated copy of his manifesto in a golden box',[16] and undertook to print 10,000 copies of this for €250,000. He also received from Daimler, free of charge, an armoured vehicle valued at €300,000. Niyazov died in 2005, but his style of government has not changed significantly under his successor, Gurgbunguly Berdymukhamedov.

The determination of prices for the country's gas as it came on stream in the 1990s and was exported to Ukraine was largely handled through ITERA, a company founded by Igor Makarov, a native Turkmen. Its vice chair, Valery Otchertsov, was also vice chair of the Turkmen Parliament from 1989 to

1991, and Minister of Energy and Finance from 1991 to 1996. However, ITERA was registered in 1994 in Jacksonville, Florida, as the 'International Institute for Energy', which in turn was the subsidiary of a company in the Dutch Antilles. Although some of its role as an intermediary was subsequently adopted by RosUkrEnergo, it continues to exist, and in 2009 signed an agreement to develop a block in the Caspian Sea. In 2010, leaked diplomatic cables suggested that ITERA had in 2008 presented a €60 million yacht to Berdymukhamedov.

The strategic issue of energy supplies to western Europe has strengthened the strategy of the EU in seeking Turkmenistan's support for the Nabucco pipeline project – designed to carry gas directly from Turkmenistan to Austria, and by-passing Russia. However, while from 2008 to 2011 the parameters of Nabucco were still being finalized, in 2009 China and Turkmenistan successfully completed the largest energy pipeline in the world, running through Uzbekistan and Kazakhstan to Xian in northern China. The diminishing interest in nuclear energy in western Europe after the Fukushima crisis in Japan in 2011 suggests that Turkmenistan's reserves will, in fact, become ever more central to the EU's energy needs, further compromising any stand on corruption there.

This combination of strategic competition for gas supplies, and price manipulation of the product, has established a pattern in which any position by the EU, or its member states, in relation to corruption has long since been cast aside.

Sudan: division of the spoils

In Africa, Sudan demonstrates the contradictions the West has faced in addressing corruption in the context of a country where Islam and Christianity both thrive, though in different regions, and where China has a major presence originating in oil. At independence in 1956, Sudan inherited a non-viable legacy of a massive country with an animist and Christian south and an Islamic north. The civil war fought from 1955 to 2008 (with an interregnum from 1972 to 1983) reflected these divisions, which were accentuated by the discovery of oil in the border region of Abyei.

By 1999, the government of President (and former general) Omar al-Bashir in Khartoum was ready to invite international companies to invest in production and in a pipeline which would bring the oil from Abyei to the Red Sea. The pipeline was built by a consortium which included the China National Oil Corporation (CNOC). By 2007, controversies surrounding the drilling and lifting of the oil led the Canadian company, Talisman, to pull out and sell its stake to CNOC. As a result, Chinese companies have become the key investors in Sudan's oil sector. The existence of the oil resource became central to the conflict between north and south. In the peace settlement of 2008, the possibility of the south voting to secede from Sudan was built into the negotiated settlement, and became a reality in the referendum of January 2011, leading to independence in July 2011.

Alongside its ill-fated war with the south, the government in Khartoum became embroiled, after 2005, in an equally tragic bush war with pastoralist groups in Darfur, Sudan's most westerly province. Using *Janjawid* mounted horsemen as intermediaries, the Sudanese military command carried out a scorched earth campaign over 20,000 square miles, designed to drive pastoralist groups off their traditional grazing lands and into highly restricted compounds without either grazing or farm land. This was to ensure that the fruits of future mineral exploitation would accrue to the specific 'embedded network' close to the Khartoum government, and that a repeat of the secession, which appeared imminent following the referendum in the south, would stand no chance in Darfur. This is the context which saw the International Criminal Court (ICC) charge al-Bashir with the violation of human rights on a criminal scale.

Although there are complex religious and ethnic factors which have driven the conflicts in Sudan, corruption has played a major part in ensuring that they have been long drawn out and led to deaths (in the south alone) of at least a million people. While the ICC's mandate restricts its remit to the abuse of human rights, the underlying factor is the corruption which lies behind the atrocities. The response of western governments to this situation has been profoundly ambivalent, torn between the need to see the conflicts end in both the south and Darfur, to moderate Islamic radicalism in the regime, and to curb the growing impact of China through its investments in oil and infrastructure. Different parts of the US Government have taken different lines: the State Department has given primacy to controlling the fighting in Darfur, the CIA has given primacy to finding ways to source intelligence on Islamic extremists from the government in Khartoum. The UK and other European foreign aid agencies have restricted themselves to making grants directed at poverty alleviation, regardless of corruption. Export credit agencies from the west have continued to support investment by their own companies, and the World Bank alone has lent US$1.5 billion between 2000 and 2010. Sovereign wealth funds from the Gulf have continued to invest – as they have done for the last 35 years – in both agribusiness and in Khartoum's booming high-rise developments. These circumstances have created a situation where networks in and around the government can engage in corruption without either domestic or external restraint. Sudan's position at both geographical and religious crossroads has enabled it to allow unfettered corruption to flourish.

Throughout this period, levels of corruption in Sudan have remained very high. Although in principle Islamic *sharia* law contains heavy penalties for corruption, especially those which exploit poorer and weaker citizens, this has not been sufficient to reduce levels of corruption as seen by the public. In the south, following the peace settlement of 2005, as revenue flows from oil have come close to US$1 billion per year, local corruption levels have been rising just as donors prepare to support the new state and have committed an additional US$500 million per year to support its budget.

Afghanistan and Iraq: wired to fail?

The wars in Iraq and Afghanistan provide dramatic case studies of how military intervention, and the contracts associated with it, can unleash new forms of corruption, even when the objective is to build improved and democratic government. In the case of Afghanistan, the objective was to destroy the regime of the Taliban which had hosted Osama bin Laden and Al Qaeda, and in the second to 'take out' Saddam Hussein, allegedly also as an active accomplice to Al Qaeda but actually for complex political reasons driven by domestic politics in the USA. In both cases, the primacy of the objective of 'regime change' was allowed to override a strategy of containing corruption in the successor regimes, and in fact in both cases US strategy undoubtedly increased the incidence of corruption of the successive governments.

The contradictions which have plagued relations between the government of Hamid Karzai and all its Western backers can be traced to American support from 1980 onwards for the mujahideen in their struggle against the Russian-backed regime of Mohammad Najibullah. In addition to the funds received from the USA and from Saudi Arabia, which committed itself to tripling those from US sources, mujahideen were also active traders in opium across the border to Pakistan where weapons were easy to purchase. In this process they facilitated the growth of an export trade with international linkages in as many as 20 countries of the region, as well as the rich markets of Europe. The fall of Najibullah's government ushered in a period when power was divided between warlords who vied for control of Kabul, which ultimately fell to the Taliban in 1996. At first the

USA was not necessarily hostile to the new government. In fact, in 1997 the California-based energy company UNOCAL was engaged in a serious negotiation with the Taliban government, which would have seen a large-scale oil pipeline project running through Afghanistan[17] carrying oil from Turkmenistan to Pakistan (in order to avoid Iran).

One year later, however, Osama bin Laden, a guest of the Taliban's leader, Mullah Omar, commissioned the attack on US embassies in both Dar es Salaam and Nairobi, in the latter case killing more than 350 people. However, it was only after the destruction of the Twin Towers in New York on 11 September 2001 that the USA fashioned a strategy of renewed support for several of the warlords whom they had supported in the fight against the Russians. The warlords had vied for power when the Najibullah regime fell, and now confronted the Taliban regime which had not yet secured control of the whole country.[18] When the Taliban regime eventually fell, and the Karzai government came to power in 2002, the USA continued to support the warlords and their militias as separate entities, even when they were formally part of the government. The ambiguity in this situation was reinforced by Karzai's first Minister of Defence, Mohammed Fahim, who was more interested in ensuring that the warlords were maintained as individual forces through the government payroll rather than in building a national army. As Ahmed Rashid has commented: 'the warlords were seen (by the USA) as a cheap and beneficial way to retain US allies in the field who might even provide information about Al Qaeda'.[19]

In fact, some of the warlords were also busy taking over the poppy production system partially developed (though suspended in 2001) by the mujahideen. By 2005, total heroin exports from Afghanistan were estimated at US$4 billion and accounted for about half of GDP, engaging about 2.3 million Afghans or 14 per cent of the population in the trade. In 2007, UNODC concluded that about 30 leading traffickers controlled the trade, each of whom had more than 500 individuals working for them in the trading chain, collecting up to about 80 per cent of the border value of the crop. In a good year such as 2002, farmers could still earn US$13,000 from a hectare of land under poppy. Not surprisingly, funds on this scale are the basis of power, and are used to fund elections, buy official positions, invest in ornate property and export capital to 'safe havens'. The Kabul-based analyst, Andrew Wilder, concluded that the parliament brought to power in the 2005 elections included 17 recognized drugs traffickers.[20]

US strategy was to leave Kabul ineffectively protected by a weak national army, relying on the warlords to control the countryside, and allow US forces free to hunt down Al Qaeda. The CIA therefore set up the Afghanistan Militia Force (AMF), whose commanders received cash and weapons, many of which were sold on local markets and purchased by the Taliban using resources from the drugs trade. The warlords' revenue was not restricted to financial support for their own militias: in some cases, such as General Agha Sherzai in the south, they became important organizers of supplies to the US Army. Recognizing the self-destruction implied by this, Senator, later Vice President, Joe Biden, was quoted as saying in May 2008: 'Not only is the US failing to rein in the warlords, we are actually making them the centre piece of our strategy.'[21]

A huge aid programme was superimposed on both government, NGOs and local *jirgas*. In 2006, total US aid was US$3.2 billion; by 2007, it was more than US$7 billion. The UK, as the second largest donor, had ramped up its aid (excluding military costs) to more than US$190 million by 2010, and intended to increase it further. In 2002/3, British aid included US$80 million committed to the compensation of farmers for the eradication of poppies, paid at a rate of US$1,250 to US$1,500 per hectare. However, aid flows on this scale into countries recovering from civil war are particularly difficult to control. US aid officials hardly left their highly fortified compound in Kabul, disbursing grants through American NGOs with local partners. The poppy elimination fund was channelled through local governors who acquired large parts of it for themselves; significant sums were leaked to the Taliban militias who were re-grouping and used it to buy weapons; and some of the cash was actually used to expand production at the farm level.

Formal government appointees were part of this picture. In Helmand Province in the south – later the scene of major NATO military commitments – Governor Mohammad Akhundzada encouraged poppy cultivation, especially by his own Alizai tribe which dominated the province. Reportedly under pressure from British prime minister Tony Blair, President Karzai removed Akhundzada from office; Wali Karzai, the president's younger brother, subsequently acquired a great deal of informal power in the south, only to be assassinated in 2011. Under both leaders the position of Chief of Police in poppy areas could be auctioned off to the highest bidder, raising fees of up to US$100,000 for six months of office.

Search for quick income by local officials has also come to characterize the arrangements for providing security to US military supplies programmed to reach bases all over the country. In June 2010, a US House of Representatives Committee[22] published a devastating report (Warlord Inc) on the security arrangements surrounding the convoys which deliver these supplies. At the heart of the problem is a Host Nation Trucking Contract (HNT), costed at US$2.16 billion and intended to fund contractors capable of providing ground transport for 70 per cent of the *materiel* required by US Armed Forces. Six contracts were awarded under this arrangement in March 2009. The selected contractors then paid off local warlords including Taliban militia, or employed private security guards to do the same. This was confirmed by Secretary of State Hillary Clinton who, in giving evidence to the Senate Foreign Relations Committee in December 2009, said: 'One of the major sources of funding for the Taliban is the protection money.'

A separate report by a team at New York University[23] concluded:

> The illicit taxation of private security providers escorting convoys and other scams on private transport and security are also an important source of funding for corrupt police and insurgents … Although it is transportation and construction companies … who are the main source of 'protection money', private security escorts also pay Taliban not to be attacked.

Equally, if not more disturbing, is the requirement that the larger security providers pay substantial monthly bribes to every governor, police chief and local military unit along the route. The Congressional Report concluded: 'This arrangement has fuelled a vast protection racket run by a shadowy network of warlords, strongmen, commanders, corrupt Afghan officials, and perhaps others.' Other major contributors to the war effort, including Italy, Netherlands, Australia and the UK, make comparable payments through their own contractors. Although at the time the report was written Admiral Mike Mullen, Chairman of the Joint Chiefs of Staff, had formed a Task Force to look into this process, its impact remains unclear. This tragic situation has grown out of the tradition of deals with warlords pursued by the USA and its allies since the overthrow of the Taliban. In this context it is impossible to build an institutional framework for fighting corruption. The acceptance of anti-corruption legislation, and the measures which go with it, can only attract public support when the government can be seen to be serious about its implementation.

Iraq: new corruption for old

Early mistakes of policy created a comparable outcome after the invasion of Iraq. On 15 May 2003, Donald Rumsfeld, US Secretary of Defence, appointed L. Paul Bremer III, a little known former mid-level US Ambassador,[24] to be 'responsible for the temporary government of Iraq'. In a first phase, the official source of funding was designated the Iraq Relief and Reconstruction Fund (IRRF), which operated for 14 months from April 2003 and was then replaced by the Development Fund for Iraq (DFI), the latter being supervised by an International Advisory and Monitoring Board (IAMB), whose establishment was approved by the UN Security Council. Responsibility passed in turn to the Iraq Inspector General (IIG) in May 2004. The sources of funds available to fund these entities were Iraq's funds frozen in US banknotes, cash seized by coalition forces, and oil and gas revenue raised under the 'Oil for Food' programme operated while Saddam Hussein remained in power. The IRRF had funds which totalled US$70 billion, but were administered in a manner which was so cavalier that personal self-enrichment became a key characteristic of the programme.

These funds were directed to both meeting the recurrent costs of government and to attempting to resuscitate infrastructure at both the local and national level. Meeting recurrent costs involved transporting US$12 billion in cash, weighing a total of 237 tonnes, from New York to Baghdad, from which it was largely disbursed in pallets from vaults subject to little security. As one military controller[25] stated at his trial for embezzlement: 'The vault had pallet upon pallet of laundered dollar bills – when you work around that it becomes "so what – it's just paper".' When the DFI's life came to an end in May 2004, it approved the disbursement of more than US$11 billion in six weeks, apparently in order to avoid handing it to the IIG. As an accountant employed by the IAMB stated in his assessment of an internal DFI report: 'You have one paragraph, half a page for US$70 billion. You had to say that's not good enough.'[26] In fact, by the end of 2008 there had been 35 convictions of US military officers for various forms of fraud.

The pattern established by this system of funding necessarily compromised the manner in which the incoming civilian Iraqi government handled the resources which it inherited. In fact, Iraq's first post-war prime minister, Nouri al-Maliki, referred to a 'second insurgency' in which 'institutions were undermined by the widespread association of political elites with corrupt activities'. Under US pressure, the government established a Commission on Public Integrity (CPI) and an army of Inspector Generals. The first commissioner to lead the CPI was Judge Radhi Hamza al-Radhi, who ensured that it investigated more than 40 ministers and senior civil servants. These investigations carried a heavy political backlash. A long-standing clause in the Penal Code had stated that no ministry official can go on trial without permission of the responsible minister. This caveat was suspended by the CPI in 2004, but reinstated so that 48 cases were blocked from September 2006 to February 2007.

The opposition to Judge Radhi's strategy and objectives was so strong that he had to seek political asylum in August 2007 in the USA, where he gave evidence to a Congressional committee. With reference to the arrest of a minister by the CPI he told Congress: 'cases like this influenced strong opposition to the CPI, with demands for the curtailment of its powers'. An over-burdened court was unable or unwilling to devote attention to the 3,000 cases forwarded to the Courts by the CPI from 2004 to 2007. Verdicts were pronounced in only 8 per cent of the cases, although Radhi estimated the cost to the economy of the underlying corruption to be 'as high as US$18 billion'.[27] The professional staff of the CPI were even more harshly treated: between 2004 and 2007, 31 CPI employees were assassinated and 12 family members murdered. As one local Inspector General commented: 'If I do my job well they will kill me.'[28] This is the background to the fact that Iraq has languished at the bottom of TI's Corruption Perception Index since its first inclusion in 2005.

In each of these cases – Turkmenistan, Sudan, Iraq and Afghanistan – factors which are geopolitical and strategic have formed the basis for actions by the West. In each case, although there have been attempts to mitigate corruption, they have not struck at the underlying forces that drive it, and in fact have been overwhelmed by them.

Corruption and growth

The balance of the debate about corruption over the last 20 years has been largely 'won', at least in policy-making and civil society circles, by the view that corruption undermines development in the ways discussed. Numerous analyses, many with impressive statistical evidence, have demonstrated the negative impact of corruption on equality, growth, and local and foreign investment. Perhaps the leading analyst of this perspective is Daniel Kaufmann, formerly head of the World Bank Institute, and from 2010 at the Brookings Institute in Washington. His valuable contributions to this critique of corruption have included the notion of 'state capture', where corrupt networks gain control of political decisions, ensuring that resources are consistently deployed in their direction.

There have always been dissenters from this analysis of corruption's impact. Some of these have echoed the critique of an earlier period, and sustained the argument that corruption is simply one method of facilitating the creation of a wealthy elite which will invest its resources productively. Others have delved deeper into the nature of corruption in different national contexts and argued that the relationship between corruption and growth depends on the social and political context in a specific country. Mushtaq Khan, a professor at the School of African and Oriental Studies in London, is the leading exponent of this second school of thought. This revisionist view of the relationship between corruption and growth is likely to gain ground in the coming years simply because the rapid growth rates achieved by China and India in the last decade have occurred in spite of levels of corruption, which can confidently be described as 'endemic'.[29] Their success mirrors the earlier success of South Korea and Malaysia in kick-starting industrialization.

The key argument which underlies the 'corruption can be compatible with growth' case is as follows. The forms of economic development which make a major and sustainable impact on a country's GDP are those which deploy resources, such as labour, land and financial savings, which would otherwise be idle or underemployed. In the cases of the 'Asian Tigers' in the 1970s and 1980s, and of China in the 1990s and 2000s, these resources were mobilized effectively, often as the instrument of corrupt deals. The surpluses the investments generated were re-invested in similar resource-activating deals, many of which were also corrupt. On the other hand, in Africa a great deal of corruption has focused on the extraction of public revenue for private gain, or on phoney projects which have minimal impact. Countries such as Indonesia and Thailand fall between these two extremes.

Economists have for many years used the concept of 'rents' to describe the profits achieved from early entry into new industries, but also the fruits of corruption – where this means excess income over the 'next best' opportunity. Where the concept applies to corruption its use can be broad and embrace 'monopoly profit, politicised subsidies, illegal mafia organised transfers, short term super profits, oligopolistic property deals',[30] and the mispricing of exports and imports. Mushtaq Khan suggests that it is possible to distinguish between 'useful' and harmful rents, where the former adds value to the economy, even after allowing for the resources – such as public finance – which corruption burns up. In Khan's analysis, South Korea's long-time ruler from 1960 to 1979, General Park Chung-hee, used 'licensed corruption' as one of the incentives to build the *chaebol*[31] economy, through maintaining control over the ways in which 'rents' were allocated – and maintained a healthy flow into his own pockets.[32] The opportunities given to the *chaebol* were carefully structured, enabling them to generate 'rents' as they bought into new technologies from abroad – especially Japan – but which were carefully phased out over time.

The fact that this situation could be manipulated under Park Chung-hee in a strategic way also depended on the fact that there were very few competing interest groups in Korea at the time – since the Japanese occupation of the 1930s and during World War II had destroyed the land-owning aristocracy. In the era initiated by Roh Tae-woo from 1987 the situation changed, as a growing economy created a stronger private sector beyond the *chaebols,* and corruption became a much more diversified phenomenon. In fact, Roh Tae-woo and Chun Doo-hwan were both themselves prosecuted on corruption charges in 1996 and imprisoned. The subsequent regimes of Kim Dae-jung and Roh Moo-hyun handled the economy successfully, but presided over an era in which 'unlicensed corruption' was rampant and any use of corruption as a 'strategic asset' had long evaporated. In fact, Roh Moo-hyun, after leaving the presidency in 2008, was investigated on bribery charges and committed suicide in 2009. In the case of South Korea, corruption, which had once been compatible with mobilizing untapped resources, had by the 1990s become a major source of public contention and of political fragility. This is a major qualification of Khan's argument that economic growth is compatible with corruption.

China

In China, the Communist Party has effectively tolerated corruption with recurrent partly rhetorical campaigns to stamp it out. Its nature is largely determined by two factors: first, about one-third of public expenditure is 'off budget'; and second, a large part of public expenditure is allocated at provincial, city and township levels. Much 'off budget' expenditure is raised through local levies determined by the party leadership. On the other hand, the proportion of these tax receipts invested in creating public assets is much higher than the average for the industrialized countries of the OECD (except for South Korea). Further, the banking system, still dominated by the state, has been guided by the party at national level to channel a target level of funds to each of China's 31 provinces, ensuring the huge flow of resources which have created China's infrastructural miracle.

Managing this mainly resource-enhancing process has created many opportunities for graft within the party. Land has been one of them: officials at the level of city, county and townships have been able to achieve high illegal incomes from the allocation of land, and have often been a 'shareholder' in its subsequent development. The loan programme gave the party leadership at Provincial level the means to execute the new infrastructural investment programme in their own domain, but plenty of scope to siphon off personal rewards. The scale has been large: since 1982, between 130,000 and 190,000 party officials have been disciplined annually for corruption-related offences.[33]

Very high-profile leaders have not been immune from the attack on corruption. The case of Chen Liangyu, party secretary for Shanghai, is an example of this. However, most of the US$1 billion he appropriated from Shanghai's Social Security Fund was invested in buildings with a very high income-generating potential, creating a huge number of jobs and demand for building materials sourced within China. In the finance sector, two successive chairmen of the China Construction Bank, Wang Xuebing and Zhang Enzhao, received extensive jail sentences for corruption in 2002 and 2005 respectively.[34] Clearly, there have been major personal kickbacks from this system. Analysing the scale of corruption in the construction sector, Minxin Pei, writing in the *Financial Times* in 2002,[35] estimated that kickbacks in the industry accounted for 3 to 5 per cent of China's GDP.

At the same time as the opportunity for corruption in infrastructure has been thriving, the provincial and even county leadership has been engaged in a highly competitive bid for both domestic and foreign investment. Given the authority to set the business terms for their domains, and with a highly decentralized fiscal system, provincial leaders have been able to attract 'resource enhancing' investment in China's fastest growing regions – extending to the western cities of Chengdu and Kunming in the 2000s. Steven Cheung, an economist with many years' experience in China, comments that a city with 300,000 residents may have as many as 500 people whose activities are focused entirely on sourcing investment.[36] In these ways, corruption in China has been compatible with 'resource enhancement'.

However, this is not universally true. China has also been plagued by the massive flight of corruptly gained capital overseas. The Central Bank of China estimated in 2011 that $124 billion had been laundered overseas since 1995 (see footnote 35). In 2003, the *People's Daily* stated that 8,300 officials had fled China in the first six months of the year, and 6,500 had 'disappeared' within China[37] with their financial assets secreted in the domestic or 'offshore' banking system. Two-thirds of these individuals were senior executives of state-owned companies. 'Suspicious' payments are a major headache for the banking system: in 2003 the regulatory authorities, working to the Central Bank of China, stated that they had identified 2.6 million suspicious and large-sum transactions amounting to a staggering US$600 billion[38] – or 90 per cent of China's official foreign exchange assets. Of the thousands of officials who choose and are able to leave each year, only a handful are successfully repatriated to China: of the 8,300 who left in 2003, only 600 were repatriated.

Corruption on this scale and of this type is 'resource reducing' in relation to China's economy, and its impact has to be balanced against the other types of corruption. However, the impact of the latter is clearly predominant and operates in such a way that buys the loyalty of party officials while being an integral part of China's phenomenal economic growth. Richard McGregor, author of an in-depth study of the party in contemporary China, concludes that corruption 'becomes the glue that keeps the system together'[39] without derailing economic growth.

India

In the case of India, where society comprises an innumerable series of interest groups, the scope for government policy to use 'licensed corruption' as a means of directing the economy is non-existent. The government of Jawaharlal Nehru, which came to power in 1947, chose to develop a planned economy, based more on Soviet experience than on western market economics. The planning system, designed to create a heavy industrial sector, was sophisticated and based on an intricate licensing system which reached down to very low levels of small-scale business. This 'licence raj', especially at the local level, became legendary for its propensity for corruption. As an individual of high personal integrity, Nehru would never have contemplated using corruption as a strategic weapon to initiate specific industrial investments. Further, India's leading existing conglomerate – Tata – was recognized as operating on the basis of strong ethical principles, frequently espoused by one of its leading chairmen, J.R.D. Tata.[40] However, the physical rationing of resources, which was integral to India's planning system, proved to be easily subverted by the bribery of the 'licence raj'. The system also depended on employment-creating subsidies, at first deemed strategic, but later regarded as a political right by the teeming interest groups whose lobbying power dominated politics. The possibility of withdrawing a subsidy to a particular project, once awarded, has seldom been achieved.

In response to the poor record of the planned economy, India adopted a strategy of liberalization in the 1980s and

1990s. This was driven by a perception that it would greatly reduce corruption through challenging monopolies and vested interest groups. Initiated on a modest basis by Prime Minister Rajiv Gandhi in 1984, the policy was reinforced from 1991 under the successor government of Narasimha Rao whose finance minister was Manmohan Singh.[41] The liberalization programmes of subsequent governments have been very successful in generating unprecedented growth rates of GDP of more than 8 per cent from 2005 to 2010, but have not succeeded in addressing corruption. In fact, the same five-year period has witnessed corporate corruption scandals on a huge scale. For example, in the case of the computer company Satyam, these have involved falsified accounts omitting US$1 billion of assets, or one-third of the total. In the case of the 2G mobile phone contracts awarded in 2008, these concerned the underpricing by nearly US$40 billion of fees payable to government.

The growth achieved by the Indian economy in the last decade has been the result, for the most part, of successful private and corporate investment, with a significant contribution from foreign direct investment. While this has not been seriously distorted by corruption, it has co-existed with extensive corruption in public services, including procurement at all levels. The existence of powerful Maoist, or Naxalite, groups in ten of India's 26 states is confirmation of the response to corruption in the country's more backward eastern and north-eastern districts. The case of contemporary India indicates that corruption is compatible with growth but that it is growth of the kind which further heightens inequality and generates very dangerous political outcomes.

Africa

Corruption in Africa has seldom been of the 'licensed' variety, and has rarely added value to basic resources. It lies at the opposite end to South Korea in Mushtaq Khan's classification, and has been 'value reducing'. The cases of corruption in Nigeria, for example, consist almost exclusively of instances of exploitation of public finances from simple theft, exchange rate manipulation, or diversion of resources (notably oil) outside the formal economy. There is significant investment in industry and agribusiness in Nigeria, much of it associated with corruption, but it has scarcely been the subject of government direction or strategy. In Cameroon in the 1960s and 1970s, a significant attempt at state-led industrialization – through SNI,[42] a government-owned investment company – initiated a series of corporate ventures which were weighed down by the corruption which was built into their operations. The scope for serious economic development policy was also undermined by the existence of a special presidential account which received most of the oil revenue due to government from the late 1970s onwards, and was deployed arbitrarily in the interests of domestic politics and the private fortune of Ahmadou Ahidjo, Cameroon's first president.

A similar fate characterized more than 400 companies which were initiated by a similar state investment company – the National Development Corporation – in Tanzania. These early post-independence attempts at industrialization, seriously distorted by corruption, were superseded by a strategy of extreme liberalization from the mid-1980s onwards. This agenda was largely driven from Washington, where the World Bank was in thrall to the renewed emphasis on the market triggered by President Reagan and Prime Minister Thatcher. A secondary, though not explicit, objective of this policy was to minimize the corruption which now characterized many developing economies, not least those in Africa.

This economic liberalization programme of the 1980s and 1990s focused particularly on the privatization of state-owned corporate assets. In many countries, this was a large-scale operation, involving the sale of hundreds of companies, but often on terms which were scandalously beneficial to the purchaser. Kickbacks to the agencies handling the privatization were common. In many instances, the buyers saw this as an opportunity to obtain assets which would continue to be protected through tariffs or price guarantees. In some cases, such as the mining sector in Zambia, the buyers were able to negotiate very favourable corporate tax regimes which appeared particularly outrageous when the price of copper began to climb to unprecedented levels after 2005. Many of the deals were concluded on the basis of a joint venture between foreign and local investors, with the latter acting as insiders able to see the opportunities to collect from the government and regulatory agencies.

If there has been a guiding hand in the orchestration of these deals in Africa, it has been to boost, placate or undermine specific ethnic interest groups. In Kenya, the successive governments of Presidents Kenyatta and Moi guided the fruits of corruption to their own ethnic groups, heightening ethnic tension while failing to trigger high levels of domestic investment. Similar ethnic politics dominated the situation in nearly every sub-Saharan African state. In some cases, such as the Ivory Coast under President Félix Houphouët-Boigny, the system was managed with considerable economic success for at least 30 years, but in ways which privileged one ethnic group at the expense of another. A notable African exception to this was Botswana, where its first president, Seretse Khama, set high personal standards but had the advantage of running a country with only one predominant ethnic group.[43]

In broad terms, corruption in Africa has seldom triggered investment capable of enhancing resources by adding value. The 'rents' gained in Africa have been deployed elsewhere, leaving Africa's growth rate at only 30 per cent that of east Asia from 1970 to 2010. In the case of Africa, the analyses of both Kaufmann and Khan converge: there has neither been an appropriate formal institutional structure to control corruption nor a social and political framework which can ensure that, if it exists, it is a net contributor to growth.

*   *   *   *   *

While anti-corruption champions and initiative takers – both individual and institutional – make progress on limited fronts, they confront not only embedded networks but also serious institutional and political constraints on the international front. The first of these is the structure of economies with 'black holes', which channel a significant percentage of GDP into offshore centres, where it lies in a limbo with no impact on growth in the country of origin (though it is perhaps channelled back for political purposes or is sometimes recycled as private investment). The second is the priority which the west has attached to regime stability in very corrupt regions – such as central Asia – where energy and related assets are so valuable that anti-corruption has been virtually ignored as a policy objective. In this same category of 'geopolitical' objectives lies the cavalier attitude to state rebuilding, and the indiscriminate support for corrupt leaders and contractors, which has characterized post-invasion policies in both Afghanistan and Iraq. The third constraint is an inescapable reappraisal between corruption and economic growth, triggered by the record of the Asian Tigers and now by that of China and India. This reappraisal makes the policy 'line' of the major aid donors – that corruption always undermines economic growth – more difficult to sustain.

10

Corruption and Global Warming

There is now a broad consensus, with important dissidents, as to the need to ameliorate climate change, undoubtedly the most important issue confronting humanity. However, nearly all the measures proposed to address climate change on a global basis, with actions in both the 'north' and the 'south', involve the expenditure of huge sums of money, both to 'mitigate'[1] the impact of climate change and to help countries 'adapt'[2] to it. If these resources are mis-spent, the consequences, unlike those of mis-spent development aid, extend throughout the world, and in the long run could be catastrophic for the planet.

The huge international conferences that began with Rio in 1992, went on to Kyoto in 1997 and to Copenhagen in 2009, triggered a series of complex action plans with the common objective of achieving a dramatic reduction in the release of carbon dioxide into the environment. The broad direction of these action plans was confirmed and expanded at the summit held in Durban in December 2011.

The International Panel on Climate Change (IPCC) – an international body with over 600 member scientists – has been at the forefront of this process, confirming that a continuing rise in global temperatures by at least 1°C is inevitable. The IPCC argued that it was not possible to counteract the impact of the greenhouse gases which had already been released, and which are the current source of global warming, but that it was possible to devise measures which would prevent an increase in gases beyond this level.

It suggested that the maximum increase which the world can tolerate is a rise of 2°C by 2050, of which 1.4°C is already certain to occur. Even at this level there are very serious consequences for agriculture and food security, the availability of water, the spread of disease vectors, and for a rise in sea level sufficient to drown whole countries – such as the Maldives – and swamp parts of others, such as Bangladesh. Even the relatively modest target of holding the average global temperature increase to 2°C involves a reduction in emissions of 30 per cent by 2030, and 80 per cent by 2050.

Putting flesh on these broad targets, a report written by Professor Nick Stern[3] in 2007 and commissioned by the British government, proposed a set of international policies which would achieve the 2°C limit, at a cost of 'only' 1 per cent of overall consumption of energy per head per year. The means to this objective in the 'developed' world ranged from domestic insulation, to renewable and nuclear energy systems, to new energy-saving technologies for vehicles, to the imposition of 'caps' on industrial emissions which could only be exceeded if the polluter bought 'credits' which could be invested in the developing world in programmes which 'saved' a corresponding amount of carbon. In India and China, where demand for energy is expected to double by 2030, it means a huge emphasis on renewable and nuclear energy, and a major reduction of dependence on coal. Both countries are committed to reducing carbon emissions from their industrial systems by 25 per cent by 2020 in comparison to 2005.

In order to realize these goals, a series of funds have been established to finance either the capping of existing commissions or investments which directly or indirectly lead to the restriction of carbon emissions. These include the Kyoto Protocol Adaptation Fund, the Joint Implementation and Clean Development Mechanism (CDM), at least six funds financed by bilateral aid donors, and REDD.[4] The Joint Implementation Fund is based on proposed collaborations between emitters and a country of the same region (for example, Italy and Romania), and the CDM is based on collaboration between an emitter and a low-income 'developing' country. The funds available through REDD are only available for initiatives that restrict deforestation or promote forestation, and priority has been given to countries with big forests, such as the DRC and Brazil.

The policies and institutions which are integral to this set of initiatives incur a huge risk of being subverted by corruption and fraud. The centrepiece is the 'cap and trade' system, which is the basis of carbon trading on several world stock exchanges, such as Bluenext in Paris, LCH Clearnet in London, and the Chicago Climate Exchange. A comparable system with the objective of reducing acid rain had previously been (successfully) launched in the USA for sulphur dioxide, reducing emissions by nearly 50 per cent from 1991 to 2000. The 'cap and trade' system in the EU[5] was launched in 2007: aggregate emissions for all member states were calculated for specific industrial sectors by the EU Commission, and then allocated in the form of numbered 'allowances' to more than 10,000 individual companies. If under-fulfilled, these allowances could be sold to surplus emitters; if over-fulfilled, the company concerned could purchase allowances from other emitters. In the subsequent years the European system became the world's largest, with an annual turnover of about €90 billion,[6] the lion's share of a global market of about €140 billion. For the period 2005–13 it was agreed that the registration of credits in this market would be handled by national governments, resulting in registers of very varied quality and accuracy. These discrepancies have paved the way for serious fraud in the market.

One set of companies, in the energy sector, were able to take early advantage of the mistake made in the issue of the credits in 2008. The number of emission allowances exceeded their needs, causing a dramatic fall in the price of the credits. This enabled four companies to buy at the low price in the market but base their charges to customers on the much higher 'guide' price which the European Trading Scheme (ETS) had projected before the allowances were issued. As a consequence, their aggregate 'windfall' profits were €6–8 billion. In November 2010 the Swiss cement company, Holcim S.A., found that it had lost 1.6 million allowances, equivalent to 1.6 million tonnes of carbon dioxide and worth about €20 million. These had been stolen by cyberthieves able to hack into Holcim's computer system.[7] The allowances, which had been registered in Romania, were sold on to companies in Italy and Lichtenstein. This was a prelude to a wider attack on the market three months later when allowances held in several national registries were attacked, and a total of €30 million was stolen, leading to a suspension in trading on the EU exchanges lasting more than one week. The software which facilitates this kind of attack is readily available on 'underground' internet forums, and costs as little as €35. In Germany in 2010 allowances were bought and exported in order to facilitate 'round tripping' on VAT payments; in the same year in Hungary used allowances were reissued and resold. The suspension of trading in early 2011 shook the market, and caused the EU Commission to find that security of the register was below par in 14 of the member states.

The principle underlying the carbon market – by which credits are transferred from low-carbon emitters to high-carbon emitters – also characterizes the Clean Development Mechanism (CDM), though in this case the transfers are between high-income and low-income countries. The scale of the task in ensuring that projects funded under the CDM are corruption-free and effective is enormous: in 2010 the CDM reviewed more than 5,300 projects, more than half of which were in India and China. The assessment is carried out by a small number of accredited verification companies, numbering only 30 from 2008 to 2010. The process too has been the subject of major abuse. In 2006 the Board of the CDM,[8] led by its chairman Hans Jürgen Stehr, admitted that up to a fifth of the projects it had supported were suspect, and their impact was not 'additional' to those which were already launched or in the pipeline. In fact, by 2008–9, 76 per cent of all projects registered under the CDM had been fully prepared and were ready to go *before* being submitted to the CDM – implying that they might well have been implemented regardless of CDM support.

One of CDM's consultants, Axel Michaelowa, found that 52 CDM projects in India financed up to 2006 failed this criterion. In India, the majority of certified emissions are greenhouse gases, nearly 40 per cent of which originate in coal mining. There is good evidence that investments have been planned and made in coal mines with high emission levels in order to collect payments from the CDM as emissions were later reduced. In Bangladesh, when the Bangladesh Climate Change Resilience Fund was established, which had as one of its objectives the improvement of dyke systems, no fewer than 150 MPs set up dredging companies in which they had a major share. Four of the verification companies accredited to the CDM were disaccredited between 2008 and 2010.

Governments that contribute to the funding of the CDM have become very conscious of these problems. Both the US Government Accounting Office and the Federal Trade Commission have published reports criticizing the whole principle of carbon offsets under these programmes, and citing further major abuses of the system to date. Within low-income countries the problems have been acute.

The carbon offset framework is clearly susceptible to high-level financial fraud of a very sophisticated variety. The REDD programme is not based on offsets, but does depend on the identification of viable projects which will not be subverted through corruption. Its objective of minimizing deforestation is complex, but now extends to the 'possibility of sustainable forest management, conservation and an increase in the forest carbon stock',[9] thus creating a new asset class of stored carbon. However, it will make grants not only to state-backed forest authorities who restrict logging, but also to corporate promoters of managed forestry concessions. The key geographical focus of REDD are the ten countries with the world's largest forests, led by Brazil, Indonesia and the DRC, although this does not exclude a number of countries with a smaller forest base, such as Tanzania and Kenya. In each case, in order to access the funds, the country concerned must prepare a REDD plan which deals with 'governance' issues as well as a disbursement strategy.

The DRC is a critical country in relation to REDD, because of the scale of its forest resource which, at 145 million hectares, covers half of the country and contributes to the livelihood of 40 million people out of a total of 70 million. The potential reduction of emissions from a successful programme has been estimated at 2.2 to 2.5 gigatonnes of CO_2 equivalents, on a cumulative basis, between 2010 and 2030.[10] But the forestry sector is dominated by the informal economy which supplies 1.7 million cubic metres of timber to the informal Kinshasa market per year, whereas formal sector operators supply less than a fifth of this. Further, the formal sector itself is notoriously corrupt. In 2006, prompted by the donor community, the government of the DRC reviewed all its formal forestry concessions, reducing these from 156 concessions on 22 milllion hectares to 65 on 9 million hectares. However, this process has been largely nominal since many of those cancelled concessionaries have reverted to informal exploitation. At present it seems almost certain that the REDD programme in the DRC will consist of support to a small number of large-scale plantation projects, rather than enabling the government and local communities to conserve carbon locked into forest soils.

Other countries are tackling the problem in a way which is perhaps more promising. In 2010, Indonesia established a special unit christened the 'Task Force on REDD' with antennae all over the country. In Kenya a series of very large-scale corruption scandals in the late 1990s under President Moi saw the excision of 100,000 hectares from the Mau Forest Complex on the Aberdare mountains, which was awarded to politicians, civil servants and smaller-scale farmers with a political allegiance to the government as an election year approached. However, this was not exclusively masterminded from the top: local councils played a key role. The Ndung'u Commission, established in 2004 to examine the 'land grabs', reported:

> Instead of playing their role as custodians of public resources including land, county and municipal councils have posed the greatest danger to these resources ... the most pronounced land grabbers in these areas were the councillors themselves. The corruption within central government has been replicated at the local level through the activities and omissions of county and municipal councillors.[11]

The aggregate sums committed to addressing climate change are now colossal. Public sector funds totalling US$100 billion per year are expected to flow through channels – such as REDD – which are untested and frequently unco-ordinated. This is equivalent to the level of current aid flows from all sources. Yet it is clear that the success of each of these major channels suffers from a major threat from corruption. The Joint Implementation and CDM Funds risk being led into projects which are promoted through corrupt means; REDD risks being disbursed to state-sponsored entities which cannot handle it, or to companies whose operations will not be genuinely additional, and in both cases being subverted by private and financial interests; and carbon trading is prone to outright fraud of the kind experienced in Europe in early 2011. The consequence of a 50 per cent reduction in the effectiveness of climate change measures as a result of corruption would be a failure to limit global warming to 2°C by 2050, with untold consequences.

11

The People's Voice

In Indonesia, no less than 1 million Facebook users associate themselves with the national anti-corruption agency, the KPK, and communicate messages between each other which relate to 'mafia'-type activities in Indonesia.[1] In Peru the lively young cartoon figure, 'Lupita', is the rallying icon, displayed on YouTube and Twitter, for the anti-corruption campaign of Proetica, the chapter of TI in Peru. In India the 'I paid a bribe' website had attracted, by late 2011, comments and reactions from more than 750,000 participants, many of whom detail the bribes they have been obliged to pay, or how they resisted paying.

Popular campaigning against local and international corruption has now found ways of using social media, and the Internet, which has introduced a new dimension. How much difference will this make? Is there now a real chance of widespread popular reaction against corruption (as in north Africa in early 2011), or will governments resist popular pressure for as long as possible and ride out a stream of protest (as in China), or ultimately just respond to public opinion (as in India in 2011)?

Opinion and government: from China to Tunisia

Protest in China at the local level, much of it focused on corruption, is widespread but sporadic, with demonstrations against specific targets estimated at 80,000 per year.[2] The government's response is focused on high-profile cases, often with a political slant, ostensibly to deter corruption on a wider front and at a lower income level. The large number of cases reported for disciplining by local Party officials seldom lead to prosecution and even less frequently to jail.[3] The Chinese 'blogosphere' does not believe that this amounts to a high-level attack on corruption, and certainly not on the corruption prevalent amongst party cadres, which was one of the key subjects of the Tiananmen Square rebellion in 1989. In March 2011, during the highest level of parliamentary consultation in China – the 'Two Congresses' – one blogger commented:

> Why are all these people representatives and CCP members daring to make such stupid statements in the solemn gathering of the two congresses? The answer is simple. These people are supported by a corrupt and privileged class which stands in opposition to the working class. This group of people can talk any bullshit without any consequences.[4]

In fact, although much of China's blogging is social, its scale is overwhelming, and contains many political postings. Sina Weibo, a microblog comparable to Twitter, and the country's largest web portal, has 100 million users and many millions of posts each day. Its top 100 users can attract 180 million responses. Yet it exists, according to its promoters, in constant threat of the firewall meted out to Google in China, which eventually led to Google's withdrawal.

Chinese bloggers joined the support across the world in early 2011 for Tunisia's 'jasmine' revolution. There were calls for similar anti-government demonstrations in Shanghai and

Beijing – but when events proved to be a damp squib, bloggers recorded resignation and awaited the next round of government control measures, though many suspected sympathizers were arrested. If protest in China remains well under control in both the blogosphere and the streets, the conditions necessary for real advance in rolling back domestic corruption are very limited. Individual but spectacular executions and jail sentences are likely to continue to set the tone for some years to come, even though the formal anti-corruption legislative framework is becoming tougher.

In India there is a greater chance of targeted support to address corruption, and in many communities in India this is happening on a significant scale. The most famous community-based organization – the Public Affairs Centre in Bangalore – has been successful in achieving widespread reductions in corruption in the provision of public services in the city, by producing a 'Report Card' on progress itemized by service. More recently, established websites such as 'I paid a bribe' and 'Truth About India Corruption' have exposed bribery on a heroic scale, in the former case by allowing many thousands of bloggers to recount their story and aggregating the bribes paid (though resistance to paying is also recorded). Numerous local protest groups, such as that led since 1971 by Anna Hazare in villages in Maharashtra State, have lobbied successfully against the destruction of natural resources in specific areas, and exposed corruption across a range of government services. However, those civil society groups campaigning for a bar on candidates with a criminal record standing as MPs have found it impossible to get such legislation passed, in spite of a 20-year struggle, and regardless of the fact that a third of MPs in parliament have been charged with crimes of corruption, vote rigging or violence.

However, in 2011 civil society's fight against corruption was given a tremendous lift by the hunger strike of Anna Hazare, now working on a national level, to ensure the appointment of a *Lokpal* or powerful anti-corruption Ombudsman. His team demanded that the board of the *Lokpal* should be appointed by a college comprising Nobel Laureates, judges and respected members of the electoral commission, who would then draft new tough anti-corruption legislation. Surrounded by thousands of supporters, summoned to central Delhi by a Facebook campaign, Hazare and his immediate supporters attracted national media attention on a colossal scale, boosted by the publicity given to the large-scale corporate corruption scandals that had rocked India in the preceding year. Unsure how to react to the hunger strike, the government briefly jailed Hazare, and he was strongly criticized by Rahul Gandhi, a member of parliament and son of Sonya Gandhi, chair of the dominant Congress Party, a misjudgement which the Indian government came to regret. However, there was considerable support for the government by India's elite, who rejected the idea of civil society determining the outcome of what should have been a parliamentary decision on both the composition of the *Lokpal* Board and the content of the legislation. Although the measures in question were passed by parliament, the saga created major divisions even within India's anti-corruption movement.

In Russia, the extreme courage of the leaders of anti-corruption protests reflect the depth of the issue. A recognition of the role of corruption in Russia by President Medvedev was embodied in both the new Measures Against Corruption which he introduced in 2008, and in the successor National Anti-Corruption Strategy launched in 2010 which led to associated legislation. This has not proved effective in turning the tide. From the government perspective, licensed corruption is a means of securing political loyalty and lining the pockets of the *siloviki*; from the public perspective it has a disastrous effect on everyday life. The Russian chapter of Transparency International has succeeded in widening the support base for action by civil society by creating an on-line media site (Vibor

33.ru) which maintains a running commentary on corruption-related issues in the Vladimir Region, and registers cases and complaints. An even more resounding success in the 'blogosphere' is that of Alexei Navalny, whose campaign against the ruling United Russia party and a wider corrupt bureaucracy has had a powerful impact, particularly through his LiveJournal[5] and Rospil websites, which enlists armies of volunteers to pursue specific cases. Navalny is also a small investor in a range of companies quoted on the Russian stock exchange, with a view to extracting information in relation to corrupt practices. These initiatives struck a strong enough accord with the public to make him the key figure in public protest at the announced election results of February 2012. But the strength of vested interests within the government, not least at provincial level, suggests that it will be a long time before civil society is strong enough to achieve real reform.

A different picture but a similar outcome characterizes sub-Saharan Africa, where the governments which have emerged from the multiparty elections held over the last 30 years retain the means and will to clamp down on serious anti-corruption initiatives led by civil society. Thus in Kenya, anti-corruption groups have emerged to expose on-going large-scale scams well after the revelations by John Githongo of the Anglo Leasing scandal in 2003. Yet parliament has continued to approve budgets with payments for promissory notes for the fictitious beneficiaries of these deals. In Zambia, in spite of widespread public protests and work by local civil society groups, ex-President Chiluba, who died in 2011, was released from trial by the judiciary in Zambia after he had been found guilty in a London court of corruptly acquiring US$50 million during his period in office from 1991 to 2002. In Cameroon, nominal anti-corruption moves initiated by the government of Paul Biya (in office since 1979) have been met with public criticism, but leading journalists addressing the subject, such as Pius Njawé who died in the USA in 2010, have been both morally and physically attacked and imprisoned. A lone and substantive voice of dissent in Cameroon has been that of Archbishop Tumi of Douala, now retired, who for 40 years has been an outspoken critic of corruption in both society and government, and has survived through his status in the Church. In Nigeria, a cacophony of public outrage over corruption, over several decades, and well reflected in the media, has never succeeded in forming a broad-based anti-corruption front, though specific initiatives such as 'Integrity'[6] have had some impact in the corporate sector.

In South Africa, the investigation of corruption in the arms deal of 1998 triggered public outrage and a spate of media revelations, but also a closing of ranks in the ruling ANC Party and the protection of those who could be involved at the highest level, including ex-President Mbeki and his successor, Jacob Zuma. Although there has been continuous public lobbying on the issue, both by minority parties in parliament and by civil society bodies, an effective anti-corruption front has not yet emerged, and the power of investigative bodies to address large-scale corruption has actually been weakened. This was evidenced by the abolition in 2009 of the 'Scorpions', a government agency which had been playing the lead role in the investigation of cases related to the arms deal.

In Tanzania, there is a semblance of open debate about corruption but little real progress in controlling it. The newsprint media in the Swahili language have for the last ten years or more covered corruption in depth, and explored any bone of information thrown to them by elected or unelected politicians. When the parliamentary report on the Richmond scandal in electricity generation, which fingered Prime Minister Edward Lowassa, became part of the public debate, President Kikwete was obliged to ask him to resign in 2007, along with two other Cabinet members.[7] But none of those close to this deal have been prosecuted, and Lowassa himself ran successfully in the 2010 parliamentary election – and was actively supported by Kikwete. In the 2005–10 Parliament, Zitto Kabwe, an effective and well-informed MP with a very effective anti-corruption platform, was suspended from parliament for three weeks by his fellow MPs for exposing probable corruption in the mining sector. In spite of this, 74 per cent of people polled[8] in Tanzania in May 2011 said that they think 'ordinary people can make a difference in the fight against corruption'. While there is clear support in sub-Saharan Africa for popular action against corruption, it often lacks leadership and organization, especially in the face of the government's capacity to suppress and out-manoeuvre most forms of protest.

In the countries of the European Union (EU) where existing anti-corruption legislation is a by-product of past public struggles, political leaders are not under severe public pressure to ratchet up anti-corruption measures, and by and large they are not losing office on the issue. While institutions anchored in Europe, such as the EU itself and the Council of Europe, pursue their formal attacks on corruption, the broader public focuses mainly on the very high-profile cases brought to the courts, including those against ex-President Chirac in France in 2011 (for a case involving his time as Mayor of Paris in the 1980s) and President Sarkozy[9] (for his alleged role in the Clearwater scandal involving access for political purposes to a secret account in Luxembourg[10]). Ex-Prime Minister Berlusconi in Italy has been in court on several different counts involving illegal corporate behaviour by his Mediaset empire. In Germany, civil society continues to be committed and active: as an energetic anti-corruption campaigner, the chapter of Transparency International in Germany has sections in 12 cities, which have proved highly effective in campaigning against corruption in municipal procurement and in relation to bribery in the pharmaceutical sector. But much of this campaigning has served to show the size of the problem: in Bavaria alone there are 50 full-time prosecutors of corruption cases.[11] The Global Corruption Barometer indicates that in the 27 countries of the

EU, more than 70 per cent of the public consider that corruption had become worse between 2007 and 2010.[12]

The corporate consolidation of the media has certainly played a part in this public pessimism. A relationship of mutual dependence between the news media and government, such as exists in Italy and France, is not conducive to media exposés of government corruption. In the UK, the exposure by other newspapers of the 'hacking' by the *News of the World* into the personal mobile phones of a range of celebrities and politicians from 2005 onwards gestated for six years while the political establishment and Metropolitan Police sought to play it down. It was only when incontrovertible evidence that the hacking had involved more than 4,000 individuals came to light that News International, the parent company of the *News of the World*, acknowledged its responsibility, and its chairman, Rupert Murdoch, agreed to appear before a committee of parliament. The public was particularly incensed that the former editor of the *News of the World*, Andy Coulson, had been appointed to be Communications Director in the office of Prime Minister David Cameron in May 2010; he was obliged to resign a year later.

In the USA, progress in fighting corruption is often made through the courts and on a case-by-case basis as precedents are established. However, public support for these prosecutions varies and can become very politicized, especially in a context in which state level Attorney Generals are elected. Eliot Spitzer and Patrick Fitzgerald, as State Attorney Generals, have in the decade since 2000 attacked corruption in New York and Illinois respectively, in the latter case resulting in the prosecution and imprisonment of two Governors of the State of Illinois between 2005 and 2010. On the other hand, charges against ex-Senator Ted Stevens of Alaska, whose five terms were ended by a flurry of charges by the State Prosecutor of Alaska, have not been upheld in Court. In contrast to these cases, as a result of the successful action and appeal to the Supreme Court in 2010 by the pressure group Citizens United, the increased scope for corporate political funding raises the leverage that corporate donors can apply to legislators in return for finance. Although in the USA a combination of focused legislation and effective prosecution has kept the anti-corruption momentum moving, corruption remains a continuous threat to both the business and political systems. Further, although civil society in the USA is vibrant, it is a force that is as likely to indirectly facilitate corruption – as in the Citizens United successful appeal to the Supreme Court – as to roll it back.

In contrast, the extraordinary events of the 'Arab spring' of early 2011 may be regarded as one of the most dramatic popular responses to corruption in history. Taking only the cases of Tunisia and Egypt, it is clear that the public anger which led to the overthrow of the governments of Zine El Abidine Ben Ali and Hosni Mubarak was fuelled by the massive resentment of the huge wealth acquired by the leaders of both regimes, as well as by the denial of effective political opposition for nearly 50 years. Although both human rights and democratic processes were part of the agenda of those calling for the overthrow of the governments, it was the recognition that the leadership had looted enormous wealth that was the most tangible basis for the public to rally for their overthrow. Mubarak was tried in August 2011 on corruption charges. The discovery of US$23 million in cash in a cupboard in one of Ben Ali's palaces in June 2011 illustrated the reality of the kleptocracy. Further, in both Tunisia and Egypt the public understood that the leaders involved constituted a network which was cohesive, and that corruption would not be rolled back unless the network itself was eased out or expelled from office. However, this would not be an easy task: by mid-2012 in Egypt it was clear that the elite group, the Supreme Council of the Armed Forces, that had supported the Mubarak regime for so long would be likely to retain a high degree of political and economic power.

The role of social media in north Africa in the 2011 uprisings needs to be considered in the context of a broader communications revolution.[13] Between 2005 and 2010 there had been a massive increase in access to satellite TV and to cell phones. In Algeria, Egypt and Morocco, the number of households with TV increased by one-third in these years, with access to satellite TV accounting for at least one-third of this.[14] In Egypt, the proportion of the population owning such phones rose during this period from 18 per cent to 67 per cent, and in Tunisia, from 67 to 95 per cent. The Al Jazeera channel dominated satellite-based TV, though many viewers were also accessing the channel through cell phones. In the first half of 2011, Al Jazeera had 182,000 followers on Twitter, 80,000 on YouTube and 1 million 'likes' and 40,000 active users on Facebook.[15] Al Jazeera was able to use this wide dissemination of cell phones to take a lead in integrating photographic material taken by such phones with that of its own reporters. The integration of the two made the broadcasters active participants in the events, and greatly reinforced their momentum. The broader pattern for the future which emerges from this is a much more interactive process between the public and the media, which the editor of the UK *Guardian* newspaper, Alan Rusbridger, has called 'the mutualisation of the news', and which will be very difficult to roll back. Opposition groups in Tunis succeeded in launching a Tunileaks website based on Wikileaks, with material on both the Ben Ali family's personal wealth and on Tunisia's relations with the USA, showing that the relationship with the USA was not quite as cosy as had been assumed.

Nonetheless, a sober assessment suggests that the social media phenomenon in north Africa was building on broader support for political change which had been rising for years, and which escalated from 2005 to 2010. Acute resentment against the regimes in Tunisia and Egypt was not limited to those under 25. In this period, urban unemployment amongst older workers had increased by more than 50 per cent, and their share of the population was actually rising. The new social media tools were able to capitalize this deep resentment across the generations and capture support from it. Where the resentment is restricted to a more limited segment of the population this has not been so effective, as was the case in Iran in the protest movements of 2009 (when Mir-Hossein Mousavi is believed to have been excluded from the presidency). There are also 'downside' costs to the technologies as they may betray the identity of activists as reported from Sudan in 2010,[16] where the security services were alleged to have set up their own Facebook page to create a link to activists.

In the global anti-corruption balance sheet the role of public outrage, and its ability to find expression, can be critical. The developments derived from new technology have given this a new strength but it will not in itself be decisive. In most of those countries where corruption is endemic, the government rather than the public has the initiative, though the events in north Africa in 2011 were a partial exception to this. International action will have a key role to play.

12

Shaping the Future

This book has shown that the conditions for real progress in rolling back corruption are tough, the fight will not be easily won, and popular pressure alone will not be enough. Political, financial and criminal networks, which thrive by corruption, are deeply entrenched and can readily morph and survive a change of regime at the top. This is as true of scams at the level of petty corruption as of the national and international level. Some characteristics of the economy at national and international level facilitate this and form a roadblock to progress. Success in overcoming four of them would open the way for more specific action.

The first is the question of the persistence of 'shadow' or 'black' economies, often accounting for 40 per cent of GDP, which at the level of small-scale enterprises in the developing world are almost completely unrecorded, but survive by paying off local officials. At the level of larger incorporated companies, in countries as diverse as India and Russia, sales may be both unrecorded and recorded, with the former a convenient and sometimes virtually limitless source of bribes. This stream of unrecorded payments plays a central role in sustaining corrupt networks at both the national and local level: corralling them into the formal system is a vital step towards controlling corruption.

Achieving this change requires the tougher regulation of business, and a higher regard for the law. The first is contingent on a more effective government machine which is itself not open to bribery, and in which its representatives will not settle for a cash payment to themselves when a larger one is due to the state. The second depends on a higher regard for law-makers and the extent to which they may be suborned by money, still far from a reality in a majority of countries whether payments are direct or result from contributions to party coffers. These are long-term goals, but a progressive government could achieve them within a decade.

The second condition is that of an end to the 'secrecy jurisdictions' which facilitate so much large-scale global corruption, whether from political or organized crime sources or from mispricing by companies. The appreciation that 'on-shore' secrecy jurisdictions are as important as 'offshore' emphasizes the scale of the problem. The last ten years have seen action at the level of formal regulatory processes from Switzerland to the Caymans. However, political will in the USA, the UK and Switzerland has so far baulked at the prospect of rival jurisdictions siphoning this enormous pool of funds away from their money markets. President Obama's campaign speeches in 2008 condemning the use by American companies of these jurisdictions have not been matched either by penalties on US companies which continued to minimize tax by parking sales revenue there, or by challenging the low tax regime for company registration in Delaware and other States. Although these arrangements are not in themselves corrupt where they constitute tax avoidance, they inflate the deposit base that keeps such jurisdictions afloat.

The UK Government has continuously proved unable and unwilling to challenge in a substantial way the secrecy jurisdictions embedded in its Caribbean and Channel Island associated territories, although it is willing to commission and receive reports on their reform. The Swiss have opened their vaults to the limited repatriation of corruptly gained funds, and made some concessions on tax evasion, but continue to offer an attractive base for new injections of similar fortunes. The most likely change-maker in respect of these objectives is the recognition by governments such as those of the USA and the UK that they are net losers of corporate revenue from the continued existence of these jurisdictions. Since 2000 this issue has been taken up by international advocacy groups such as the Tax Justice Network in the UK, Citizens for International Transparency in France, and from 2010 in the UK by a grass-roots organization, UKUNCUT, which uses peaceful lobbying tactics directed against tax evasion by multinational companies. The issue for the EU is particularly complex since some member states, such as Luxembourg and Cyprus, constitute such jurisdictions themselves; others, such as Monaco, are closely controlled by another EU member state (France); and yet others, such as Zug in Switzerland, have a high degree of autonomy in the context of a federal constitution. However, a move towards a more or less common rate of corporation tax across such jurisdictions, and in line with those in the EU and the USA, would at a stroke remove the incentive to use them as secret havens for close to US$1 trillion per year, a move which would be of clear benefit to all exchequers paying for public services.

The third condition is the elimination of corruption in world trade, and particularly bribery as a means of promoting market share. While the OECD Anti-Bribery Convention has had some success in this regard, its longer-term prospects may be limited by the increasing share of the BRIC countries in world trade. The introduction of legislation outlawing foreign bribery in 2011 in China, India, Indonesia and Russia is a critical first step in implementing the common set of rules already embodied in the UN Anti-Corruption Convention. As the share of the east Asian countries in world trade increases, western companies are likely to become more supportive of anti-bribery rules as their own share is eroded, and are likely to push their governments harder for effective implementation of foreign bribery legislation everywhere.

The General Assembly of the World Trade Organization has so far resisted labelling bribery as a restraint on trade which would enable disputes to be referred to the WTO's Disputes Settlement Body. Even though the Body's findings are not binding, and issues are finally resolved between member states themselves, it has proved itself effective in relation to other areas in dispute, such as 'dumping', and a move of this kind would be far-reaching. The basis of a reference to the Disputes Settlement Body would be a pattern of continuous bribery sustained over a number of years in order to increase the market share of a set of companies. This could, for example, include the sale of counterfeit pharmaceutical products from Asia into a large African economy, such as Nigeria, or of counterfeit DVDs into the EU.

The fourth condition is the effective curbing of organized crime, whose influence is growing and whose penetration of political systems is ensured by numerous forms of corruption. At present, the attempt to regulate organized crime is vested in a range of product specific entities – such as sections of specialized national police forces – interacting with a number of international agencies[1] with overlapping agendas. In most cases the responsibility for organized crime is separate from the responsibility for fighting corruption. These institutional arrangements often fail to recognize that the real skills of the mafias concerned are in their financial and logistical capacity rather than in their product. The criminal gangs concerned may choose to move from one product to another – such as from narcotics to counterfeit products – in response to the scope for increased profits, and even into legitimate business. They are likely to use both reputable lawyers and accountants for part of their business, and to change their international associates as different business opportunities emerge. 'Secrecy jurisdictions' provide an invaluable haven for idle profits, and for their recycling into legitimate trusts in due course.

It is highly unlikely that the present framework for combating organized crime will ratchet up its impact – which focuses on seizures of product batches, or of smuggled humans – rather than to the dismantling of the gangs which have trafficked them. Further, from the standpoint of the general public, the sheer convenience of purchasing counterfeit DVDs or Rolex watches at less than the price of the genuine product ensures a high level of public indifference to the issue. It is essential that the powerful interests which drive organized crime are subject to a much higher level of exposure, which seldom occurs outside the drugs trade. In the case of drugs, the arguments for liberalization which would end the need for corruption as a weapon to protect the traffickers are very strong. The examples of partial liberalization in the Czech Republic, Portugal and the Netherlands, and now advocated by several Latin American leaders, provide a basis for wider and deeper adoption of this strategy. The issue of counterfeit products needs to be attacked through the introduction of ever more sophisticated labelling, and associated public awareness-raising, to swing demand against counterfeit goods. Given the major role of China and India in the world counterfeit market, these governments should be consistently pressurized by the G20 to suppress counterfeit production and the organized crime groups which control it.

If these four conditions – reform of the dual economy, secrecy jurisdictions, bribery in world trade and the roll back of organized crime – are met, there are some key additional steps which could tip the balance against corruption at the global level, particularly in relation to the 'new' threats of this century. These are: a clear decision that corruption by a head of state or senior politician is a violation of human rights, and as such can be referred to the International Criminal Court (ICC); a recognized institutional structure for the repatriation of corruptly gained assets; an extension of industry-wide anti-corruption agreements between companies and between governments and business; a new approach to the reconstruction of states undermined or destroyed by civil war; and an effective commitment to integrity in climate change finance.

The ICC became operational in 2002 and was set up in order to prosecute 'the most serious crimes' of genocide, crimes against humanity, war crimes and crimes of aggression. The Court is supported by 116 states, with the principal aim of bringing to account major violations of human rights, defined according to the UN Human Rights Convention. Its remit at present does not explicitly include major crimes of corruption, even when these extend to forms which have clearly deprived many citizens of their access to livelihoods, and which are covered by the Human Rights Charter.[2] The devastation wreaked on his people by a Duvalier in Haiti, a Mobutu in DRC or even an Abacha in Nigeria is clearly a direct abrogation of their human rights.

There is therefore every reason to extend the remit of the ICC to cover the crime of large-scale corruption, a process which would have to be agreed by the member states. There is significant debate about whether the charter of the ICC in its present form can be interpreted as extending to corruption. The argument turns on whether Article Seven,[3] which covers acts which cause 'great suffering or serious injury to mental or physical health', can be applied to consistent acts of corruption over an extended period. There is sufficient disagreement about this to indicate that a revision to the 'Rome Statute', which governs the Convention, is necessary if it is to embrace corruption. This will not be an easy process because there is concern that the Court has already taken on too much, and that so far all its cases relate to crimes committed in Africa. However, the logic of this revised remit is clear, and is more than justified by the size and impact of acts of corruption.

But pinning guilt on political leaders is only one part of the story. The second part is the repatriation of the stolen funds, where they have been remitted abroad, to the 'victim' country and their investment in projects with a valuable economic or social impact. Since the year 2000, the objective of making such repatriation effective has been pursued by legal authorities, working with the banking system, in key EU countries, the USA, Switzerland, and some 'secrecy jurisdictions'. The substantial success stories are very limited: the most conspicuous are the cases of Ferdinand Marcos of the Philippines, Sani Abacha of Nigeria and Vladimiro Montesinos, close associate of Alberto Fujimori of Peru. The case of Marcos dates back to his flight to exile in 1986; after a prolonged 12-year legal wrangle with the Swiss Federal Banking Commission, assets worth US$624 million were remitted to the Philippines; in the case of Abacha, a rather shorter legal process led by 2011 to the repatriation from Switzerland to Nigeria of US$1.2 billion, or about one-third of his estimated overseas assets, and in the case of Montesinos, about US$200 million has been repatriated to Peru. In Nigeria the Economic and Financial Crimes Commission, under Nuhu Ribadu, succeeded in recovering US$5 billion, mainly from State Governors, though some of this was held locally. These very limited success stories indicate how difficult it is to establish the political will and the legal basis for repatriation of this kind, and there is the further practical problem of expenditure of the funds in a still corrupt environment. The World Bank itself, working with UNODC, the UN Agency which tackles money laundering, established a new initiative – the Stolen Asset Recovery Initiative (STAR) – to address the problem in 2005, but by 2011 had not triggered a significant number of successful repatriations.

However, the development of an effective system for the purpose of asset repatriation is central to providing a disincentive to the accumulation of such corruptly gained fortunes, as formally recognized by UNCAC and now embraced by the G20.[4] There could be two key components of such a system, both based on the principle of establishing an independent Trust. The first would be an international Trust Fund into which assets could be paid and 'parked' as soon as identified, and retrieved from the financial system or property market of a 'host' country. The second would be a series of Trust Funds at national level within 'victim' countries which would be under the control of a mixed board of both local and international Trustees, who would disburse funds to both public sector projects and projects promoted by local charitable and community bodies. The latter proposal is extremely sensitive since the 'victim' country feels that the sums in question should simply be deposited in the country's Treasury and be part of the budget process. However, if budgetary processes are impaired, this may introduce a further round of corruption.[5] But earlier chapters have shown how embedded networks can easily survive regime change, as in Kenya and Peru, and the assumption that repatriation to the Exchequer of the country concerned is sufficient to ensure that the funds will be well spent is deceptive.

Real progress in addressing corruption has been made by the Extractive Industries Transparency Initiative (EITI), which has forged a new approach to making the payment and receipt of royalties and taxes transparent in energy-rich countries. Elements of a similar model are built into several other initiatives, including the Kimberley Process Certification Scheme (with diamonds), COST[6] (with construction) and IFBEC[7] (with defence companies, and excluding governments). The fundamental objective of EITI is to prevent a corrupt pact between companies and governments in which secret royalty and other payments are made to the detriment of a broader public. The fundamental objective of the schemes which exclude governments, such as IFBEC, is to create a 'level playing field' which is corruption-free, so that companies are released from the dilemma of knowing that their rivals are paying bribes which their corporate ethos forbids.

These arrangements work best where there is a limited number of corporate participants, no major partner is excluded, and there is a willing government (whether a formal partner or not). Thus the success of COST in Africa will depend on whether Chinese construction companies are prepared to join the initiative; the IFBEC agreement will depend on whether major arms-exporting companies from Russia and China can be brought into the agreement. But the experience to date suggests that these initiatives can make a valuable contribution to addressing corruption, and should be strengthened and extended. Where companies can be persuaded that the arrangements are watertight they are prepared to collaborate; governments may be reluctant when they perceive either that their technical expertise is inadequate in relation to that of the companies (and so they will be out-manoeuvred), or individuals within government may see the possibility for corruption being undermined in a way which is unwelcome. However, initiatives of this kind will not work where there are a large number of companies involved, and too many potential mavericks to form a credible common front.

The fourth area where a different approach needs to be adopted is in the area of state reconstruction after a civil war, particularly avoiding a repeat of the disasters of Iraq and Afghanistan. The key to this lies in ensuring that a new government, usually without broadly-based credentials, does not facilitate or trigger corrupt practices from the earliest days of the new regime. From a political perspective this may be particularly difficult where, in order to secure a settlement, patronage networks are embedded in the peace agreement itself, as was the case in Afghanistan. If one faction, which is in control of a patronage network, is able to secure control over a channel of corrupt funds, at the expense of other factions, this will certainly undermine the credibility of a new government. Further, it is essential to avoid unrealistic expectations of what can be funded and delivered by a new government in association with financial donors. Expectations in this area are easily raised, not only beyond what can be implemented, but also in relation to what can be sustained for more than three to four years.

The fifth and final area where – if the other conditions are met – specific additional initiatives need to be made is in relation to climate change finance. Flows to remedy climate change projected at the Copenhagen conference of 2009 and confirmed at Durban in 2011 total US$250 billion per year by 2030. Even if the reality falls well short of these targets, the sums involved are much larger than aggregate aid flows of US$115 billion in 2010, a significant proportion of which were disbursed through or to corrupt channels. Further, the carbon trading which is essential to the 'cap and trade' strategy for the control of carbon emissions, is itself subject to potential massive fraud, as occurred in 2010. These issues need to be recognized much more fully. In relation to the funds, such as REDD and the CDM, governments and donors should commit to a 'Climate Integrity Pact' which would work to a common standard, which in turn would be subject to both external reporting and external review. The carbon trading regime in the EU should be overhauled through an EU-wide central register of all participating companies, replacing national registers of varying accuracy. Given the fact that these are two of the world's most important tools for adapting to climate change, it is essential that they operate without corruption, and that they are agreed at the level of individual countries by all parties. Without measures of this kind, in relation to both the funds and the trading regimes, there is every likelihood of a major shortfall in the effectiveness of the climate change regime programme. The consequence would be a failure to restrict global warming to a further 2°C by 2050, with catastrophic consequences for the world as a whole.

* * * * *

The case for combating corruption relentlessly is that it is a force which drives poverty, inequality, dysfunctional democracy and global insecurity. Its most consistent victims are the poor who constitute a majority of the population in low-income countries; its most dramatic victims are the subjects of human trafficking. Its everyday victims are the citizens of the many countries where political funding is generated by corrupt means and where their voice is lost in the rush by elected politicians to pay off their backers. Corruption feeds failed states, the trade in nuclear weapons and their components, and the perpetuation of hunger even where harvests are plentiful. Unless checked, its major legacy will be an unjust and unstable world, tipping the outcome of uncertainties about the future in an ever more dangerous direction.

Who should act? As we move into the second decade of the twenty-first century a framework for action to combat corruption is falling into place. Since 2003 UNCAC has provided a principled basis on which the world can move forward. Its apparent active embrace by the G20 has brought its practical application nearer to reality. But this will only achieve its potential if current and future leaders in many walks of life grasp a snake which will frequently respond with poison, and will only die with repeated attack. Elected politicians will have to think again before they feast on inflated expenses, or take 10 per cent off building contracts in their electoral district; on- and off-line media editors will have to be bold enough to speak truth to power in spite of their sponsors; owners of the social media will have to pull out of countries where filters are imposed; CEOs of major companies and their staff will have to make their anti-bribery provisions work around the world and abandon the mispricing which deprives countries of badly needed revenue; NGOs in civil society will have to break down the barriers which frequently separate them and recognize that corruption is all too often a threat to their own more specific objectives.

What is the time frame for success? Concerted action by the EU, the USA and the BRIC countries, operating through the G20, could change the landscape within ten years, building on the modest success already achieved. There are, however, enemies at the gate: the power of the super wealthy for whom secrecy jurisdictions are a way of life; the strength of sophisticated mafia bosses who will hold on to their fiefdoms at all costs; the dangers of regional arms races fuelled by corruption; and heads of state whose hold on power can only be retained by bribing their electorates. They will not bend easily. The attack will have to be bold yet focused, sophisticated yet clear, courageous yet circumspect. But the snake will die only if severed at the head.

Notes

Notes to Chapter 1

1. Transfers of profits by price manipulation from a sale in one country where tax rates are deemed too high, to another location where rates are low or nonexistent. For a longer definition see Chapter 3, p.2.

2. In September 2011, such sales became the subject of lawsuits brought by buyers such as Freddie Mac, who successfully achieved repurchases by the Bank of America to the extent of nearly US$20 billion (Braithwaite, T., Scannell, K., 'Wave of lawsuits engulfs troubled lenders', *Financial Times*, 6 September 2011).

3. TI-India-CMS: *India Corruption Study 2007*: with focus on below the poverty line households.

4. Sohail, M. and Cavill, S., Water and Sanitation, *TI Global Corruption Report 2008*, p.40 (Cambridge, UK, 2008).

5. Quiroz, A., *Corrupt Circles* (Baltimore, MD, 2008).

6. *Combating Corruption in Indonesia*, p.136 (World Bank, Washington, DC, 2004).

7. *Illicit Flows from Developing Countries*: 2000–9, Global Financial Integrity, Washington, DC, Table 8.

8. World Economic Forum, *Global Competition Report*, 2003.

9. Ledeneva, A., *How Russia Really Works*, p. 38 (Cornell, 2006).

10. Retrospective parliamentary approval for the deal was sought by the Ministry of Defence in the week of 28 March to 4 April 2011, having been supported personally by President Museveni on 24 March (Source: *The East African*, 4–10 April 2011).

Notes to Chapter 2

1. Collor has served as Chairman of the Senate Infrastructure Commission since 2009; he ran unsuccessfully for the Governorship of Alagoas in 2010.

2. According to a Nigerian parliamentary report of 2004, but corroborated by other investigations in France and the USA.

3. Total of a criminal offence fine of US$402 million paid to DoJ and civil court fine of US$177 million paid to SEC.

4. *Agence Presse Francaise*, 11 March 2011.

5. And in fact wrote a biography of Nzeogwu (*Nzeogwu: an intimate portrait of Major Chukwuma Kaduna Nzeogwu*, Ibadan, 1987), explaining his motives.

6. Peel, M., *A Swamp Full of Dollars*, p.15 (I.B.Tauris, London, 2009).

7. Quiroz, A., *Corrupt Circles: A History of Unbound Graft in Peru*, p.403 (Woodrow Wilson Center Press, Washington DC, 2008).

8. El Commercio, no. 83912, 19 July 2001, quoted in Quiroz, A.: *Corrupt Circles*.

9. In addition to an agent's fee of 15 per cent.

10. Indonesian usage often uses only one name.

11. This estimate was made by John Clomey and David Liebhold for a detailed investigative article in *Time* magazine for 5 May 1999, after Suharto's fall but before his death. It was challenged by the family's lawyers.

12. *Combating Corruption in Indonesia*, p.135 (World Bank, Washington, DC, 2004).

13. *Jakarta Post*, 4 April 2010.

14. Mereu, F., 'Bureaucrat numbers booming', *Moscow Times*, 13 April 2006.

15. Ibid.

16. Myers, L., 'In Russia, bribery is the cost of doing business', *New York Times*, 10 August 2005.

17. Ibid.

18. Aslund, A., *Russia's Capitalist Revolution*, p.259 (Peterson Institute for International Economics, Washington, DC, 2007).

19. Quoted by Elena Paflinova in the *Global Corruption Report* of 2009 and based on an interview with the Prosecutor General reported in *Rossiiskaya Gazeta*, 19 June 2008.

20. Shleifer, A. and Vishny, R. W., 'Corruption', *Quarterly Journal of Economics*, 108(3): pp.359–617.

21. Aslund, A., *Russia's Capitalist Revolution*, p.157.

22. Global Financial Integrity, *Illicit Financial Flows from Developing Countries* (Washington, DC, 2000–6).

23. Baker, P. and Glasser, S., *Kremlin Rising: Vladimir Putin's Russia and the End of Revolution*, pp.86–7 (New York, 2005).

24. And in 2004 by RusUkrEnergo.

25. Preferred estimate from Global Financial Integrity (GFI), Washington, DC, which compares figures compiled on three different bases: see *Illicit Flows from Developing Countries*, GFI, 2000–6.

26. Greenhill, K., 'Kleptocratic interdependence: trafficking, corruption, and the marriage of politics and illicit profits', in *Corruption, Global Security and World Order* (ed. Robert Rotberg) (World Peace Foundation, Cambridge, Mass, 2009).

27. Glover, C., 'Bribery on the beat', *Financial Times*, 4 November, 2010.

28. *Transparency International*, 2009.

29. Xiaboo Lu, *Cadres and Corruption: The Organisational Involution of the Chinese Communist Party* (Oxford, 2005).

30. Barboza, D., 'A Chinese reformer betrays his cause and pays', *New York Times*, 13 July 2007.

31. Non-attributable source speaking at a conference on China's pharmaceutical industry and ethics at Renmin University, Beijing, May 10th, 2007.

32. Tsui, E., 'Canada to deport China's most wanted fugitive', *Financial Times*, 22 July 2011.

33. McGregor, R., *The Party: The Secret World of China's Communist Rulers* (London, 2010).

34. Institutional Revolutionary Party, or Partido Revolucionario Institutional, was originally named the National Revolutionary Party and first took power in 1929.

35. Quoted in 'Downward drift', *Financial Times*, 30 June 2010, p.11.

36. Estimate by US Attorney General, John Ashcroft, with reference 2000 quoted in Kellner, T. and Pipitone, F., 'Inside Mexico's drugs war', *World Policy Journal*, XXVII(1), Spring 2010.

37. Ezequiel 'Tony Tormenta' Guillen and Jorge Eduardo 'El Coss' Costilla Sanchez according to the US Treasury's Office of Foreign Assets Control.

38. The Bureau of Alcohol, Tobacco, Firearms and Explosives (ATF).

39. Thomson, A., 'City of darkness', *Financial Times*, 13 March 2010.

40. Guillermoprieto, A., 'The Murderers of Mexico', *New York Review of Books*, 28 October 2010, p.46.

Notes to Chapter 3

1. Rear Admiral Kevin S. Cook, Director of Prevention Policy, US Coast Guard, 15 March 2011, speaking to House of Representatives Transportation and Infrastructure Sub Committee.

2. Cawthorne, N., *Pirates of the 21st Century* (John Blake, London, 2010).

3. The Coltan Phenomenon, Mikolo Sofia, Dominic Johnson, Pole Institute/Credap, Kivu, DRC, 2002.
4. Section 2, para 2 at www.globalwitness.org/library/dodd-frank-acts-section-1502-conflict. Accessed 15 June 2012.
5. Global e-sustainability initiative published 'The social and environmental responsibility in metals supply to the electronic industry' (Brussels, 2008).
6. 2011 Supplier Responsibility Report, Apple PLC, 2011.
7. Defined by the UN as 'a structured group of three or more persons, existing for a period of time and acting in concert with the aim of committing one or more serious offences in order to obtain directly or indirectly a financial or other material benefit'. UN Convention on Organised Crime, Article 2a (1998).
8. *UNODC World Drugs Report 2010*; FATF estimates maximum value of US$280 billion.
9. Naím, M., *Illicit, How Smugglers, Traffickers and Copycats are Hijacking the Global Economy*, p.83 (Arrow Books, London, 2007).
10. www.Havoscope.com figures for Colombia 2011.
11. Lewis, D., 'High times on the Silk Road', *World Policy Journal*, XXVII(1), Spring 2010.
12. Naím, M., *Illicit*, p.83.
13. UNODC estimate 2010; *Havoscope* estimates US$54 billion.
14. *Havosccope* 2011.
15. The Sinaloa Federation, Los Zetas, and La Familia Michoacana: *World Drug Report 2010*, UNODC, p.238.
16. Greenhill, K., 'Kleptocratic interdependence: trafficking, corruption, and the marriage of politics and illicit profits', in *Corruption, Global Security and World Order* (ed. Robert Rotberg), p.52 (World Peace Foundation, Cambridge, Mass, 2009).
17. Kumar, A., *The Black Economy in India*, p.151 (Penguin, New Delhi, 1999).
18. Harding, L., 'Doing Moscow's dirty work: the gangs backed by the Kremlin', *The Observer*, 2 December 2010.

Notes to Chapter 4

1. A description of the charcoal network in Tanzania is in Chapter 9, pp.165–6.
2. *State of Corruption in the Country*, Report of the Warioba Commission, Dar es Salaam, December 1996, p.1 (based on public hearings held in every district in Tanzania).
3. *Daily Lives and Corruption: Public Opinion in Tanzania*, Infinite Insight for Gallup International (the survey covered 1006 people questioned

between 30 April and 6 May 2011 and was sponsored by Transparency International as part of the Global Corruption Barometer).

4. TI-Pakistan, *National Perception Survey, 2010.*

5. TI-India, *Corruption Survey, 2007–8.*

6. Kenya, Uganda,Tanzania, Burundi and Rwanda.

7. *Global Corruption Barometer 2010,* Transparency International.

8. *Africa Education Watch,* Transparency International, 2009.

9. *World Development Indicators,* World Bank, 2010.

10. Sohail, M. and Cavill, S., 'Water and sanitation', TI Global Corruption Report 2008, p.40, Cambridge University Press.

11. Statement by Civil Society Organisations at the AU Summit, January 2005 and quoted in the *TI Global Corruption Report 2006,* p.105.

12. Morris, J. and Stevens, P., *Counterfeit Medicines in Less Developed Countries* (London, 2006).

13. Wade, R., 'The market for public office: Why the Indian State is not better at development', *World Development,* 1985, 13(4): pp.467–97.

14. Rijsberman, F. R., 'Water for food', *Global Corruption Report,* Transparency International, 2008, p.74.

15. Birner, R. et al., *Public Expenditure and International Development: Ghana's Ministry of Agriculture* (Washington, DC, 2009).

16. Distributed by the Cotton Development Trust Fund; this sale was well publicized in the Tanzanian press.

17. South Korea, Hong Kong, Taiwan and Singapore.

18. Khan, M. and Jomo, K.S., *Rents, Rent-Seeking and Economic Development,* pp.139–41 (Cambridge, UK, 2000).

19. Ha-Joon Chang, *Bad Samaritans: The Guilty Secrets of Rich Nations and the Threat to Global Prosperity,* p.166 (London, 2007).

20. Brassiolo, M., *Administrative Recovery of a Town after Corruption Cases* (Milan, 1996).

21. Report of the Comptroller and Auditor General.

22. Based on a total cost of US$400 million and annual budgetary expenditure of US$3.4 billion.

23. Based on total embezzlement of US$5 billion and a total GDP of US$100 million over five years. Vinod, R. and Lamont, J., 'India's activist public servant hits his stride', *Financial Times,* 14 September 2010.

24. Quiroz, A., *Corrupt Circles: A History of Unbound Graft in Peru,* Woodrow Wilson International Center, Appendix Table A1 (Major Direct and Indirect Costs of Corruption) (Washington, DC, 2008).

25. Global Financial Integrity, *Illicit Flows from Developing Countries,* 2008–9, Table 3.

26. 'China officials smuggled $124 million', *Financial Times,* 16 June 2011, quoting the Central Bank of China (Money Laundering Website).

27. Kumar, A., *The Black Economy in India*; Dreher, Axel and Schneider, Friedrich, 'Corruption and the shadow economy: an empirical analysis', *Public Choice*, 144 (2012): pp.215–38.

28. Kishor, N. and Damania, R., 'Crime and justice in the Garden of Eden: Improving governance and reducing corruption in the forestry sector', in *The Many Faces of Corruption* (eds J. Campos and S. Pradhan), p.90 (World Bank, 2007).

29. 'Combating Corruption in Indonesia', World Bank, 2004.

Notes to Chapter 5

1. James, R., *E. Hoffa and the Teamsters: a study of Union Power*, p.162 (Van Nostrand, New Jersey, 1965).

2. Kennedy, R., *The Enemy Within: The McClellan Committee's Crusade Against Jimmy Hoffa and Corrupt Labor Unions* (HarperCollins, New York, 1960).

3. Hoffa was released after serving five years of his sentence in an arrangement with the Nixon Administration in 1972 rumoured to have involved a commitment by the Teamsters to switch their support from the Democratic to the Republican Party. He was assassinated in a mafia attack in 1975.

4. *Exodus*, 23, verse 8.

5. *Rig Veda Samhita*, verse 1-104-3, vol. II, pp.338–9, New Delhi.

6. Iqbal, Z. and Lewis, M., 'Governance and corruption: can Islamic countries and the west learn from each other?', *The American Journal of Islamic Studies*, 19(2): p.8.

7. Iqbal and Lewis, *The American Journal of Islamic Studies*, 19(2): p.9.

8. Noonan, J., *Bribes*, p.347 (University of California Press, 1984).

9. Noonan, J., *Bribes*, p.360.

10. McFarlane, A., 'Political corruption and reform in Bourbon Spanish America', in *Political Corruption in Europe and Latin America* (eds W. Little and Eduardo Posada-Carbo), p.42 (London, 1996).

11. Juan, J. and de Ulloa, A., *Discourse and Political Reflections on the Kingdoms of Peru* (ed. and trans. by J.J. Tepaske and B.A. Clement), p.247 (Oklahoma University Press, 1978).

12. Tylden, D., *Boss Tweed: The Story of a Grim Generation*, p.50 (London, 2002).

13. Carlyle, T., *Past and Present*, p.339 (Chapman and Hall, London, 1843).

14. The play was updated in 2008 with corruption casting a wider net by the Israeli playwright Joshua Sobol and performed at the Cameri Theatre in Tel Aviv.

15. Crew, A., *The Law Relating to Secret Commissions and Bribes* (London, 1913).

16. Verein gegen des Bestechungsunwesen, identified in Crewe, p.136, based on a report by Sir Francis Oppenheimer, UK Commercial Attache to Germany, January 1913.

17. World Development Report, *The State in a Changing World*, p.105 (World Bank, 1997).

18. Cross-party legislation under the Presidency of Chester Arthur (Republican) steered through the Senate by Sen. George Pendleton (Democratic Senator for Ohio). The legislation was controversial and cost Arthur a nomination by the Republican party for a second term in 1884.

19. Described in the press as 'cash for questions'.

20. Bank of Credit and Commerce International, accused of money laundering in several jurisdictions.

21. Davey, M. and Healy, J., 'Illinois Governor charged in scheme to sell Obama's seat', *New York Times*, 12 October 2008.

22. Senator Edward E. Kaufman, 21 January 2010.

23. Pettit, P., *Republicanism, A Theory of Freedom and Government*, pp.201–11 (Oxford, 1997).

24. Barstad, A., 'Culture of corruption? Interpreting corruption in Soviet and Post Soviet contexts', MA Thesis, University of Bergen, 2003; quoted in Karklins, R., *The System Made Me Do It: Corruption in Post Communist Societies*, p.67 (M.E. Sharpe, New York, 2005).

25. Originally established in the early 1950s.

26. Such as legislation which adopts the 'reverse burden of proof': wealthy individuals may have to explain their acquisition of assets without any formal charge.

Notes to Chapter 6

1. Dallek, R., *The Lost Peace: Leadership in a Time of Horror and Hope*, p.275 (HarperCollins, New York, 2010).

2. Hatta, M., *The Co-operative Movement in Indonesia*, pp.84–5 (Cornell University Press, Ithaca, 1957).

3. Karanjia, R.K., The Mind of Mr Nehru, p.61 (London, 1960), quoted in Myrdal, G., *Asian Drama*, vol. II, p.941 (London, 1960).

4. Report of the Committee on the Prevention of Corruption (*The Santhanam Report*), Ministry of Home Affairs, New Delhi, 1964, pp.6–7.

5. *Santhanam Report*, p.108.

6. They include: raising the pay of low-paid civil servants; strengthening police departments; modifying and extending legislation to ensure that action against corrupt officials is punitive; taking measures against the

private sector who corrupt civil servants; forbidding contributions by business to political parties; protecting genuine whistleblowers – and ensuring that newspapers which make unfounded allegations can be prosecuted.

7. Myrdal, G., *Asian Drama*, p.956 (Penguin, London, 1986).
8. Myrdal, G., *Asian Drama*, p.946.
9. Quiroz, A., *Corrupt Circles*, Table A.6, p.447.
10. Wrong, M., *In the Footsteps of Mr Kurtz*, p.98 (Fourth Estate, London, 2000).
11. Wrong, M., *In the Footsteps of Mr Kurtz*, p.148.
12. Lankester, T., *The Politics and Economics of Britain's Foreign Aid: The Pergau Dam Affair* (Routledge, London, 2012).
13. *Sunday Times*, 20 February 1994.
14. Overseas Development Administration.
15. Department for International Development.
16. People and Development, given on 1 October 1996 in Indonesia.
17. OECD Membership in 1997. In 2012 all 34 member states and five others are members of the Convention.
18. In India, The Prevention of Bribery of Foreign Public Officials and Officials of Public International Organisations was passed in March 2011, with a penalty of up to seven years in jail. The Chinese measure is an amendment to the Criminal Law, passed on 1 May 2011, and carries a penalty of up to ten years in jail plus a fine. It applies to all companies registered under Chinese law regardless of where they are operating.

Notes to Chapter 7

1. National chapter of Transparency International in Kenya.
2. Wrong, M., *In the Footsteps of Mr Kurtz* (Fourth Estate, London, 2000)
3. Johnston, M., *Syndromes of Corruption*, p.178 (Cambridge, UK, 2005).
4. Known in Italian as *manu polite* and *tangentopolli*.
5. However, his British lawyer David Mills was found guilty on bribery charges in 2008, a finding later rescinded on appeal by the Court of Cassation.
6. Adelstein, J., 'Yakuza', *World Policy Journal*, XXVIII, Summer 2010.
7. O'uchi, M., *Japan: An Illustrated Encyclopedia* (Kodansha, 1994).
8. Kumar, A., *The Black Economy in India*, p.277 (New Delhi, 1999); The Cost of Elections, Commonwealth Parliamentary Association, London, 2000, p.9.
9. www.plunderofindia, TruthAboutIndiaCorruption. Accessed 15 June 2012.
10. Department Related Parliamentary Standing Committee on Personnel, Public Grievances, Law and Justice (2007).

11. Source: Association for Democratic Reform, Lok Sabha 2009, National Level Analysis, Full Details of Pending Criminal Cases of MPs' at www.adrinda.org. Accessed 15 June 2012.

12. Transparency International-India, Satyagrah Brigade and Common cause.

13. Public Interest Litigation under art. 32 of the Constitution of India seeking issuance of appropriate writ/directions for the eradication of the 'Criminalisation of Politics', para. 4.

14. Chama cha Mapunduzi, or Party of the Revolution.

15. At the 2002 exchange rate of £1=US$2.

16. Power, T. J. and Taylor, M. M., *Corruption and Democracy in Brazil: The Struggle for Accountability*, p.33 (Notre Dame, 2011).

17. Partido dos Trabalhadores.

18. Down from 31 per cent and 26 per cent respectively in 1992, at the time of the impeachment of Collor. Source: Opiniao Publica 2006.

19. Alfredo Nasciemto (Transport), Wagner Rossi (Agriculture), Nohn Johim (Defence), Orlando Silva (Sports), Pedro Novais (Tourism).

20. Centre for the Study of Democracy (for the EU), *Examining the Links Between Organised Crime and Corruption*, p.40 (Bulgaria, 2010).

21. Greenhill, K., in R. Rotberg et al., *Corruption Security and the World Order*, p.113 (World Peace Foundation, Cambridge, Mass., 2009).

22. McDonald, N. and Wagstyl, S., 'Higher aspirations', *Financial Times*, 13 January 2010.

23. McDonald, N. and Wagstyl, S., 'Higher aspirations'.

24. The Corruption Perception Index is published annually by TI and measures the degree to which public sector corruption is perceived to exist around the world. In 2010 the Index covered 178 countries, scoring them on a scale from 10 (very clean) to 0 (highly corrupt). Its sources include the Economist Intelligence Unit, the Asian and African Development Banks, and the World Competitiveness Survey.

25. Power, T. J., *Corruption and Democracy in Brazil*, pp.236–7 (Notre Dame, 2011).

26. *UNODC Annual Report* 2009.

27. Naím, M., *Illicit: How Smugglers, Traffickers and Copycats are Hijacking the Global Economy*, p.162 (London, 1960).

28. Clark, P., 'Lethal Counterfeits', *World Policy Journal*, June 2010.

29. *Small Arms Survey 2003*, Graduate Institute of International and Development Studies, University of Geneva, p.286.

30. *Washington Post*, 19 March 2005.

31. Naím, M., *Illicit*, p.44.

32. Kennedy, R., *The Enemy Within: The McClellan Committee's Crusade Against Jimmy Hoffa and Corrupt Labor Unions*, p.240 (HarperCollins, New York, 1960).

33. See Chapter 7 for discussion of the OECD Convention on Illicit Payments of 1997.
34. In this settlement BAE Systems accepted guilt in relation to its deals in Saudi Arabia, the Czech Republic and Hungary and admitted the existence of a series of offshore companies which served as vehicles through which to make payments, leading to a fine of US$400 million (see www.justrice.gov/criminal/pr/documents/o3-01-10%20bae-sentencing-memo.pdf).
35. Leahy, J., 'Satyam accounts understate scams woe', *Financial Times*, 29 September 2010.
36. Global Corruption Report 2009, TI, Berlin, p.137.
37. Braithwaite, T. and Scannell, K., 'Wave of lawsuits engulfs troubled leaders', *Financial Times*, 6 September 2011.
38. Baker, R., *The Achilles Heel of Capitalism: Dirty Money and How to Renew the Free Market System* (New York, 2005); Baker, R. and Joly, E., 'Illicit money can it be stopped?', *New York Review of Books*, 3 December 2009.
39. An amalgam of niobium and tantalum used to regulate voltage and store energy in a range of electronic devices.

Notes to Chapter 8

1. *OECD Working Group on Bribery*, 2010 Annual Report.
2. Githongo, J., 'Report on my findings of graft in the government of Kenya' conveyed by letter to President Kibaki of Kenya, dated 22 November 2005 and subsequently made available on BBC website (bbc.com). The total value of the deals in question, some of which were more spurious than others, was c.US$600 million.
3. Suberu, R., The Travails of Nigeria's Anti-Corruption Crusade, in *Corruption, Global Security and World Order*, p.268 (ed. R. Rotberg) (Washington, DC, 2009).
4. Tobs Agbaegbu, 'Nnamani's 20 Foreign Accounts' and Andrew Airahuobhor, 'EFCC versus Nnamani' *Newswatch* (Lagos), 19 May 2008, quoted in Suberu, R., The Travails of Nigeria's Anti-Corruption Crusade, p.268.
5. Suberu, R., The Travails of Nigeria's Anti-Corruption Crusade, p.264.
6. 'Exit Ribadu', Wole Soyinka at www.nigerianmuse.com/openssays. Accessed 15 June 2012.
7. Jean-Christophe Mitterrand was prosecuted on corruption related charges in France in 2001 and given a 30-month probationary jail sentence.
8. Counting the EU as 27 states.
9. Managing Director of the World Bank from 2007 to 2011.

10. Corruption Eradication Commission.
11. The number of formal (fee paying) members of the Global Compact has varied since 2008, and in 2009 there was a fairly radical excision of non-compliant companies.
12. A series of related initiatives with overlapping objectives were launched after 2000 including the Global Reporting Initiative, the International Business Leaders' Forum and the Principles for Responsible Investment.
13. James Giffen: he was alleged by the Department of Justice to have channelled US$78 million in bribes to the President of Kazakhstan and his associates, but in November 2010 was exempted by a Federal District Court in New York on the grounds that he had rendered service to the USA through the CIA.
14. SNEPCO also pleaded guilty on the same case to the Nigerian Economic and Financial Crimes Corruption Commission (EFCC).
15. *Transparency in Reporting on Anti-Corruption: A Report on Corporate Practices*, TI, Berlin, 2009.
16. Johnson, M. and Smithy, A., 'Critical mass is vital to hold groups to account', *Financial Times*, 29 March 2011.
17. Cockcroft, L., 'Corporate Corruption: challenges in a changing world', ICC Commercial Crime Services, 8th Annual Economic Crime Lecture 2008.

Notes to Chapter 9

1. World Bank, Sustainable Development (Africa Region), *Enabling Reforms: A stakeholder based analysis of the poitical economy of Tanzania's charcoal sector and the poverty and social impact of proposed reforms* (Washington, DC, 2010).
2. World Bank, Environmental crisis or sustainable development opportunity? Transforming the charcoal sector in Tanzania, 2009.
3. Ledeneva, A., *How Russia Really Works*, pp.148–9 (Cornell, 2006).
4. Schneider, F. and Kepler, J., 'Shadow economies and corruption all over the world; new estimates for 145 countries', *Economics (Open Access)* 24/7, no. 2007-9.
5. The estimate for Singapore, which is largely free of domestic corruption, is 12 per cent.
6. Prani, S., Stern, J. and Yafimava, K. *The April 2010 Russo-Ukrainian Gas Agreement and its implications for Europe*. Oxford Institute of Energy Studies, June 2010, p.7, Table 1.
7. Initially by the UK-based Tax Justice Network, which defines such jurisdictions as 'places that intentionally create regulation for the primary

benefit and use of those not resident in their geographical domain. That regulation is designed to undermine the legislation or regulation of another jurisdiction ... and create a deliberate, legally backed veil of secrecy that ensures that those from outside the jurisdiction making use of its regulation cannot be identified as doing so.'

8. Shaxson, N., *Treasure Islands*, pp.98–102 (Bodley Head, London, 2011).
9. Shaxson, N., *Treasure Islands*, p.142.
10. Hollingshead, A., *Privately Held Non Resident Deposits in Secrecy Jurisdictions* (Washington, DC, 2010).
11. Hollingshead, A., *Privately Held Non Resident Deposits in Secrecy Jurisdictions*, Table 4, p.11.
12. Cayman Islands, Antigua, British Virgin Islands, St Kitts and Nevis, Turks and Caicos, Grenada.
13. Guernsey, Jersey, Isle of Man and Gibraltar.
14. Foot, M., Final Report of the Independent Review of British Offshore Financial Centres (H.M. Treasury, October 2011).
15. Foot, M., Final Report of the Independent Review of British Offshore Financial Centres, p.55.
16. US Department of Justice, Deferred Prosecution Agreement with Daimler, 24 March 2010, p.56.
17. Rashid, A., *Descent into Chaos*, p.189 (Penguin, London, 2009).
18. In the north these forces consisted of the 'Northern Alliance' led by Ahmad Shah Masud, Karim Khaliki in the central highlands; in the west, Rashid Dostum and Ismail Khan; and in the east, Abdul Qadir.
19. Rashid, A., *Descent into Chaos*, p.129.
20. Rashid, A., *Descent into Chaos*, p.329.
21. *Los Angeles Times*, 17 May 2002.
22. Warlord Inc., SubCommittee on National Security and Foreign Affairs, Committee on Oversight and Government Reform, US House of Representatives, Washington, DC, June 2010.
23. Sherman, J. and DiDomenico, V., *The Public Cost of Private Security in Afghanistan* (NYU, New York, 2009).
24. Bremer had served as Ambassador to the Netherlands.
25. Bowen, Stewart, Inspector General, 'Hard Lessons: the Iraq Reconstruction Experience' quoting W. Stein, Robt Jnr Controller for South-Central Region in 2003–4, US Government Printing Office, 2 February 2009, Washington, DC.
26. Bowen, S., 'Hard Lesson', quoting Neil Hawkins.
27. Bowen, S., 'Hard Lesson'.
28. Bowen, S., 'Hard Lesson'.
29. In the Corruption Perception Index for 2010 the 'score' of China was 3.6, Brazil 3.5 and India 3.4.

30. Khan, M.H. and Sundaram, J.S., *Rents, Rent Seeking and Economic Development: Theory and Evidence in Asia*, Chapter 1 (Cambridge, UK, 2000).

31. Manufacturing companies such as Daewoo and Samsung which were resourced and guided by the state but legally independent.

32. On trial in 1995 Roh admitted accumulating a personal fortune of US$650 million. Jamil Anderlini, 'China Officials smuggled $124bn', *Financial Times*, 16 June 2011.

33. McGregor, R., *The Party: the Secret World of China's Communist Rulers*, p.267 (Allen Lane, London, 2010).

34. *New York Times*, 22 April 2005.

35. Pei, M., 'The long march against graft', *Financial Times*, 12 December 2002.

36. McGregor, R., *The Party: the Secret World of China's Communist Rulers*, p.176.

37. *People's Daily*, 12 September 2003.

38. *China Daily*, 24 July 2004, quoted in Governance in China, OECD-China Programme of Dialogue, Paris, 2005, p.113.

39. McGregor, R., *The Party: the Secret World of China's Communist Rulers*, p.267.

40. Tata, J.R.D., *Keynote*, Bombay, 1986 is an edited edition of J.R.D. Tata's views on ethics and business.

41. However, Gandhi's premiership was dogged by corrupt payments associated with the sale by the Swedish armaments company Bofors of howitzer guns to the Ministry of Defence.

42. Société Nationale d'Investissement.

43. Botswana continues to have the most favourable 'score' in all Africa in TI's Corruption Perception Index at 5.8 in 2010.

Notes to Chapter 10

1. By, for example, reducing carbon emissions.

2. By, for example, building flood prevention works.

3. Stern, N., *The Economics of Climate Change: The Stern Review* (Cambridge, UK, 2007).

4. 'Reducing Emissions from deforestation and forest degradation in developing countries'.

5. Which extended to Norway, Iceland and Lichtenstein.

6. Including both spot and futures contracts.

7. *Financial Times*, 21 January 2011, p.8.

8. Davies, N., 'Abuses and incompetence in the fight against global warming', *The Guardian*, 6 June 2007.

9.   Carbon Trade Watch 2010.

10. Ministry of the Environment, Nature Conservation and Tourism, REDD Readiness Preparation Proposal for 2010–11, 2 March 2010, Kinshasha.

11. Southall, R., The Ndungu Report: Land and Graft in Kenya, *Review of African Political Economy*, 103, March 2005, pp.142–51.

Notes to Chapter 11

1.   Through the Ganyang Koruptor Facebook page.

2.   Fenby, J., *The Fall and Rise of a Great Power, 1850–2008*, p.978 (Allen Lane, London, 2008).

3.   McGregor, R., *The Party: the Secret World of China's Communist Rulers*, p.267 (London, 2010).

4.   'Brightstar' comments recorded in relation to PCC member Hu Kailin from Kunming, who had called for a more unequal society.

5.   The Cyrillic version has an average readership of 2 million.

6.   'Integrity' is a programme launched in 1997 which requires companies to sign up to a corporate ethics charter and has about 15 companies as members.

7.   In fact, the whole cabinet was asked to resign but the majority were reappointed.

8.   Global Corruption Barometer, December 2011; poll carried out by Infinite Insight for Transparency International.

9.   The case was brought by ex-Prime Minister Dominique de Villepin, widely described as an arch rival to President Nicolas Sarkozy.

10. The Clearwater account funds originated from the Elf arms deal with Taiwan of 1991.

11. Source: Joachim Eckert, Penal Court Judge, Munich, speaking at IACC, Bangkok, November 2010.

12. Global Corruption Barometer 2010, Transparency International, Appendix C, Table 1.

13. Information drawn from Tully, C., *North Africa and the Role of the Social Media in 2011's Political Movement* (London, 2011).

14. www.odgersberndtson.com/en/knowledge-insight/article/human-capital-media-and-the-middle-east-3485. Accessed 6 April 2011.

15. http://interactiveme.com/index.php/2011/05/how-did-al-jazeera-channel-become-number-1-arab-social-brand-in-the-middle-east/. Accessed 15 June 2012.

16. http://www.reuters.com/article/2011/02/08/technology-protest-spies-idUSLDE7161WF2011020. Accessed 15 June 2012.

Notes to Chapter 12

1. Such as Interpol, Europol and UNODC.
2. The Human Rights Charter embraces three Human Rights Conventions, one of which is devoted to economic rights.
3. Article 7(1)(k) of the Rome Statute recognizes a category of 'other inhumane acts of a similar character intentionally causing great suffering or serious injury to mental or physical health'.
4. The G20 Working Group on Corruption accepted this as part of its agenda in 2011.
5. This issue was perfectly reflected in a tussle between the UK SFO, BAE Systems and the government of Tanzania in 2011 when the Tanzanian government sought successfully to channel a US$40 million payment arranged in a plea bargain between the SFO and BAE Systems to its budget rather than through grants to a series of NGOs.
6. The Construction Sector Transparency Initiative, launched by the UK's Department for International Development in 2006: it requires companies to comply with a set of disclosure and transparency arrangements and in 2011 was active in seven countries.
7. International Forum for Business Ethics, includes BAE Systems, EADS, Northrop, Saab, Thales and a majority of members of national aerospace and defence company associations in Europe and the USA.

A Note on Sources

Throughout this book I have drawn on a variety of sources, which include newspapers and websites as well as academic articles and books. The most important sources are listed below.

Chapter 2: Fernando Collor de Mello and P.C. Ferias, *Peter Cobb: A Death in Brazil* (a brilliant and colourful overview of past and present Brazil); Indonesia: Robert Elson's book *Suharto* is a masterly overview of his career, well complimented by the World Bank's *Combating Corruption in Indonesia*; Peru: Alfonso Quiroz: *A History of Unbound Graft in Peru* covers more than 400 years of corruption in Peru and is one of the most important books available on corruption; Russia: Anders Asland's *Russia's Capitalist Revolution* is an authoritative account of the whole liberalization process in Russia; it is well complemented by Alena Ledeneva's *How Russia Really Work*; China: the cases of Zheng Xiaoyu and Chen Liangyu are well documented in reports by Reuters; Richard McGregor's *The Party: The Secret World of China's Communist Party Rulers* paints an accurate context; Mexico: various media sources including *World Policy Journal, The Economist* and the *Financial Times* supported by interviews with senior Mexicans.

Chapter 3: Somali pirates: knowledge shared by Juvenal Shiundu of Kenya; DRC and coltan: regular Annual Reports by the UN Security Council Mission, specific reports by Global Witness and Human Rights Watch; context of organized crime set by Moisés Naím's overarching *Illicit*, Misha Glenny's *McMafia* and UNODC; the relations between organized crime and politics are well analysed worldwide by Kelly Greenhill in *Corruption, Global Security and World Order* (edited by Robert Rotberg) and in the EU by the Sofia-based

Centre for the Study of Democracy's *Examining the Links Between Organised Crime and Corruption*.

Chapter 4: The story of Ali Juma is my own based on nearly 50 years of visiting Dar es Salaam and its townships. Other material on the impact of corruption on the individual is drawn from numerous reports, particularly by TI and its national chapters; on the wider economic impact from a series of studies many of which are particularly well summarized in *Corruption, Institutions and Economic Development* by Dr Toke Aidt, published in the Oxford Review of Economic Policy. My preferred source on the debate about the relationship between economic growth and corruption is Dr Mushtaq Khan's *Rents, Rent Seeking and Economic Development: Theory and Evidence in Asia*.

Chapter 5: Sources on ethics include a valuable text on Hindu sources from S.J. Sharma, a resilient sage associated with Gandhian causes in India; on the historical figures discussed, I am particularly indebted to Judge John Noon's exhaustive *Bribes*, certainly the most detailed study of the subject yet written. Albert Crew's *The Law Relating to Secret Commissions and Bribes*, dealing with a civil society campaign against bribery from 1890 to 1913 in the UK, is available in the British Library.

Chapter 6: Attitudes to corruption in Asia in the 1950s are particularly well captured by the celebrated sociologist, Gunnar Myrdal, in his panoramic study, *Asian Drama*; a remarkable insight into US attitudes to Latin America in the late 1940s is provided by the *Memoirs 1925–1990* of the American statesman, George Kennan; an invaluable perspective on Western attitudes to Mobutu in his heyday is Michela Wrong's *In the Footsteps of Mr Kurtz*. The changes initiated by Jim Wolfensohn at the World Bank are reflected in his own speeches from 1996 onwards.

Chapter 7: The role of the 'black economy' and organized crime in Indian politics has been covered for many years by Professor Arun Kumar, most extensively in *The Black Economy in India*; contemporary websites such as *Ipaidabribe.com* add current flavour but confirm Kumar's analysis. The Tanzanian material is drawn from current media coverage and reports by a committee of Tanzania's parliament. Material on bribery cases involving multinationals is drawn from TI's Annual Report on the OECD Anti-bribery Convention, the richest source available on this topic. The section on 'mispricing' reflects the work of Raymond Baker and Global Financial Integrity.

Chapter 8: Reports on the work of Eva Joly and John Githongo reflect personal knowledge; information on Nuhu Ribadi is summarized by Rotimi Suberu in *Corruption, Global Security and World Order*; John Dickie's *Cosa*

Nostra provides an excellent account of the courageous stance of Giovanni Falcone and Paolo Borsellini. The story of the development of Global Witness is based on conversations with two of the founders (Patrick Alley and Simon Taylor) and of TI from personal knowledge. The text on corporate initiatives is drawn partly from my own work as initial Chairman of a group developing the 'TI Business Principles for countering bribery' and subsequent follow-up initiatives.

Chapter 9: In relation to the 'shadow economy' I have relied extensively on the work of Professor Friedrich Schneider of Linz University in Austria; information on coltan in DRC has been sourced from UN reports and those of Global Witness and Human Rights Watch; sources on 'secrecy jurisdictions' have included Nicholas Shaxson's *Treasure Islands,* the UK Treasury Report by Michael Foot on British Offshore Centres, and work by the GFI. The discussion of realpolitik in Turkmenistan relies on reports by Global Witness, on Sudan on my own knowledge, in Afghanistan, partly on Ahmed Rashid's invaluable *Descent into Chaos* and on the extraordinarily frank report by a US House of Representatives committee entitled *Warlord Inc,* and in Iraq by the similarly frank report by Stewart Bowen, the Inspector General for Iraq appointed by the US Government. The discussion in relation to corruption and growth in China, India and Africa is based on my own background knowledge.

Chapter 10: The material on global warming is based on TI's report on *Corruption and Global Warming* (the Global Corruption Report for 2010), on the report on REDD and corruption issues made by the U4 centre at the Christian Michelsen Institute, and relevant media articles.

Chapter 11: This chapter relies on reports from TI national chapters, and (for north Africa) on a report on the impact of social media on the events of early 2011: *North Africa and the Role of Social Media in 2011's Political Movements,* by the consulting group From Overhere.

Chapter 12: This chapter relies on material discussed earlier in the book.

Bibliography

Books

Aburish, S., *The Rise, Corruption and Coming Fall of the House of Saud* (London, 2005).

Akbarzadeh, S. and Saeed, A., *Islam and Political Legitimacy* (London, 2003).

Aslund, A., *Russia's Capitalist Revolution: why market reform succeeded and democracy failed* (Washington, DC, 2007).

Baker, R., *The Achilles Heel of Capitalism: Dirty Money and How to Renew the Free Market System* (Chichester, 2005).

Bhushan, P., *Bofors: The Selling of a Nation* (New Delhi, 1990).

Bker, P., *Kremlin Rising: Vladimir Putin's Russia and the End of Revolution* (New York, 2005).

Burnett, S.M., *The Italian Guillotine: Operation Clean Hands and the Overthrow of Italy's First Republic* (Oxford, 1998).

Cawthorne, N., *Pirates of the 21st Century* (John Blake, London, 2010).

Champion, D., *The Paradoxical Kingdom: Saudi Arabia and the Momentum of Reform* (New York, 2003).

Chang, H.-J., *Bad Samaritans: The Guilty Secrets of Rich Nations and the Threat to Global Prosperity* (New York, 2007).

Chene, M.J., *Islamic Approaches to Corruption* (Bergen, 2007).

Chetwynd, E., Chetwynd, F. and Spector, B., *Corruption and Poverty: A Review of Recent Literature* (Washington, DC, 2003).

Chubb, J., *The Mafia and Politics: The Italian State under Seige* (Occasional Paper 23) (Cornell, 1989).

Dallek, R., *The Lost Peace; Leadership in a Time of Horror and Hope* (New York, 2010).

Dickie, J., *Cosa Nostra: A History of the Sicilian Mafia* (London, 2007).

Eigen, P., *The Web of Corruption: How a Global Movement Fights Graft* (Frankfurt, 2008).

Eisenstein, L., *The Printing Press as an Agent of Change* (Cambridge, UK, 1979).

Elson, R., *Suharto: A Political Biography* (Cambridge, UK, 2001).

European Bank for Reconstruction and Development and World Bank, *Business Environment Survey* (London, 2001–10).

Feinstein, A., *The Shadow World: Inside the Global Arms Trade* (London, 2011).

Gittings, J., *The Changing Face of China: from Mao to Market* (Oxford, 2005).

Glenny, M., *McMafia: Crime without Frontiers* (London, 2008).

Gong, T., *The Politics of Corruption in Contemporary China* (Westport and London, 1994).

Hale, H., *Why Not Parties in Russia? Democracy, Federalism and the State* (Cambridge, UK, 2006).

Harris, R., *Political Corruption: In and Beyond the Nation State* (London, 2003).

Heidenheimer, A., *Political Corruption: A Handbook* (New Brunswick, 1989).

Hors, I.E., *China in the Global Economy: Governance in China* (Paris, 2005).

Hsu, L., *The Political Philosophy of Confucianism: An Interpretation of the Social and Political Ideas of Confucius, His Forerunners and His Early Disciples* (London, 1975).

Jain, A., *Economics of Corruption* (London, 1998).

Jenkins, R., *Democratric Politics and Economic Reform in India* (Cambridge, UK, 1999).

Johansen, E., *Political Corruption: Scope and Resources: Annotated Bibliography* (New York and London, 1991).

Johnston, M., *Syndromes of Corruption* (Cambridge, UK, 2005).

Jopshi, S., *Corruption in India: Ramifications and Remedies* (Mumbai: Prakashan, 2005).

Juan, J.A., *Discourse and Political Reflections on the Kingdoms of Peru* (Oklahoma, 1978).

Karklins, R., *The System Made Me Do It* (M.E. Sharpe, New York, 2005).

Kennedy, R., *The Enemy Within: The McClellan Committee's Crusade Against Jimmy Hoffa and Corrupt Labour Unions* (New York, 1960).

Khan, M., *Rents, Rent Seeking and Economic Development* (Cambridge, UK, 2000).

Kishor, N.D., 'Crime and justice in the Garden of Eden: improving governance and reducing coruption in the forestry sector', in J. Campos, *The Many Faces of Corruption*, pp. 90–100 (Washington, DC, 2007).

Kochan, N., *Corruption: The New Corporate Challenge* (London, 2011).

Kumar, A., *The Black Economy in India* (Penguin, New Delhi, 1999).

Kwong, J., *Political Economy of Corruption in China* (M.E. Sharpe, London, 1997).

Lambsdorff, J., 'Corruption in comparative perspective', in A. Jain, *Economics of Corruption*, pp. 81–111 (London, 1998).

Lankester, T., *The Politics and Economics of Britain's Foreign Aid: The Pergau Dam Afffair* (Routledge, London, 2012).

Larmour, P., *Interpreting Corruption: Culture and Politics in the Pacific Islands* (Australia, 2011).

Larmour, P., *Corruption and Politics in the Pacific Islands* (Canberra, 2011).

Ledeneva, A., *Russia's Economy of Favours: Blat, Networking and Informal Knowledge* (Cambridge, UK, 1998).

Ledeneva, A., *How Russia Really Works* (Cornell, 2006).

Ledeneva, A. and Lovell, S., *Bribery and Blat in Russia* (MacMillan, London, 2000).

Leigh, D.V., *Sleaze: The Corruption of Parliament* (London, 1997).

Leonard, R., *The War against Bribery* (London, 1913).

Little, W., *Introduction to Political Corruption in Europe and Latin America* (London, 1996).

Lu, X., *Cadres and Corruption: The Organisational Involution of the Chinese Communist Party* (Oxford, 2005).

Lynch, D.T., *Boss Tweed: The Story of a Grim Generation* (New Brunswick, 2002).

McFarlane, A., 'Political corruption and reform in Bourbon Spanish America', in W.-C. Little, *Political Corruption in Europe and Spanish America*, pp.42–52 (London, 1996).

McGregor, R.,*The Party: The Secret World of China's Communist Rulers* (Allen Lane, London, 2010).

Meredith. M., *Mugabe: Plunder and Power in Zimbabwe* (New York, 2007).

Moody-Stuart, G., *Grand Corruption* (Oxford, 1997).

Myrdal, G., *Asian Drama* (Penguin, London, 1968).

Naím, M., *Illicit: How Smugglers, Traffickers, and Copyats are Hijacking the Global Economy* (London, 2007).

Neild, R., *Public Corruption: The Dark Side of Social Evolution* (London, 2002).

Noonan, J., *Bribes* (New York, 1984).

Obasanjo, O., *Nzeogwu: an intimate portrait of Major Chukwuma Kaduna Nzeogwu* (Ibadan, 1987).

Office of Democracy and Governance Bureau for Democracy, Conflict and Humanitarian Assistance, *Money in Politics Handbook: A Guide to Increasing Transparency in Emerging Democracies* (Washington, DC, 2003).

O'uchi, M., 'Political corruption and Japanese corporate donations', in S. Vishwanathan, *Japan: The New Challenges* (New Delhi, 1982).

Peck, L., 'Corruption and political development in early modern Britain', in A.E. Heidenheimer, *Political Corruption: A Handbook* (New Brunswick, 1989).

Peel, M., *A Swamp Full of Dollars* (London, 2009).

Pettit, P., *Republicanism: A Theory of Freedom and Government* (Oxford, 1997).

Porta, D., 'A typology of corruption networks', in Junichi Kawata, *Comparing Political Corruption and Clientelism* (Aldershot, 2006).

Power, T., *Corruption and Democracy in Brazil: The Struggle for Accountability* (Notre Dame, USA, 2011).

Quah, J., *Combating Corruption Singapore Style* (Maryland Series in Contemporary Asian Studies, Vol. 2007, No. 2, Article 1).

Quiroz, A., *A History of Unbound Graft in Peru* (Washington, DC, 2008).

Rashid, A., *Descent into Chaos* (Penguin, London, 2009).

Rose-Ackerman, S., *Corruption and Government: Causes, Consequences and Reform* (Cambridge, UK, 1999).

Rotberg, R., *Corruption Security and World Order, World Peace Foundation* (Cambridge, Mass, 2009).

Schlesinger, A., *Robert Kennedy and his Times* (London, 1978).

Scott, J., *Comparative Political Corruption* (Englewood Cliffs, NJ, 1972).

Sidorenko, K., *Robert F Kennedy* (New York, 2000).

Stockton, D., *Cicero: A Political Biography* (London, 1971).

Suberu, R., 'The travails of Nigeria's anti corruption crusade', in R. Rotberg, *Corruption, Global Security and World Order*, pp.264–69 (Washington, DC, 2009).

Tata, J., *Keynote* (Mumbai, 1986).

Tay, S., *The Enemy Within – Combating Corruption in Asia* (New York, 2003).

Thoebald, R., *Corruption, Development and Underdevelopment* (Durham, USA, 1990).

Thomas, J., *Informal Economic Activity* (Hemel Hempstead, 1992).

Tylden, D., *Boss Tweed: the story of a grim generation* (London, 2002).

Williams, R., *Party Finance and Political Corruption* (Houndmills, 2000).

Woods, N., 'Governing climate change: lessons from other governance regimes', in N.H. Helm, *The Economics and Politics of Climate Change* (Oxford, 2009).

Wrong, M., *In the Footsteps of Mr Kurtz* (Fourth Estate, London, 2000).

Yew, L.K., *From Third World to First: Singapore and the Asian Economic Boom* (Singapore and London, 2000).

Zimbardo, P., *The Lucifer Effect* (Random House, USA, 2007).

Published reports and articles

Adelstein, J. (2010). Yakuza. *World Policy Journal*, XXVII (Summer).

Baldwin, R. (2008). *Rise of Emissions Trading.* Department of Economics and Law Society. London: London School of Economics.

Bowen, S. (2009). *Hard Lessons: The Iraq Reconstruction Experience.* Washington, DC: US Government Printing Office.

Callisters, D. (1999). *Corrupt and Illegal Activities in the Forestry Sector: Current Understandings and Implications for World Bank Forest Policy.* Washington, DC: World Bank.

Clark, P. (2010). Counterfeit drugs. *World Policy Journal*, XXVII (Summer).

Centre for the Study of Democracy (2010). *Examining the Links Between Organised Crime and Corruption.* Sofia: Centre for Study of Democracy.

Dasgupta, N. (2011). *Evidence on the Economic Growth Impacts of Corruption in Low Income Countries and Beyond: A Systematic Review.* EPPI-Centre, Social Science Research Unit. London: Institute of Education.

Foot, M. (2009). *Final Report of the Independent Review of British Offshore Financial Centres.* London: HM Treasury.

Global e-sustainability initiative. (2008). *The Social and Environmental Responsibility in Metals Supply to the Electronic Industry.* Brussels, 2008.

Global Financial Integrity. (2010). *Illicit Flows from Developing Countries 2008–9.* Washington, DC: GFI.

Global Financial Integrity. (2010). *Privately Held Non Resident Deposits in Secrecy Jurisdictions.* Washington, DC: GFI.

Global Witness. (1998). *A Rough Trade.* London: Global Witness.

Global Witness. (2010). *The Hill Belongs to Them.* London: Global Witness.

Graduate Institute of International Develoment Studies. (2003). *Small Arms Survey.* Geneva: Graduate Institute of International Development Studies.

Guillermoprieto, G. (28 October 2010). The murderers of Mexico. *New York Review of Books*, p.46.

International Food Policy Research Institute. (2009). *Public Expenditure and International Development: Ghana's Ministry of Agriculture.* Washington, DC: IFPRI.

Iqbal, Z. (2002). Governance and corruption. *American Journal of Islamic Studies*, 19, part 1.

Iqbal, Z. and Lewis, M. (2002). Governance and corruption. *American Journal of Islamic Studies*, 19, part 2.

Kellner, T. (2010). Inside Mexico's drug war. *World Policy Journal,* Spring (XXVII).

Lewis, D. (2010). High times on the Silk Road. *World Policy Journal,* Spring (XXVII).

Lintott, A. (1990). Electoral bribery in the Roman Republic. *Journal of Roman Studies,* 1–16.

Ministry of the Environment, Nature Conservation & Tourism, Democratic Republic of the Congo. (2010). *REDD Readiness Preparation Proposal for 2010–11.* Kinshasha: Government of DRC/REDD.

Ministry of Home Affairs, India. (1964). *Report of the Committee on the Prevention of Corruption (Santhanam Report).* New Delhi: Government of India.

OECD. (2010). *Annual Report of Working Group on Bribery.* Paris: OECD.

Olken, B. (2011). *Corruption in Developing Countries.* Cambridge, MA: National Bureau of Economic Research.

Schleifer, A. (1993). Corruption. *Quarterly Journal of Economics,* 108(3), 99–617.

Schneider, F. (2007). Shadow economies and corruption all over the world: new estimates for 145 countries. *Journal of Population Economics,* 3, 495–526.

Schneider, F. (2010). Corruption and the shadow economy: an empirical analysis. *Public Choice,* 144, 215–38.

Sherman, J. (2009). *The Public Cost of Private Security in Iraq.* New York: Centre on International Co-operation, NYU.

Southall, R. (2005). The Ndungu Report: land and graft in Kenya. *Review of African Political Economy,* 103, 142–51.

Sub Committee on National Security and Foreign Affairs, US House of Representatives. (2010). *Warlord Inc.,* Washington, DC: US House of Representatives.

Tegera, A. (2002). *The Coltan Phenomenon.* Pole Institute, Goma: DRC.

TI-India. (2009). *India Corruption Survey 2007–9.* New Delhi: TI-India.

TI-India. CMS. (2007). *India Corruption Study.* New Delhi: TI-India.

TI-Pakistan. (2010). *National Corruption Perception Survey.* Karachi: TI-Pakistan.

Transparency International. (1995–2010). *Corruption Perception Index.* Berlin: TI.

Transparency International. (1999–2011). *Bribe Payers Index.* Berlin: TI.

Transparency International. (2003–2010). *Global Corruption Barometer.* Berlin: TI.

Transparency International. (2008). *Global Corruption Report 2008 (Water and Sanitation).* Berlin: TI.

Transparency International. (2009). *Africa Education Watch.* Berlin: TI.

Transparency International. (2009). *Global Corruption Report (Corruption and the Private Sector)*. Berlin: TI.

Transparency International. (2009). *Transparency in Reporting on International Corruption: A Report on Corporate Practices*. Berlin: TI.

Transparency International. (2010). *Global Corruption Barometer*. Berlin: TI.

Transparency International. (2011). *Daily Lives and Corruption: Public Opinion in Tanzania*. Berlin: TI.

Treisman, D. (2000). Causes of corruption: a cross national study, *Journal of Public Economics*, 76, 399–457.

TruthAboutIndiaCorruption in www.plunderofindia.org (2012).

United Nations Office for Drugs Control. (2010). *World Drug Report*. Vienna: UNODC.

Wade, R. (1985). The market for public office: why the Indian state is not better at development, *World Development Report*, 13(4), 467–97.

Warioba Commission. (1996). *The State of Corruption in the Country*. Dar es Salaam: Government of United Republic of Tanzania.

Williams, A. (2009). *Climate Change and REDD*. Bergen: U4 Anti Corruption Resource Centre & Christian Michelsten Institute.

World Bank. (1997). *World Development Report: The State in a Changing World*. Washington, DC: World Bank.

World Bank. (2004). *Combating Corruption in Indonesia*. Washington, DC: World Bank.

World Bank. (2009). *Environmental Crisis or Sustainable Development Opportunity? Transforming the Charcoal Sector in Tanzania*. Washington, DC: World Bank.

World Bank. (2010). *A Stakeholder Based Analysis of the Political Economy of Tanzania's Charcoal Sector and the Poverty and Social Impact of the Proposd Reforms*. Washington, DC: World Bank.

World Bank. (2010). *World Development Indicators*. Washington, DC: World Bank.

World Economic Forum. (2003). *Global Competition Report*. Geneva: WEF.

Index